DEFENDING THE
ENEMY

JUSTICE FOR THE WWII JAPANESE WAR CRIMINALS

DEFENDING THE
ENEMY

JUSTICE FOR THE WWII JAPANESE WAR CRIMINALS

ELAINE B. FISCHEL

MEMBER OF THE AMERICAN DEFENSE
TEAM - TOKYO TRIALS

Bascom Hill Books
212 3rd Avenue North, Suite 290
Minneapolis, MN 55401
612.455.2293
www.bascomhillpublishing.com

ISBN - 978-1-935456-03-2
ISBN - 1-935456-03-2
LCCN - 2009936364

Cover Design by Jenni Wheeler
Typeset by Peggy LeTrent

Printed in the United States of America

BASCOM HILL
PUBLISHING GROUP

Contents

 # DEDICATION

TO MY WONDERFUL MOTHER, EDITH D. TOW FISCHEL

During the months I spent in Japan, I wrote to my mother nearly every day and she lovingly saved my letters. As the years passed, it remained my intention to revisit my memories of the time I spent in Tokyo working as a legal secretary for the defense during the International Military Tribunal for the Far East (IMTFE).

Like many mothers in those days, mine worried constantly about my health, my abundance of male suitors, and my close proximity to the enemy. I valued her opinion more than anyone else's, so I spent endless hours crafting letters to reassure her that I was being virtuous and still searching for a nice Jewish boy.

I described the joys, pressures, and difficulties of my work as a legal secretary, and the idiosyncrasies, brilliance, and sincere dedication of my bosses. I also wrote to her of the wonders of Japan. I sincerely tried to convey to her my growing affection for the Japanese people. I shared the cultural mannerisms, some of my social interactions, and my encounters with the ordinary and extraordinary people of this country—from the beautiful maids that assisted me, to some within the royal lineage. I gave her the details of my daily life on and off the job.

To the wonderful woman who worried, advised and guided me, I dedicate this book as a testament of my deep love and respect—my mother.

Edith D. Tow Fischel

ACKNOWLEDGMENTS

In 1948, I came home after working for two-and-a-half years at the War Crimes Trials in Tokyo, Japan, and wanted to tell others about the historic events I witnessed, and what it was like to be part of the Occupation of Japan by the United States. I started to write a book, but then put it away after completing only sixty-two pages.

One day, while visiting my friends Eileen and Sam Rifman, I found myself once more resisting Sam's entreaties to get a computer and write a book about what practicing law was like in the days when there were so few female attorneys. I told Sam about the book I had already started and that if I were to write any book, it would focus on my experiences in Japan.

Sam was kind enough to ask to read what I had written so many years ago. After he did, he chastised me for stopping. He said he wanted to read more. Right then and there he ordered my computer. So my first thanks are to Sam and Eileen for their encouragement.

I also owe a great deal to Julia Venkateswaran. Much of my writing was based on the letters I had sent my mother. Julia read those letters and guided me in selecting excerpts to be placed in the book. Later Janelle Killingsworth and I met weekly at the Balboa Bay Club in Newport Beach, which was an ideal place to have a delicious lunch and then work in a spacious library. There Janelle told me what she thought would bring my experiences to life. She handed me a weekly assignment, which many times meant reading the letters again and making further selections.

Janelle and Julia each stressed how important it was for people to know about this trial. Today we hear of war crimes trials taking place throughout the world. But other countries are not like Japan was after World War II; victors occupying defeated countries are not likely to ever be as welcomed as Americans were in Japan.

When we hear about war criminals, it is difficult to visualize them as human beings. I cannot imagine making a friend of Saddam Hussein, just as I could not have imagined becoming friends with Hideki Tojo. However, the commander of the Japanese Forces who fought the Americans did become my friend. This story illustrates how we can never really know where our experiences and feelings will take us.

If my story has merit, it is because my mother encouraged me to always do my best. She had patience and wisdom and endured the hardships that befell many Americans during the days after World War II when I was so far away from home. She wanted me to know that my being part of this historic event meant that I had to justify the trust given to me to carry out my job. I thought of her often as my adventures unfolded.

# INTRODUCTION

On December 7, 1941, I sat in the miniature grandstand at the Lincoln Park Tennis Courts in Santa Monica, California, waiting for a court to open up. I was listening to a portable radio when the announcer interrupted with breaking news: "The United States is being attacked. Bombs are falling on Pearl Harbor." The games came to an abrupt halt.

Like so many other Americans, my life took a new direction that day. It is still an amazing story, even to me, when I look back and see how pieces of my life's puzzle fit together so perfectly in order to take me to Japan in the spring of 1946. It would have been impossible that day to imagine myself going to the country of our former enemy less than six years later to be part of an historic event about which little is known even today: the trial of the leaders of Japan for war crimes.

My participation in the trials was on a daily basis for two-and-a-half years. I interacted with the accused war criminals who masterminded the attack on Pearl Harbor. I spoke with the accused, met their families, shared their hospitality, and enjoyed the tradition of "presentos." Many of these people became my friends, and some of those friendships have lasted to this day.

The "puzzle pieces" first began to take shape in New York City, U.S.A. My father died when my sister was nine, and I was eight. My wonderful mother, a widow at twenty-seven, was left alone to raise the two of us. She decided to leave New York, the only home she knew, to raise her girls in California. In 1932, we gathered our few possessions and moved to Santa Monica to be there in time for the Olympic Games in Los Angeles.

My mother had never been more than one hundred miles outside of New York City. Throughout our cross-country trip she regularly pulled into gas stations and asked, "Which way is it to California?"

When we finally got here, the strain of this undertaking caused her to briefly consider returning to New York where she had family. Instead, she found an apartment and we quickly became Californians. Our lives were filled with school (A's were the standard), tennis, and swimming. In tennis, I worked up to the rank of number one in Southern California in the juniors, and at the University of California,

Los Angeles (UCLA) I was the runner-up in the National Intercollegiate Championship. In swimming, I performed with the Aquacade.

My thoughts of being a top tennis player faded when I had transitioned from "18 and under" to the seniors circuit. While I was in the same age group as Jack Kramer, who went on to become a famous professional in the tennis circuit (and I even knew Bobby Riggs), my skills could not give me a life in the professional tennis circuit.

I turned nineteen in April of 1940 and graduated in June from UCLA with a major in political science for which I credit the professors who were so bright and made the subject so interesting.

I was considering law school, so I sought admission to Boalt Hall in Berkeley and was granted an interview. Their conclusion was that I was summarily too young and completely unsophisticated. At loose ends, I did not know what else to do except find a job.

My first job was a secretarial position in a doctor's office in Santa Monica, California. Maybe it was the competitive spirit I learned in tennis that made me so driven, but I set a goal to be the best secretary anywhere. I was still a novice in some key areas: dating, socializing and learning to horseback ride. However, I loved to dance, play Ping-Pong, swim and travel.

The attack on Pearl Harbor turned life upside down for every American. Our country was at WAR! Jobs became plentiful. My strongest asset was that I could type one hundred words a minute. It was no problem finding a typist job on the swing shift at Lockheed Aircraft. Electric typewriters were brand new and toy-like for a "speed demon" like me. My working hours were 4 p.m. to 12 a.m., leaving me time in the morning to attend stenotype school.

When my speed reached 175-words a minute, I was promoted to secretary at the new Lockheed Flight Engineering School, where airmen trained for the newly designed aircraft—the Constellation. Being a stenotypist instead of a shorthand secretary gave me an added skill, enabling me to record lectures given in a dark room while technical slides were presented.

When the Army Air Force took over the program, I was asked to go along. The program was transferred to Sheppard Field in Wichita Falls, Texas, where engineers were trained for the new B-29 planes. I was secretary to the head of the school, Major Frost. Many young men were sent to the school. The program was so new that instructors were scarce, as were books. Even scarcer was any formal curriculum. But, somehow it all came together.

When the first group of engineers graduated and were given their wings as flight engineers, I felt almost as if I earned those wings myself. I, too, was part of the war effort. I was proud for all of us! (I retain that same pride today.)

The school was moved to Smoky Hill Air Force Base in Salina, Kansas, where the B-29s were delivered and the crews were readied for combat. In this little town at a private airfield, I decided to complete my dream and learn how to fly. I "earned my wings."

When the school moved to Lowry Field in Denver, Colorado, I applied for entry into the Women's Air Force Service Pilots—WASPs— and was accepted. But the news came that the Air Force was discontinuing the program. This left me in Denver without a job, because I had already given my resignation to the Flight Engineering School. I figured the Air Force must have had some guilty feelings, because I was soon told I could work in Washington, D.C., in Intelligence.

While working in Washington, I enrolled in the evening program at George Washington University Law School. I met Colonel Leonard Coleman, a pilot in the Air Force and an attorney in civilian life. We became friends and stayed in touch.

When the war was over, I returned to Los Angeles and began working as a secretary in the District Attorney's Office. One day I received a call from Leonard. He asked if I were still interested in attending law school. He told me about an opening for secretaries to serve in Tokyo, Japan, at the War Crimes Trials, which were expected to last about six months. He emphasized this experience would be great preparation for law school.

So, this story begins in the spring of 1946. Like so many other Americans, I judged Japanese people by the horrific hallmark event that took place at Pearl Harbor. I had heard stories of the death march at Bataan, when the Japanese took over the Philippines. To me the Japanese were evil, subhuman people. Now here I was -- a participant in the International Military Tribunal for the Far East (IMTFE).

I had heard of the Nuremberg Tribunal and knew the two trials followed the cessation of hostilities, and also had something to do with fixing blame for the major conflicts that had dominated American life for the past five years. I was supposed to work with the lawyers who would be prosecuting the leaders of the fallen country. But it did not turn out that way. The job swiftly took a 180-degree change for me; I began working for the defense of the accused Japanese war criminals.

For the next two-and-a-half years, I interacted with "the accused" on a daily basis. I spoke with them; I met some of their families; we became friends. I remained friends with many of the Japanese people I met while working for the Occupation. I traveled to all four islands; each had spectacular shrines, parks, cities, and people. When not traveling, I frequented those tennis courts that were still playable at Hibiya Park or at the almost burned-out Tokyo Tennis Club and later at the Dai Ichi Hotel.

At the end of the trials, three of those I regarded as "enemy-friends" were sentenced to be hanged. Others were imprisoned and later freed. Those who were freed went on to make meaningful contributions to the rebirth of their country and regain their former stature as leaders within the new government. One eventually became prime minister.

In the remotest corners of the four islands of Japan there was not a single Japanese person who did not know about the "Tokyo Saiban" and the role played by the American defense counsel. It was many, many months before those millions of unbelieving eyes and ears could begin to comprehend that the presence of American attorneys was living proof of the greatness of our nation—a nation whose doctrines and teachings could be trusted and followed to the benefit of a defeated country.

It is my wish for this account to bring forth some measure of understanding of the human side of this historic trial, and provide recognition for the efforts and struggles of the American attorneys who so vigorously guarded our ideals of fair play and justice for even the most hated of defendants, and who struggled to bring lasting understanding and benefit to the Japanese people.

Today, so many decades later, wars of aggression are still fought. There are winners and losers. Historians and learned scholars have written about the Nuremberg Trials, and a few have written about the International Military Tribunal for the Far East. In 1970, American moviemakers, in collaboration with the Japanese, made *Tora, Tora, Tora*, describing the Pearl Harbor attack from its conception to its delivery. Other movies since then have portrayed the attack in an attempt to recreate the social and political culture of our country before, during, and immediately after the Pearl Harbor attack.

However, for those who lived through the war, every year on December 7th, there are reminders of the attack and memories are stirred. The mind plays funny tricks, but still brings us back to where we were when the announcement was made on that fateful day. We can almost hear the voice of President Franklin D. Roosevelt addressing the nation: "December 7th, a date that will live in infamy."

My story is not a treatise on the legality of the trial or the lessons it may have taught. This is simply my story written with the hope it will bring some understanding of why American attorneys defended the leaders of their most recent enemy—Japan. For those of us who were part of the defense, the enemy leaders took on a new dimension. They became "clients with a story to tell."

Whether this trial proved they were right or wrong, justified or unjustified, is not half as important as the visual indoctrination of the Japanese people with the American concept of democracy. The old and familiar expression, "One picture is worth a thousand words," was never more evident than in the courtroom of the War Ministry Building where every day for two-and-a-half years, the Japanese spectators' section was crammed to capacity with unbelievers who watched American attorneys fighting sincerely and earnestly in defense of Japan's former leaders.

When I finally came home, I had a completely different perspective of these people and their culture; and those experiences continued to broaden my life through all these years. That is why I felt compelled to write this story and invite you, the reader, to join me in seeing two sides of the Occupation—the American demonstration of democracy in action and the old Japanese culture competing with the new.

Japanese spectators awaiting entry to trial:
A note card was distributed to all spectators stating the rules of the court.

During the two-and-a-half years of the trial, some 200,000 spectators attended the sessions.

MEMOIRS OF THE JAPANESE WAR CRIMES TRIALS
THE PEOPLE, THE NATIONS, THE FRIENDS, THE ENEMIES

THE HIGH AND MIGHTY

EMPEROR HIROHITO ascended to the throne in 1926 and ruled Japan continuously until his death in 1989. His subjects regarded him as a god. He became less of a deity and more of a human being during the Occupation of Japan by the United States, following the cessation of World War II hostilities. He met with General Douglas MacArthur at the American Embassy in Tokyo on September 27, 1945.

GENERAL DOUGLAS MACARTHUR, a five-star general, became Supreme Commander of the Allied Powers (SCAP) during the American Occupation of Japan. He signed the surrender agreement aboard the U.S.S. Missouri in Tokyo Bay on September 2, 1945, and arrived in Tokyo three days later, moving into the United States Embassy with his wife and son. His headquarters were in the Dai Ichi Building directly across from the Imperial Palace grounds. It was primarily his decision that Emperor Hirohito not be tried as a war criminal.

PRINCE NOBUHITO TAKAMATSU was the younger brother of Emperor Hirohito. He was often thought of as the "eyes and ears" of the emperor. He had been a captain in the Japanese Navy. He was of invaluable aid to the American lawyers who were striving to defend the three admirals of the Japanese Navy who were among the accused war criminals standing trial at the International Military Tribunal for the Far East (IMTFE).

ADMIRAL ISORUKU YAMAMOTO was born in 1884. As a young man he was accepted into the Japanese Navy where he pioneered in the new field of naval aviation. He was stationed in the United States in 1919 and 1923 and was the naval attaché at the Japanese Embassy in Washington, D.C. In 1939, he became commander-in-chief of the Combined Fleet of the Japanese Navy. When the Militarists appeared hell-bent on war with the United States, he warned his admirals that Japan could not defeat the U.S. in a long war. He conceived the Pearl Harbor attack as a way to immobilize the United States Fleet for one year to give the Japanese a chance to achieve enough victories to make a negotiated settlement that would not destroy Japan.

THE ELEVEN NATIONS SITTING IN JUDGMENT OF THE JAPANESE, AND WHY THEY WERE THERE

THE UNITED STATES OF AMERICA

A fleet of U.S. ships was destroyed by the Japanese in the attack on Pearl Harbor, which was considered to be a violation of international law. That law required advanced notice before the commencement of hostilities. Pearl Harbor was struck before notice reached the White House; therefore, further negotiation to avoid war was not possible.

CHINA

China's land had been ravaged by the Japanese for many, many years. This hostility was punctuated by a series of aggressive attacks against its people, the most notorious of which was the massacre at Nanking. Japanese warriors also conquered Manchuria, though not quite as brutally as in the Nanking attack.

THE NETHERLANDS

Japanese aggression against the Dutch East Indies and Japan's refusal to negotiate peaceful settlements of their disputes led to that country's participation in the trial.

THE PHILIPPINES

From 1942-45, the Japanese committed the most horrific atrocities, killing soldiers and civilians in an effort to dominate the islands into submission to Japanese rule.

THE SOVIET UNION

On August 5, 1945, a few days before the surrender of Japan, the Soviet Union declared war. Ostensibly, their reason was that Japan failed to cease hostilities after the Germans capitulated. But there was some evidence that the U.S. had "invited" the Soviets to declare war in order to bring the war to a swift end.

INDIA

Though not a signatory to the Instrument of Surrender and not a sovereign state until 1947, India had a great desire to be part of the proceedings; it had suffered thousands of casualties in Hong Kong, Malaya, Singapore, and Burma. The Far Eastern Commission permitted India to send a judge to the Tribunal.

FRANCE

France participated in the Pacific Theater of War for four-and-a-half months. It had colonies in Laos, Cambodia, and Vietnam; but they were governed by the Vichy government, which had collaborated with the Nazis. In 1945 after the collapse of the Vichy Government, Japan occupied the whole of French Indochina. France was considered one of the Big Four and thus was invited to participate in the trial.

THE BRITISH EMPIRE

The capture of Singapore and the mistreatment of its inhabitants were grounds enough for the British to sit in judgment. There were judges from Great Britain, Canada, Australia, and New Zealand, giving the Empire a great presence in the trial.

THE ACCUSED WAR CRIMINALS

THE MILITARY – THE ARMY

GENERAL HIDEKI TOJO was a general and a prime minister (1941-44). The best known of the accused, his nickname was "Razor" to denote the sharpness of his mind. The armies he commanded were likewise infamous for razor cutting through any and all kinds of materials and opposition. He was loyal to the emperor and the Army. He assumed responsibility for the war and was the most compelling witness at the trial. Despite the atrocities committed by his forces, he was not charged with committing any horrors himself. Even a tough United States colonel, who was in charge of guarding the prisoners, could not help but admire him. In addition, by all appearances, he was a favorite of all of the military police responsible for his safety.

Generals Araki, Doihara, Hashimoto, Hata, Itagaki, Kimura, Koiso, Matsui, Minami, Muto, Sato, and Umezu each wielded immense power as the Japanese armies ran all over the Far East, the Dutch East Indies, French Indochina, China, Manchuria, and the Philippines. Seven, including Tojo, were sentenced to death by hanging. Some appeared very, very old; some were still quite young.

Araki   Doihara   Hashimoto   Hata   Itagaki   Kimura

Koiso   Matsui   Minami   Muto   Sato   Umezu

THE MILITARY – THE NAVY

OSAMI NAGANO was an admiral and former navy minister (1936-37), chief of the General Naval Staff (1941-44), and a leader of the attack on Pearl Harbor. He was outspoken in his dislike of going to war against the United States. He had been a superior officer to Admiral Yamamoto and a great admirer of that man's genius. He died during the trial.

SHIGETARO SHIMADA was an admiral and Navy minister (1941-44). He is the man supposedly brought into the Tojo cabinet so that the vote for commencement of hostilities could be unanimous.

TAKASUMI OKA was an admiral and chief of the General and Military Affairs Bureau of the Navy Ministry (1940-44).

THE DIPLOMATS

KOKI HIROTA was a career diplomat. He had been foreign minister (1933-36) and prime minister (1936-37). He was the only non-military man to be hanged. Many historians have questioned the severity of the verdict against him and expressed opinions that he did not bear guilt for the crimes for which he was found guilty.

SHIGENOI TOGO was a career diplomat and former ambassador to Germany and also to Moscow at various times. His wife was German. The testimony at trial was mixed as to his true nature. He had been foreign minister from 1941-42 and again in 1945. He was very much involved in the negotiations leading to the transmittal of the final message from Japan to the United States securing peace negotiations—which failed. Pearl Harbor followed.

HIROSHI OSHIMA was an Army officer, but better known for being the ambassador to Germany (1938-39) after having been a military attaché there in 1936. He bore some of the responsibility for Japan entering into the Tripartite Alliance with Germany and Italy in 1940 (i.e., the Axis Alliance). He was most arrogant and unpleasant.

MAMORU SHIGEMITSU was a career diplomat and foreign minister (1943-45). He was also the man designated to sign the Instrument of Surrender aboard the U.S.S. Missouri at the end of hostilities. He received the lightest sentence of the accused (seven years). When he was released he became prime minister of Japan.

TOSHIO SHIRATORI was a career diplomat and ambassador to Italy in 1939.

TEICHI SUZUKI was characterized as being a "minister without portfolio" (1941-43). He was mentioned infrequently during the trial.

MARQUIS KOICHI KIDO was a special defendant who did not fit into a category. He was the Lord Keeper of the Privy Seal. The power of that position was often debated. To some, he was the one closest to the emperor and responsible for policy decisions; to others he was a high-functioning messenger with limited inflence. His 5,000-page diary was a primary source of evidence for the prosecution.

BARON KIICHIRO HIRANMA was a member of the Privy Council (1924-39) and considered a major proponent of war in each post he held through the years. But in 1943 he became a peace advocate.

NAOKI HOSHINO held many cabinet posts and was heavily involved in the drug trafficking in Manchuria. He was considered a hard-liner, enthusiastic for war against the U.S. and Britain.

OKINORI KAYA was finance minister at different times in different cabinets. He was involved in exploiting China, from pushing drugs to taking the natural resources to enrich the Japanese war effort.

THE JUDICIARY

There were three leading members of the International Military Tribunal for the Far East.

CHIEF JUSTICE WILLIAM WEBB, from Australia, ruled the court in an abrasive way, and was rude to the prosecution as well as the defense. He was almost brutal in his rulings on the exclusion of evidence that would have assisted the defendants in pleading their cases.

JUSTICE B.V.A. ROLING, from the Netherlands, was considered one of the more brilliant judges with a fine background in international law. It was never possible to come close to guessing what his true feelings were about the evidence presented, though he did write certain opinions and articles on the trial. He had an illustrious lifelong career.

 JUSTICE RAHABINOD PAL, from India, wrote a dissenting opinion appearing in a 700-page book in which he declared no one should have been convicted, and wherein he joined authors, along with commentators, who stated the trial was an example of "victors' justice."

THE ATTORNEYS

PROSECUTION PRIMARY ATTORNEYS

 JOSEPH KEENAN from the United States had been head of the Criminal Division of the Justice Department. He was a graduate of Harvard Law School and known to be a person with influence in the inner circles of Washington D.C. Yet behind his back were frequent criticisms stating he knew almost nothing of Asian affairs and was an alcoholic. During the trial he did not do well when he examined General Tojo; most everyone agreed Tojo got the best of the American.

 SIR ARTHUR COMYNS CARR of Great Britain was the other leading prosecutor. Carr was a man with a sterling reputation who acquitted himself very well in his presentation.

DEFENSE ATTORNEYS

 CAPTAIN BEVERLY COLEMAN was a captain in the U.S. Navy and the second of the defense counsel. He left after only a few months, leaving a large gap in the staff. He was sorely missed, but stated he had his reasons for not continuing.

COMMANDER DICK HARRIS was a commander in the Navy and the first defense counsel on the scene. He spoke fluent Japanese and was extremely helpful to one and all. He was no longer involved in the trial after the first few months.

THE BRILLIANT ONES

Four outstanding American attorneys were capable of the finest work expected of top attorneys defending clients in capital cases:

JOHN BRANNON, from Kansas City, Missouri, was a skilled attorney with a successful practice when he was called into the Navy during World War II. After the war, he assumed the defense of the Japanese Navy, as well as being the attorney to whom the other attorneys turned for advice on strategy and law. He was a member of Phi Beta Kappa, a five-star athlete in college, and was much loved by the Japanese. Some time later, he served in the U.S. Senate representing Missouri, finishing the term for a senator who had fallen ill.

WILLIAM LOGAN was from New York City, practicing with the firm of Hunt, Hill and Betts. He and George Yamaoko represented many Japanese corporations prior to the war. He was the attorney for Marquis Koichi Kido, who willingly surrendered his meticulous diary to the prosecution at the time of his arrest.

GEORGE YAMAOKA was a Nisei from New York City who spoke fluent Japanese and was a great help in furthering communications for and between the Japanese and American lawyers. He was skilled in presenting arguments and extremely well thought of by all.

BEN BRUCE BLAKENEY was a major in the U.S. Army who spoke fluent Japanese and was often spokesperson for the defense in court. Upon completion of the trial, he wrote the appeal to General MacArthur, stating, "The verdict was not fair; not based on the evidence; guilt had not been proven beyond a reasonable doubt; and the verdict was not actually the purpose of the Allied Powers, which was to show aggression was a crime."

These men were ferocious in the defense of their clients and their attacks on the legality of the trials and the participation by the Soviet Union. They had many clashes with the judges and prosecutors, but they always knew exactly what they were doing. They worked extremely long hours and were always prepared.

THE NEXT TIER

Other defense attorneys made their marks on the Tribunal (even though they did not succeed in obtaining favorable rulings).

 OWEN CUNNINGHAM, an attorney from Des Moines, Iowa, clashed many times with the judges and wrote legal pieces criticizing the trials. He had been counsel for Ambassador Oshima, who he thought did not belong in the company of the other defendants—after all, he had been ambassador to Germany.

ARISTEDES LAZARUS – a former Marine.

GEORGE FURNESS, a captain in the U.S. Army, had also served in the Manila trials of General Yamashita and General Homma.

DAVID SMITH was an attorney who fought too hard, to the point where he was banned from appearing in front of the Tribunal after a notable battle in which he refused to apologize for criticizing Sir William Webb for interfering in the questioning of his witness.

OTHER ATTORNEYS came from all over the United States. Meyer Levin was from Milwaukee, Floyd Mattice from Indianapolis, Buck

Freeman and Roger Cole from the South, Albert Brooks from Kansas City, Ned Warren - an Army colonel, Larry McManus from New York, and George Blewett from Philadelphia.

FRIENDS

There were many special people that came into my life; a few are named here.

JAPANESE FRIENDS

 KICHISABURO NOMURA was the special envoy chosen to deliver the message to Cordell Hull, the American secretary of state. He, along with Ambassador Kurusu, arrived at the White House after Pearl Harbor was struck. He was never charged as a war criminal.

 CAPTAIN YASUJI WATANABE was a former aide to Admiral Yamamoto. He was extremely helpful to John Brannon in defending the Japanese Navy. Also, he was a friend of Prince Takamatsu and assigned as chief of the Japanese Coast Guard during the Occupation.

 JUJI ENOMOTO, both a historian and statistician, was the consultant for the Japanese Navy. He was a wonderful human being, much loved by all. He was truly a kind gentleman and always helpful with my Japanese language lessons, as well as teaching me a great deal about events that led to the war.

HIROKO KAWANO, the daughter of Admiral Shimada, was a young girl when she first came to Ichigaya to visit her father in the holding room. She later visited me in California and we are friends to this day.

CHEOKO, KAZUKO, HIROKO, and the many Japanese female employees of the Occupation with whom I came in contact also became my friends.

THE JAPANESE ATTORNEYS worked alongside their American counterparts to provide the best legal defense for their clients. They were hardworking and diligent and had a true work ethic that kept them going when the language barrier would have discouraged those with less heart.

NON-JAPANESE FRIENDS

COLONEL AUBREY KENWORTHY was a colonel in charge of the military police responsible for the safety of the prisoners. We become good friends when I was given the job of visiting our clients in the holding room each day to coordinate their requests to their attorneys, both Japanese and American. He was a tough career soldier, yet he had a compassionate heart for his prisoners.

CLAUDE WALL was the supervisor of the United Airlines station in Tokyo. The Occupation authorities had contracts with United to bring in supplies and personnel from the U.S. to Tokyo. Claude was the "host supreme" and permitted me the distinct honor of being hostess at many fine dinners and functions at his beautiful residence. Claude was a true friend.

HERBERT NORMAN was the chief of the Canadian Legation with an extraordinary knowledge of the history of Japan and the aims of the Occupation. He held a high position in the administration of General MacArthur and was instrumental in having Marquis Kido added to the list of war criminals. Many years later, to the shock of all who knew him, he committed suicide when he was exposed as a KGB agent.

DAVID HORNSTEIN was the young naval officer who headed the Language Section of the International Military Tribunal. He was fluent in Japanese and, although very young, commanded the interpreters as if he were a five-star general. For many months at the beginning of the trial he was referred to as the star of the courtroom. He "conducted" the court proceedings with his pencil.

COLIN CAMPBELL was an officer with the cavalry unit in Tokyo. He was an extraordinary, gifted young man and the first American serviceman with whom I had a close association. My special name for him was "Cog." He was an excellent horseman and, through his efforts and friendship, I learned how to ride horses. His service with the Army ended a few months after our meeting, much to my sorrow. He constantly warned me to not take the Occupation too seriously and to always remember that the life presented to those who served at this period in history was not reality.

FRITZI BERGER (NISHIKAWA) was a world champion ice skater married to the grandson of Mikimoto, the Pearl King. Though she had been in Tokyo all during the war, she never lost her zest for life. She took the time to teach me ice-skating, and I helped teach her tennis.

COLONEL FROST, formerly MAJOR FROST, was the officer in charge of the B-29 Flight Engineering School during World War II. He was responsible for the training of service men to assume the newly created commissioned post of flight engineer for the B-29 airplane. That position continues to this day as cockpits in large planes today are occupied by pilot, co-pilot, navigator and flight engineer.

CORRESPONDENTS VICTOR BOISEN and GOHL OBEAH were stationed in Tokyo during the Occupation. Victor was employed by Liberty magazine and Gohl by Air India. They were interesting and knowledgeable gentlemen who reported the happenings during the Occupation.

JAPAN

This lovely land with its gracious people will always represent the happiest days of my life. I was privileged to have enjoyed these people, their country, their beautiful culture and traditions, and to have been present when that culture, which went back thousands of years, underwent a major change.

Japan emerged from isolation at the time of the Meiji Revolution in the late 19th century, which propelled the country into the modern world. The Occupation changed the country from one so focused on war and expansion, to one destined to keep peace in Asia. Japan became an example for its neighbors in embracing the principals of democracy, which the Occupation offered, always keeping in mind that parts of that democracy would fit in with the New Japan and other parts would not. The choice was, appropriately, that of the Japanese people.

CHAPTER 1 ~ DEPARTURE AND ARRIVAL

1946. World War II had ended and the United States was to occupy Japan. "Occupation" meant soldiers were stationed in every part of that country. The United States had ambitious plans to assist Japan in her reformation and rebirth. The occupying forces planned to help write a new constitution and, in the process, break up the huge trusts that fueled the Japanese military machine. These trusts had provided the resources used by Japan for its ten-year prolonged war efforts in China and its occupation of many countries in Southeast Asia.

The War Department started a large-scale recruiting program for civilians to work overseas. I was one of the ones recruited. I would leave for Japan with little information about what I was actually going to do, where I would live, or any other specific details.

Paperwork came and, before I knew it, I was on my way from Los Angeles to San Francisco with a set of official orders assigning me to "Project K"—the War Crimes Commission.

My assignment was for the duration of the trial, in the capacity of legal stenographer. I had hoped to qualify as a court reporter, but everything happened so fast there was no time to argue with the powers in charge.

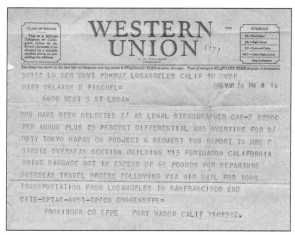

Telegram of assignment

1

During the war, I had obsessed about Hitler, Tojo, and Mussolini—the "big three" on my personal "hate parade." Like many Americans, I was happy the war was over; I was unhappy these "monsters" brought so much devastation into the world's arena.

Following the cessation of hostilities and the demise of Mussolini, the War Crimes Trials of the German leaders commenced with considerable publicity. Not until later did newspapers report that the Japanese war hero, General Hideki Tojo, had tried to commit suicide. Aside from that, there was practically no information reported about the Japanese leaders, let alone that they would be tried as war criminals.

What excited me was the idea of being a part of the prosecution of the Japanese. Working for the 20th Air Force (which was training flight engineers to man the B-29s that were to participate in raids on Tokyo) during the war was exciting. Being secretary to Colonel Frost, the commanding officer of the school, put me in close contact with the students who were to be named as "flight officers"—a new rank for the Air Force. As time went by, many of those young men were killed, wounded or listed as "missing in action."

I was bitter and uncompromising in my hatred for the Japanese people. The only concrete emotion I felt about the assignment I received was that, no matter how tiny a share I might have in this trial, I would get even in some way for the misery and heartbreak of the Pacific conflict. It never occurred to me that less than ten days after leaving the U.S., I would be part of the *defense* of Tojo and company—an endeavor that lasted two-and-a-half years. I could not fathom then that at the trial's end I would leave many of the accused war criminals with sadness, regret, and tears.

Imagine a group of Americans traveling some eight thousand miles to defend the lives of their recent enemies (the Japanese). These American lawyers embarked on a task for which there was no victory, little thanks, and an initial repugnance on the part of their fellow countrymen. I was in awe of these men, and I remain so.

Preceding my departure for Tokyo, my physical activities were confined to preparation for the trip and the anticipated six-month stay. For all my skepticism and cynicism, I was much more excited than I wanted to be. The Army's mysterious and devious channels tended to prevent any outright rejoicing or exultation. My attitude was, "When I'm in Japan, I'll believe it."

At 6:44 p.m. on the night of March 30, 1946, I was on a plane leaving Hamilton Field in San Francisco. All the information I had was contained in my set of official travel orders.

On the flight from Hamilton Field, we were classified as VIPs (very important persons) complete with the highly sought-after "Number One Priority." The Army must have wanted us in a hurry. The passengers on our flight included three pilots transferring duty stations, a major general, his aide, and three civilians en route to China. Along with two others, I only knew my eventual destination was something known as the War Crimes Commission in Tokyo. I was so impressed with these flight companions (high-ranking officers, combat pilots, important civilians), that I did not have time to think about my own lowly status. I likened myself to Cinderella on her way to her first "military ball."

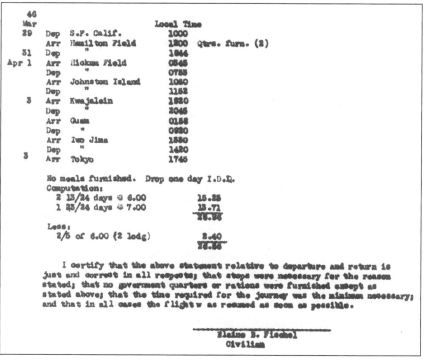

Schedule

The flight was smooth and quiet, but very cold; the plane's heating apparatus failed. A cruising altitude of 10,000 feet did not improve the freezing temperature in the plane's cabin. We all bundled up, our loudly chattering teeth and shaking limbs adding to the general discomfort. At 4:45 a.m. we arrived at Hickham Field in Honolulu, Hawaii. The heavenly Hawaiian breeze restored our equilibrium. Following some food and a shower, we took off again at 7:45 a.m. for points east.

Four hours out of Hickham Field, we made a refueling stop at Johnson Island. How could these pilots find that hunk of rock in the middle of a huge ocean? I knew something about navigation from my days as a flight student, but it still seemed like a miracle when our pilot set the huge four-engine plane down on that tiny strip of coral (I think it was coral) in the middle of nowhere.

Thirty minutes later we were off again for Kwajalein. This leg of the flight lasted some eight or nine hours, yet it seemed to pass quickly. I felt a sense of wonder at the clouds surrounding the plane. For once, I was in the translucent beauty of the present moment.

My new life in Tokyo (whatever form it would take) had not yet begun to unfold. Because there was no way of knowing what might happen to me in the months ahead, I decided the wisest course of action was to relax. I drifted in and out of sleep. While awake I could hear the pilots navigating by means of radio reception. Later they invited me to the flight deck to watch their use of the instrument panel, larger than any I had seen in my limited flying days.

These pilots filled the endless hours of the journey by recounting wartime anecdotes to one another, and I provided a fresh audience for their stories. At various stops along the way, new passengers boarded. A special kinship grew among those of us who had been together from the journey's beginning. By the flight's end, we were like family.

Kwajalein came next (another hunk of rock, so it seemed to me). We were there for two hours. I jumped at the chance to make use of the Ping-Pong table in the very primitive lounge. By the time I played a few games, it was time to leave for Guam, our next destination, another eight hours away.

Guam was not only historic, but also beautiful with tropical foliage, waving palms, sunny skies, and unpredictable showers. The military residents of these island outposts could never understand what was beautiful about them. Their standard comment to remarks of admiration for the tropical setting was, "If you had to live here you wouldn't think it was so beautiful."

Off again at 8:15 on the morning of April 3rd for the final leg of the trip. I was separated from the rest of the passengers and placed on a mail plane with another secretary and a court reporter. The three of us comprised the passenger manifest. In four hours, we were lunching on the island of Iwo Jima and looking at famous Mount Suribachi.

Iwo Jima had become famous due to the picture of the American flag being raised on that desolate piece of land. I remembered reading of the fierce battle to capture that island and its importance in the planning for the invasion of Japan.

Once we left the cabin and stepped onto the soil of Iwo Jima, it seemed as if we were on another Air Force base. There were so many planes on the runways. We were taken to a simple little building and given our lunch, which included ice cream. I could not help but think how strange it was to be eating American ice cream on the land where such fierce battles had been fought so recently. To me, it looked and seemed like nothing but a huge rock with no way to sustain life. Yet this island had played a major part in the war.

Up until this point, my thoughts centered on the many landmarks to which our flight had brought us; the social aspects of mixing with fellow passengers and the crews; and the visual impression of the various cloud formations, vast stretches of ocean, the moon and stars. Suddenly, I realized I was more than seven thousand miles from home and, in four more hours, I would be in Tokyo, Japan.

From the moment we left Hamilton Field I had been literally and figuratively up in the air, having the time of my life. The long hours of flying time were so rapidly consumed in fascinating conversation, sleeping between landings and stops at the various islands; it never occurred to me how each passing hour took me further and further away from my homeland. So far, this whole experience reminded me of an airplane ride at an amusement park rather than the beginning of a new and exciting venture. Finally, on the island of Iwo Jima, the realization came to me how, like Dorothy in *The Wizard of Oz*, I was "not in Kansas anymore."

My new adventure began.

I was in the flight deck area when we sighted land. As the ocean disappeared, the pilots began a play-by-play travelogue, which included an illustrated lecture on the topography of Tokyo Bay. They explained the route followed by the famous Doolittle Flyers whose daring raids on the city had electrified the American public. All I remember was the odd combination of densely populated areas, waterways, deep green hills, and Mt. Fuji, looking magnificent in the distance.

We landed at Atsugi Airfield at 5:45 p.m. April 3, 1946. I, Elaine Betty Fischel, was in Japan! Looking out the cabin window I saw American flags, American jeeps, American soldiers, and lots of airplanes that reminded me of the landing fields at the air bases where I worked during the war.

Atsugi had been a special field for the Imperial Japanese Navy. When Japan's surrender was announced, American military leaders met in the Philippines with high-ranking Japanese to plan the physical occupation of Japan. Small units of the Army and Navy landed at Atsugi and in the bay near Tokyo, followed by the Navy ships, preceding the entry of General MacArthur. An American C-47 carried the first American to set foot in Japan. As this first man to launch the Occupation stepped off the plane, he was met by a group of Japanese officials who identified themselves as those chosen to welcome him to their country. Hundreds of Japanese lined the runway for his arrival. Imagine how this man's heart must have been racing!

The next day, paratroopers landed and took charge of the field. In the afternoon of August 25, 1946, General Douglas MacArthur landed, having been flown to Atsugi from Okinawa. Somehow a caravan of cars was found to take the general to Yokohama. High-ranking officers accompanied him to a fine hotel that survived the bombing and was soon taken over by the Americans, just as planned.

All the activities and planning preceding my arrival made it safe for me to be in Japan.

As the cabin door of my plane opened, the first thing I saw was the portable stairway rolled up by six smiling Japanese who alternately bowed and grinned at the deplaning passengers. I grinned back. We were given directions to the Operations Office where I met the others I was separated from during our flight from Guam. After checking in, we were loaded into a large "Stateside" bus and driven to Tokyo.

First impressions can be tarnished by time, but I clearly recall the women and children along the road smiling and waving as our bus drove by. There were infants, babies, tots, and children everywhere—more than I had ever seen at one time (or in one place) in my life. They appeared happy and unconcerned about anything other than greeting us.

I was enthralled by everything I saw from the first moment I debarked. I was wishing for another set of eyes to gather in all these impressions—the wooden houses, the carts and cattle, the crowded street cars with people hanging out the windows and doors, the kimonos, the bombed buildings, the flatness of the city, the wheat growing in the cracks in the sidewalks, the people walking in the streets, and the Americans in uniform. Hundreds of these "pictures" made up my first impression.

Handcart and bike occupy the same street as an American jeep.

Rickshaw driver

Street scene

Caught up in the richness of the urban landscape, it was hard to abandon the sights and sounds of the city streets. We were transported to the Billeting Office, assigned quarters for the night and told where to report the following day. The office was in the Forestry Building, adjacent to a main street and completely unmarred by signs of bombing. What an amazing sight with so much destruction all around! Office buildings and billets surrounded the area. These, too, seemed in perfect condition.

When newspapers talked of precision bombing used in certain air raids, I had not known what they meant. Now, seeing several buildings intact on certain streets, brought the realization that precision bombing was just that—precise! Buildings the U.S. planned on using during the Occupation stood ready for immediate occupancy, enabling the Americans to enjoy the comfort and convenience of home—only Japanese-style.

Quarters, Kanda Kai Kan Building

On the flight over, I became friends with Audrey Davis and Daphne Spratt, who were also assigned to the trial. After receiving our preliminary instructions, the first thing we girls did was to invade the GI mess hall at the Dai Ichi Building in search of lemons to rinse our hair. (Hooray, we found them!) We might have been travel weary, but the boys on duty made us feel more than welcome.

This building appeared to be a functioning office building complete with elevators and spacious offices. I learned that "dai ichi" means "life insurance."

War Ministry Building

Our next stop was the snack bar of the Uraku Hotel where we feasted on hamburgers and soft drinks served by smiling Japanese waitresses amidst a general atmosphere of gaiety and noise. We attempted to pay our bills in American nickels and dimes, but soon discovered that Japanese currency was the order of the day. Fortunately, two officers approached us with 100-yen notes and insisted on treating us. We were "rich," comfortable, and sleepy; life could not have been better.

A jeep drove us to our quarters for the night at the former YWCA, also called the Kanda Kai Kan. The brick building with nice lobbies and sleeping rooms was only twenty-five minutes from the Imperial Palace. Within moments of settling into my new home, I was fast asleep in Tokyo.

Room at Kanda Kai Kan

CHAPTER 2 ~ I DIDN'T FLY 8,000 MILES TO BE IN THE TYPIST POOL

The next morning, in accordance with instructions, I reported to the administrative officer of the International Prosecution Section armed with my shorthand machine, travel orders, personnel file, and a sales talk designed to effect a change in classification from legal stenographer to court reporter. Before accepting the assignment in Japan, I had spoken by phone to the authorities in Washington. They informed me that the only immediate openings were for legal stenographers, but I could simply request court-reporting duties upon my arrival in Tokyo. The promise of obtaining work in the field of court reporting was part of my motivation for traveling thousands of miles; however, I soon discovered that reclassification to the job of court reporter was not easily accomplished. This was the Army. My official orders read "legal stenographer;" so legal stenographer I was destined to be!

Following a brief interview with the colonel in charge (who bluntly stated, "Report to the stenographer's pool"), any delusions or illusions of grandeur I might have had faded rapidly. The colonel was not the least bit concerned about my arrival or that of any other female employee working for the War Department.

I was assigned a desk-one of several in a large room filled with some twenty or twenty-five stenographers so busily engaged in their own work that the arrival of any new girls to the pool went unnoticed.

My only consolation was that Audrey shared my disappointment. She came to Tokyo with the promise of a plum secretarial assignment to one of the chief prosecutors. But it was the "pool" for her, too. Daphne joined the other court reporters, as her position had been set from the beginning. I was a bit envious.

Audrey and I took our places while muttering nasty remarks about the lieutenant in charge of the crew. We did not like his battle jacket, his boots, or his assumed air of authority. We decided the closest he had probably ever come to combat was bossing a few girls around. However, we determined that for one week we would remain silent and carry out our assignments. Then, if the situation continued to disintegrate, we would start searching for a way out. Any visions we

11

had of plush jobs, glamour, and excitement flew out the door. We had to remain hopeful that better days would come.

My first assignment in the pool consisted of typing index-sized cards containing comments about incidents that occurred in China in 1937. People and places were referred to that had no meaning to me whatsoever. The second day, I typed Tojo's name on a document analysis form; but most of the time I sat and watched everyone else work. These were the "old-timers" who had arrived in Tokyo before me. I could not help feeling a little jealous of their familiarity with the office routine.

As yet, I had no idea what I was doing there, who was on trial, if there ever was going to be a trial, or where the location of the court-room was. Is this a mystery? I wondered. This operation, staffed en-tirely by Americans, was ironically called the International Prosecution Section. Perhaps if I had been more enthusiastic, someone might have explained to me the way things worked, but I was still in mourning for my unrealized ambition to be a court reporter. I was a mere typist and I refused to do anything until I was asked. Occasionally, I was sent out to take dictation from an attorney. These brief, routine, and uninteresting assignments demanded little ability and less ingenuity.

On the third day, I learned there were thirty or more Japanese war criminal suspects lodged in Sugamo Prison. They would be indicted during the month and tried for Class-A crimes. Prior to my arrival, the corps of stenographers, all working for the prosecution, had been reporting to the prison daily with the assigned prosecution attorneys and the necessary interpreters. While there, they recorded detailed interrogations of the prisoners. These were already completed as part of the preparation of the actual case. It appeared to me that the prosecution section had been there forever.

The prisoners were bused to court from Sugamo Prison.

One day when I reported for dictation, I was introduced to the Philippine prosecutor, Major Pedro Lopez (the first non-American I met who was connected with the trial). The talk concerned the drafting of the indictment, evidently being handled by the British. I was in the same room as an American and Philipino, listening to a legal discussion about the British! For the first time since my arrival, I felt there was something international about the project and I might get to see history in the making after all.

There were rumors that our office would be transferred to the War Ministry Building, the site of the actual trial. In the meantime, I met the chief court reporter to whom I more or less poured out my tale of woe regarding not being assigned to his staff. He advised me to bide my time and wait until the prosecution staff moved to the War Ministry Building. He promised he would do everything in his power to secure an assignment for me as secretary to one of the eleven judges or to one of the defense attorneys.

The fact that the Japanese would be defended had not occurred to me, probably because all I had been hearing was "prosecution, prosecution, prosecution." I liked the idea that new jobs would be available. So, why not me? Anything would be better than what I was doing. I was excited and intrigued with the possibilities. Yet there had been no mention of staffing for the Japanese defense, only that there was such a thing as a "defense."

Rumors abounded of choice jobs with either the judges or the general secretary. Yet they were only rumors. I wanted to be someplace far away from the "pool" of typists, as far away as I could get. I was discouraged and pessimistic, yet somehow I had a feeling the War Ministry Building would change my situation.

Because the most urgent portion of the stenographic work for the prosecution had been completed, there was a surplus of stenographic personnel. Ten of us were sent to the International Military Tribunal for further assignment. It was without regret (and many thanks) that I left to report for duty at "Ichigaya." In retrospect, the day I was selected to leave the International Prosecution Section turned out to be my lucky day. Many weeks later, the entire section was transferred there.

Elaine at International Military Tribunal

Ichigaya had been the headquarters of the Japanese War Ministry during the war. Under the direction of General MacArthur the old auditorium in the building was transformed into a modern courtroom venue. The design included a high platform for the judges, a glass-enclosed booth for the translators and tiers for the defendants, with tables and lecterns for the attorneys in the well. Many weeks passed before I saw the courtroom. The business of the trial was conducted in the offices scattered throughout the building.

My good fortune was in being declared "surplus," which somehow rescued me from being part of the prosecution section. I wanted to make the most of what I considered a privilege and an opportunity simply to be in Japan. But a fulfilling assignment in Tokyo was what I wanted most. Home was a long way away and I was too stubborn to settle for a job that was not meaningful and interesting. Ichigaya was my ticket out of obscurity.

On April 5, 1946, the Defense Division was officially established. On April 12, 1946, I reported to the Personnel Office of the general secretary. Following a brief interview, I was temporarily loaned to this embryonic section—the defense. After my first day, I requested permanent assignment to the Defense Section. I did not think for a moment it meant working for the enemy. To me, it meant a job with some punch to it. To my elation, I was officially appointed as Captain Beverly Coleman's personal secretary. I did not know anything about him, yet I wrote to my mother that day.

> *The gods must be smiling alright. I was notified of my assignment to Captain Beverly M. Coleman. I'm about the happiest girl in Tokyo right now.*

Captain Coleman was tall, distinguished, handsome, and a gentleman. He was equivalent to a full colonel in the Army and had been appointed chief of the Defense Section. In civilian life, he was an attorney. He was on active duty with the Navy when he was selected for this position. I never learned how that all happened; I was just so happy it did.

Captain Coleman with General Hideki Tojo and Valentine Deal, defense attorney

Captain Coleman with Japanese attorneys

Captain Coleman came from Virginia and had the nicest Southern accent. I asked him if his middle name—Mosby—had any particular meaning. His answer was that during the Civil War one of the relatives for whom he was named led a famous brigade known as Mosby's Raiders. He was proud of being named Beverly Mosby Coleman. He was gracious and a fine, hard-working attorney/administrator. With a pleasant twinkle in his eyes, he called me "the sweetest, nicest girl in the world." This was the beginning of our friendship. Years later, when I was an attorney and wanted to qualify to practice before the Supreme Court of the United States, Captain Coleman sponsored me.

Given this break from the day-to-day monotony of the "typist bullpen," I was determined to make a superior impression.

I knew that several high-ranking officers I met casually, before I began this wonderful position, were very influential, including Lieutenant Commander Dick Harris. For a short time, prior to Coleman's appointment as chief defense counsel, Harris acted as head of the Defense Section. With his fluent Japanese, he conducted many meetings with the Japanese lawyers who were in and out of our offices. I asked him how, being a boy from Brooklyn, he spoke Japanese. He said he had always been interested in Japan and had made up his mind to learn the language. The Japanese attorneys loved him. He was always in a huddle with them.

As secretary to the chief defense counsel, I felt pressure to dress up and make an appearance worthy of my title. I felt different and my whole attitude was upgraded. My letters home were full of descriptions of my clothes, hair, and makeup. There was always something I needed—lipstick, nail polish, fashion magazines. I wanted to look like "The Secretary" to a very important person. What a pain I must have been to my mother to whom my requests were often addressed!

There appeared to be no organizational structure, no directives telling Captain Coleman what kind of staff he would oversee, or where he could obtain books or office supplies. He was on his own, pioneering each step of the way. With the exception of three or four men in naval uniform, few people on the scene knew what needed to be organized or accomplished.

Technically, my first assignment consisted of sorting and filing documents dealing with the general law problems encountered at the Nuremberg trials, and typing a few letters relating to personnel problems. These assignments, however trivial, were the first opportunity I had to gain some insight into what might be in store for the defense.

I did know that the Nuremberg trials were different from these trials. While there were eleven nations trying the Japanese, in Germany there had been only four: the United States, Great Britain, France, and Russia. The eleven nations in Japan each had one judge representative. The countries they represented were Australia, Canada, China, France, Great Britain, India, the Netherlands, New Zealand, the Philippines, the Soviet Union, and the United States. There were more differences I learned about later. It was commonly said that the Nuremberg trial was a true war crimes trial and thus a precedent for the Japanese trial.

At Nuremberg there were three acquittals (even though the prosecution sought the death penalty for all defendants). The verdicts were reached while our trial was progressing. Our defendants were silent when they learned of the fate of the accused Germans. Of course, that was not a surprise, as their attorneys would not let them speak. But Owen Cunningham (the American lawyer defending former Ambassador to Germany Oshima) expressed some optimism as to the possible fate of some of our defendants, saying four things were obviously different from the German war activities:

1. There was nothing comparable to the German's slaughter of the Jews.
2. There had been no continuous government ruling in the years leading to the war.
3. In China, Chiang Kai Shek was not able to achieve peace after the Japanese left, so perhaps the actions of the Japanese were not one hundred percent to blame for the devastation caused in that country.
4. The Chinese Communists had taken over Manchuria. This might mean the Japanese were right in asserting that their activities in that country had prevented a Communist takeover while they were there.

Maybe if there had been a real chance of acquitting the defendants, the trial would not have taken place. But take place it did. Individuals were held to answer (first and foremost) for crimes against peace. The indictment described a "criminal militaristic clique" domi-nant within the Japanese government between January 1, 1928 and September 2, 1945, whose "policies were the cause of serious world troubles, aggressive wars, and great damages to the interests of peace-loving people, as well as to the Japanese people themselves." The ac-cused had formed a "conspiracy."

The language of the indictment stated that the conspiracy led to the commission of crimes against peace, the war crimes, and the crimes against humanity. This was truly a strong indictment against the lead-ers of Japan. There was so much the attorneys needed to know to be able to answer these charges.

The most startling information I came across was that a group of American lawyers were due to report to Tokyo from Washington, D.C. and other places to aid in the defense of the Japanese. Leading Japanese lawyers were also being hired to defend the war criminals.

Commander Harris told me the chief Japanese defense coun-sel, Dr. Ichiro Kiyose, was brilliant; he would make his mark on the Tribunal. When I first met him I was amazed at how small a man he was. I thought of the old adage, "Good things come in small packages." I would hear more and more about him.

Other Japanese lawyers appeared who were chosen by the Japanese due to their stature in legal circles. Some were professors, others advisors to cabinet ministers. All appeared to be hard working and appreciative of the help of the American lawyers.

The defense personnel present on the scene, though few in num-ber, went into "high gear." They borrowed files from the prosecution to make copies of the interrogations that had already been conducted at the prison. At a later date, the defense team members conducted their own interrogations. It seemed perfectly natural that the Japanese should be given all the help available to ensure they received a fair trial. The term "fair trial" took the edge off any amazement or regret an American might have at the elaborate preparations underway to provide counsel for the accused men.

The Potsdam Declaration, issued on July 26, 1945, which preceded the surrender of Japan, carried the provision that justice would be meted out to the defeated leaders of the enemy country. The Japanese had a choice: surrender or risk annihilation. Those in power had not responded. The dropping of the atomic bombs on Hiroshima and Nagasaki followed.

I learned from listening to the attorneys there had been a lot of discussion among the Allied Powers on just how you mete out "stern justice." The United States' advocacy for the judicial method was the beginning of the formation of the International Military Tribunal for the Far East.

American justice stressed the rights of defendants to respond to charges against them. This situation was no different. The entrenched American judicial method almost demanded an adequate defense for the wartime leaders of Japan.

Lieutenant Commander Dick Harris was on the scene from the beginning. He was so gracious to me when he learned that I wanted to study the language and learn about the country. I constantly admired his interest in the many problems of the Japanese lawyers. His conduct set a pattern and example for my own behavior and sense of concern. I realized, as an employee of the U.S. government, that it was my duty to assist in as many ways as I could. Pure logic dictated that this historically significant trial must be fair and without prejudice.

By the end of the first day on the defense side, I reoriented my thinking along these strictly legal lines. The accused Japanese lodged in Sugamo Prison were entitled to the finest legal assistance if the words "fair trial" were to have any meaning. I was proud and happy to be associated with the defense, despite the bitterness many of my countrymen felt about providing assistance to people who they considered barbaric murderers.

Potsdam Declaration
July 26, 1945

The Potsdam Conference brought together the British Prime Minister Winston Churchill, US President Harry S Truman, and Soviet leader Josef Stalin. During the conference, general election in Britain removed Churchill's Tory Party from power. Clement Atlee, leader of the Labor Party, replaced Churchill as prime minister and joined Truman and Stalin at the conference. After the conference, President Truman and Prime Minister Clement Atlee issued the following proclamation outlining the terms under which they would halt their war against Japan. Note the assertion that the President of the Republic of China, Chiang Kai-shek, endorsed the plan. [Introduction corrected, Jan. 31, 2004]

(1) We-the President of the United States, the President of the National Government of the Republic of China, and the Prime Minister of Great Britain, representing the hundreds of millions of our countrymen, have conferred and agree that Japan shall be given an opportunity to end this war.

(2) The prodigious land, sea and air forces of the United States, the British Empire and of China, many times reinforced by their armies and air fleets from the west, are poised to strike the final blows upon Japan. This military power is sustained and inspired by the determination of all the Allied Nations to prosecute the war against Japan until she ceases to resist.

(3) The result of the futile and senseless German resistance to the might of the aroused free peoples of the world stands forth in

The Postdam Declaration 1 of 3

awful clarity as an example to the people of Japan. The might that now converges on Japan is immeasurably greater than that which, when applied to the resisting Nazis, necessarily laid waste to the lands, the industry and the method of life of the whole German people. The full application of our military power, backed by our resolve, will mean the inevitable and complete destruction of the Japanese armed forces and just as inevitably the utter devastation of the Japanese homeland.

(4) The time has come for Japan to decide whether she will continue to be controlled by those self-willed militaristic advisers whose unintelligent calculations have brought the Empire of Japan to the threshold of annihilation, or whether she will follow the path of reason.

(5) Following are our terms. We will not deviate from them. There are no alternatives. We shall brook no delay.

(6) There must be eliminated for all time the authority and influence of those who have deceived and misled the people of Japan into embarking on world conquest, for we insist that a new order of peace, security and justice will be impossible until irresponsible militarism is driven from the world.

(7) Until such a new order is established and until there is convincing proof that Japan's war-making power is destroyed, points in Japanese territory to be designated by the Allies shall be occupied to secure the achievement of the basic objectives we are here setting forth.

(8) The terms of the Cairo Declaration shall be carried out and Japanese sovereignty shall be limited to the islands of Honshu, Hokkaido, Kyushu, Shikoku and such minor islands as we determine.

(9) The Japanese military forces, after being completely disarmed, shall be permitted to return to their homes with the opportunity to lead peaceful and productive lives.

The Postdam Declaration 2 of 3

(10) We do not intend that the Japanese shall be enslaved as a race or destroyed as a nation, but stern justice shall be meted out to all war criminals, including those who have visited cruelties upon our prisoners. The Japanese Government shall remove all obstacles to the revival and strengthening of democratic tendencies among the Japanese people. Freedom of speech, of religion, and of thought, as well as respect for the fundamental human rights shall be established.

(11) Japan shall be permitted to maintain such industries as will sustain her economy and permit the exaction of just reparations in kind, but not those which would enable her to re-arm for war. To this end, access to, as distinguished from control of, raw materials shall be permitted. Eventual Japanese, participation in world trade relations shall be permitted.

(12) The occupying forces of the Allies shall be withdrawn from Japan as soon as these objectives have been accomplished and there has been established in accordance with the freely expressed will of the Japanese people a peacefully inclined and responsible government.

(13) We call upon the government of Japan to proclaim now the unconditional surrender of all Japanese armed forces, and to provide proper and adequate assurances of their good faith in such action. The alternative for Japan is prompt and utter destruction.

The Postdam Declaration 3 of 3

Years later, in a Washington, D.C., interview, Captain Coleman described it this way: "I thought that our role was the most delicate in the whole setup. If the U.S. was going to provide defense counsel, the U.S. must see to it that it was the best defense available. If we sent people to defend our enemies and they did a bum job, the good name of the U.S. in history would be marred."

Toward the end of April, Captain Coleman officially took over the position of chief defense counsel. There was still no concrete legal plan or even a sufficient number of attorneys to start the legal machinery. I tried to establish some kind of working order for our offices. Every few days, an American in uniform drifted in from some outfit stationed in Tokyo and became attached to the section. These drifters could hardly be said to constitute a legal staff. Eventually, we did have what could pass for a staff but it was always "not enough" of anything—lawyers, secretaries, clerks, copy machines, etc.

Talk centered on Indictment Day, the actual date the indictment would be delivered to the Class-A suspects who were to stand trial. The Japanese defendants needed court representation. However, for the moment, general legal issues had to be addressed.

The defense filed many routine motions and arguments questioning the Tribunal's jurisdiction over the accused. They raised cogent questions such as: "Was aggressive war a crime under international law? Did killing during the course of an aggressive war constitute murder? Were individuals responsible for acts formulated by heads of state?"

Each time an attorney went into action and presented his argument to the court, the hope was that the Tribunal would listen and react favorably. Unfortunately, the Tribunal never did.

Most of my available time was spent doing legal research. I was searching for precedent from the Nuremberg trials that could impact our defense of the Japanese. I was more eager and enthusiastic about this job than I had ever been about anything in my life. It was a wonderful opportunity to learn about the people of Japan and to understand the complex cultural and political differences that had escalated into a war with not only the United States, but all the other countries. Those eleven nations all had their own violent tales to tell.

In the Nuremberg trials, the defense counsel was German and the four prosecuting nations were England, France, the U.S., and

Russia. At this trial, eleven prosecuting nations from various areas had been victims of the Japanese expansionist war machine. The battles in China and the Philippines were the most well known.

Defense counsel included both Japanese and Americans. The Japanese legal system was neither Anglo-Saxon nor Continental; I honestly did not know what form it took. Most of the Japanese attorneys were unfamiliar with the procedures followed by the courts and countries of the prosecuting nations. Even though many of the leading Japanese lawyers had been educated in America and Europe, they had not continued practicing Western-style law after returning to Japan. The passing of years and lack of practice tended to dispel the legal training they had gathered abroad.

To insure a fair trial, guidance from the Allied nations was essential. General MacArthur and the acting president of the Tribunal, Justice Northcroft, recognized this immediately.

Earlier, at the trials of Generals Yamashita and Homma in Manila, the Philippines War Crimes Commission had consisted of five generals—no lawyers. The American defense counsel, all from the military ranks, sincerely and earnestly carried out their assigned tasks. Despite their efforts, however, Yamashita and Homma were quickly found guilty and sentenced to death by hanging. At the International Tribunal, we planned a trial of much greater scope and inquiry, not simply a trial about battlefield and civilian atrocities.

Mr. Saburo Ohta, from the Liaison Office that helped to bridge the gap between the defendants and the Americans authorities, made the first request for the presence of Allied attorneys in a letter addressed to the clerk of the International Military Tribunal for the Far East.

Serving as the temporary president of the Tribunal, Justice Northcroft of New Zealand approved the suggestions of Mr. Ohta. General MacArthur concurred with Justice Northcroft's recommendation for the presence of American counsel. These letters are reproduced from the official records of the IMTFE.

APO 500
March 15, 1946

General Douglas MacArthur
Supreme Commander for the Allied Powers

25

Tokyo, Japan

Dear General MacArthur:

Mr. S. Ohta of the Central Liaison Office, Imperial Japanese Government, acting in behalf of Japanese suspects who expect to be indicted and tried as major war criminals, appeared at a conference of the Judges of the International Military Tribunal for the Far East now in Tokyo to present certain requests for the services of British and American lawyers to be associated with Japanese counsel for the defendants in the forthcoming trials.

The suggestion of Mr. Ohta that the services of American or British lawyers, in association with the Japanese lawyers representing the defendants, will be necessary to an adequate defense and a fair and impartial trial of those accused is in accord with the views of the members of the Tribunal that all reasonable facilities be made available to defendants for their adequate defense and fair trial. We consider the request for American and British lawyers as a reasonable one that should be granted.

The splendid record of American lawyers who have served in various CApacities in previous trials of war criminals and the practical difficulties presented in securing British lawyers lead us to the conclusion that the appointment of lawyers from the United States will substantially satisfy the request for Anglo-Saxon counsel and the reasons urged in support thereof.

The Judges therefore suggest that American counsel be made available in Tokyo to meet the need for supplementing the Japanese counsel for the accused by Anglo-Saxon counsel and that it is desirable these counsel arrive in Tokyo at the earliest possible date to avoid undue delay. I, therefore, request that as soon as possible you set in motion the machinery necessary to gather together lawyers of suitable experience and qualifications who may be provided to Japanese defendants. An appropriate number should be secured to furnish at least one American lawyer for each defendant to be tried.

Yours sincerely,
E H P Acting President
Mr. Justice E. H. Northcroft

GENERAL HEADQUARTERS
SUPREME COMMANDER FOR THE ALLIED POWERS

19 March 1946
Dear Mr. Justice Northcroft:

The suggestion of Mr. Ohta that British and American lawyers be associated with Japanese counsel to defend major Japanese war criminals charged before the International Military Tribunal for the Far East has my full approval.

The administrative and transportation problem will be much simplified by obtaining personnel for this purpose from the United States. To that end and to avoid delay, on February 21, 1946, the Judge Advocate General's Department in Washington was requested to select from Army, Navy, or civilian personnel fifteen-to-twenty attorneys of suitable experience and qualifications to act as a panel from which might be drawn by selection or by Court appointment counsel for defendants charged. On March 7, 1946, the Judge Advocate General's Department in Washington was requested to select from Army, Navy, or civilian personnel fifteen-to-twenty attorneys of suitable experience and qualifications to act as panel from which might be drawn by selection or by Court appointment counsel for defendants charged. On March 7, 1946, the Judge Advocate General's Department advised that arrangements were being made to send fifteen defense attorneys, principally civilians, sufficient military personnel not being available.

Today a requisition has gone to the Judge Advocate General in Washington to increase from fifteen to twenty-five the number of lawyers to be sent, they to be of suitable experience and qualifications to assure the Japanese defendants proper representation and adequate defense. Appropriate travel priority will be provided to insure the presence of these attorneys in Tokyo at the earliest possible moment.

Sincerely yours,
DOUGLAS MACARTHUR

These letters contained the promise that an adequate crew of attorneys would be appointed. On April 5, 1946, in the first memorandum issued from the Office of the General Secretary, the Defense Division was officially established:

1. The Defense Division to provide Allied counsel to the major war criminals at the forthcoming trials is this date established in the secretariat of the International Military Tribunal for the Far East.
2. The chief defense counsel will be in charge of the Defense Division. He will be responsible for control and administration of the Defense Division and for coordination of Allied and Japanese defense counsels.

On April 22nd, in his second memorandum, the general secretary officially designated Navy Captain Coleman as chief defense counsel. On April 29, 1946, (in the courthouse of the Tribunal) the indictment was lodged against twenty-eight of the Japanese suspects. This was the day their enemies announced to them and to the world what crimes they believed these individuals had committed. All the research done by those attorneys working for the prosecution was rolled into that document. Once an indictment was lodged with the court, it carried with it the belief that each defendant could be convicted of the charges.

The crimes charged:

1. Crimes Against Peace—defined as the planning, preparation, initiation, or waging of a declared or undeclared war of aggression, or a war in violation of international law, treaties, agreements, or assurances, or participation in a common plan or conspiracy for the accomplishment of any of the foregoing. Conventional war crimes were defined as violations of the laws or customs of war.

2. Murder—defined as individual defendants named in different counts. Several were named in Count 39—the "Pearl Harbor Count" for ordering the attack on the United States in which about 4,000 members of the Army and Navy were unlawfully killed and Americans were murdered.

When the indictment was lodged, Joseph Keenan, the chief prosecutor, issued a press statement: *"But it is high time, and indeed was so before this war began, that the promoters of aggressive, ruthless war and treaty breakers should be stripped of the glamour of national heroes and exposed as what they really are—plain ordinary murderers."*

3. Conventional War Crimes and Crimes Against Humanity— Crimes Against Humanity consisted of murder, extermination, enslavement, deportation, and other inhumane acts committed before or during the war, or persecutions on political or racial grounds in execution of or in connection with any crime within the jurisdiction of the Tribunal, whether or not in violation of the domestic law of the country where perpetrated. Leaders, organizers, instigators, and accomplices participating in the formulation or execution of a common plan or conspiracy to commit any of the foregoing crimes are responsible for all acts performed by any person in execution of such plan.

General Headquarters of Allied Forces, Tokyo

The attorneys already on the scene knew how sweeping the charges were. The concept of trying the leaders of a fallen nation cast an awesome responsibility upon these lawyers. They knew that there was a reason for calling the Tribunals the site of the Class-A trials while Class-B and C trials were proceeding in Yokohama with the objective of bringing to justice the actual wrongdoers in the fields—the ones who participated in the killing, pillaging, raping and torturing of soldiers and civilians. Although five of the twenty-eight accused were not yet in Tokyo, all were in custody. Three of them were in the Malayan area; one was in Bangkok, and one in Manila.

The indictment named four former premiers, three former foreign ministers, four former war ministers, two former Navy ministers, six former generals, two former ambassadors, three former economic and financial leaders, one Imperial advisor, one totally radical theorist, and one colonel. What a variety of wrongdoers, I thought.

The prosecution was pressing for a speedy arraignment, while the defense, through Captain Coleman, submitted its application requesting that the date for taking the pleas of guilty or not guilty be no earlier than two weeks after the filing of the indictment. He further requested the defendants be permitted to enter pleas when they were arraigned, while reserving the right to amend their pleas and make applications and motions attacking the indictment. I was proud to show off my skills as I transcribed the words of my very important boss.

CHAPTER 3 ~ TRIBUNAL GETS STARTED

The Defense Section had its problems and troubles from the first day of the indictment, as the accused were represented by a meager total of six counsel and three secretaries. In actuality, a legal staff of thirty attorneys and fifty secretarial assistants was probably the minimum number required to adequately perform this job.

The Japanese attorneys were completely disorganized. Security regulations at Sugamo Prison severely restricted communication between the Japanese attorneys and the accused. The American defense counsel was impeded in their interviews and conferences by the ever-present language barrier. This barrier was equally detrimental in the attempts by the Americans to confer with their Japanese legal counterparts.

My admiration for Commander Harris grew each time I heard him speaking with any of the Japanese attorneys. I was determined to learn at least enough Japanese to enable me to be helpful to the attorneys who knew no English at all. There were also basic differences of understanding between the Americans and the Japanese as to the meaning of certain legal issues. All of this severely compromised the early days of the trial and prevented the growth of mutual understanding between the Japanese and American legal teams. Yet progress was slowly made.

As the trial advanced, the frequent and unjustified criticism of the American attorneys was a constant source of irritation to me. Here was a group of legal minds acting in accordance with the highest tenets of their profession, yet time and time again they were plagued with derogatory remarks emanating from both the home front and their associates in the Tokyo area. "How can you defend those Japs?" or "What kind of an American are you?" were a few of the ripostes they endured.

This attitude saddened me greatly. These Japanese on trial were clients. Most lay persons know something about the relationship attorneys develop with their clients once the attorney agrees to be that person's lawyer. Criticism only took away time and energy to answer the somewhat nasty remarks, energy and time that must necessarily be devoted to the task at hand—defending their clients.

American lawyers were impassioned in the representation of their clients, and on more than one occasion would be chastised by the Tribunal judges for being too vigorous in their defense of the Japanese. The trial's early days were chaotic for both sides. The American counsel requested a delay in the proceedings to have more time to study the indictment and get to know their clients. They also needed time to confer with their Japanese colleagues and prepare the appropriate motions.

These combined factors led to the defense's request that there be a minimum period of two weeks from the day of the indictment to that of the arraignment. Two weeks were not really enough time for a complete analysis of the indictment, but would allow the American and Japanese counsel a crucial opportunity for collaboration and discussion prior to the arraignment, which would be the day the charges were read aloud and each defendant asked to plead guilty or not guilty.

In response to this request, the prosecution urged that the issue of arraignment was a simple determination of whether or not the defendants wished to stand trial or plead guilty. The prosecution contended that the defense would have ample time to present any motions or applications to the court. However, the presiding judge directed the prosecution to serve copies of the indictment and charter on each of the accused, and fixed Friday, May 3, 1946, at 10:30 a.m. as "the time and place when the accused will plead to the charges in the indictment."

The night before the opening session of the International Military Tribunal for the Far East (IMTFE), I worked until 11:15 p.m. and was back in the office at 7:15 a.m. preparing the documents to be read in court. I had little understanding then of what those documents said or meant or even if they were important; but I knew my curiosity would help me find out as time went on.

On May 3, 1946, with the glamour and artistry of a Hollywood premiere, the trial was underway. The Japanese and Allied spectator's sections were filled to capacity. Newsreel and still cameramen were placed at vantage points throughout the courtroom while reporters were confined to a special reserved section.

The courtroom

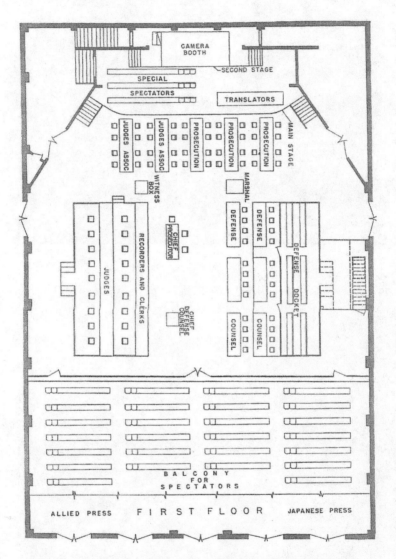

Diagram of the courtroom at Ichigaya. It was about 100 feet in length, with separate sections for the defendants, their attorneys, the prosecutors, translators, press, spectators, and of course the eleven judges.

The accused coming to court: General Doihara, Marquis Kido,
Okinora Kaya, General Anami, Admirals Shimada and Nagano,
Premier Koiso and General Tojo are among the defendants.

The marshal of the court called loudly for order and silence as the accused were led into the courtroom guarded by a host of military police. The judges ascended to the bench in solemn dignity. The four Japanese interpreters entered with their American chief. As a team of court reporters signaled their readiness, the IMTFE was called to attention. The overhead lights burned brightly. The spectators filled their section. Lawyers filled the well of the courtroom, and court reporters sat ready to come in for their shift, much like a relay team handing the baton to the next in line.

Justices of the Tribunal

Before pleas could be heard from the defendants, there was the translation of the chief judge's speech, which was an instruction that the time had come for them to plead guilty or not guilty to the indictment with which they had been served.

Baron Sadao Araki received the dubious honor of answering first. In days gone by, the Baron had been a four-star general in the Japanese Army and an education minister, famous for his long and eloquent speeches. Instead of pleading "guilty" or "not guilty," the baron commenced a dramatic speech in Japanese that was immediately cut short by President Webb's stern rebuke, "We want a plea—not a speech."

Justice William Webb looked as though he could have been given the job of chief justice by central casting for a Hollywood movie. Big and gruff, sarcastic, acerbic, and arrogant, he ruled that courtroom. As Australian War Crimes Commissioner during the war, he had been involved in an investigation of Japanese atrocities in New Guinea. The defense's opinion was he should have recused himself. They were surprised to learn Justice Webb had in fact considered that, but decided his past service did not disqualify him. He felt he was totally eligible to serve.

Justice William Webb

A few of the accused answered their pleas in English. Japanese or English, the plea was always the same: "not guilty." The attention of the spectators was drawn to the former prime minister and general, Hideki Tojo, as he awaited his turn at the microphone. General Tojo enjoyed more celebrity stature than any other defendant. To the Japanese, he was the most colorful figure of their generation and he was also well-known to the American public. Tojo's place was directly in the center of the double-rowed prisoner's dock on the lower level.

**General Hideki Tojo pleading to the indictment
at the time of the arraignment of the accused**

Immediately above Tojo sat Dr. Shumei Okawa, who was labeled by the prosecution as the Japanese Goebbels. The doctor was suffering from the effects of a severe case of syphilis, which had affected his brain to the extent of preventing appropriate behavior. He alternately crossed and uncrossed his legs as he attempted to fold them under his emaciated body in true Japanese fashion. He buttoned and unbuttoned his shirt, scratched his body, clasped his hands in prayer, wept, laughed and then climaxed his actions by reaching over and slapping General Tojo on the head. He grinned, looked around to see if his performance was appreciated, then delivered a second slap. One less defendant was in the dock when Dr. Okawa was finally removed from the courtroom.

As the trial progressed, day after day was filled with tedious translations, legal motions, objections to testimony, witnesses to atrocities, lessons in history, presentations of motions, and a myriad of legalese as expected in a trial of this magnitude.

To the Japanese, the spotlight of the opening day lay in the hands of the boyish ensign who headed the language section. David Hornstein was from the Seattle, Washington, area, and only twenty-two years old. His position held enormous power, as he was in charge of all of the interpreters. The Yomiuri Shimbun Daily Newspaper of May 4th printed an impressive article entitled, "Conductor of the Tribunal Orchestra is a Handsome Red-Headed Youth."

> ...As it is, in this Tribunal, the real power of Mr. Hornstein is reigning supreme. Even Sir William and Chief Prosecutor Keenan fix, at all times, their eyes upon each and every movement of the tip of the pencil gripped in his right-hand fingers and have to address him. Whenever the speaking comes to a pause, the tip of his pencil gives the command to stop. Then and there. The tip of the pencil is pointed at the face of the Japanese interpreters and the English speech is interpreted into Japanese. When it is finished the tip is again directed toward Sir William and Mr. Keenan to go on with the proceedings. The great actor in this historical and dramatic scene of the age is neither Sir William Webb, nor Chief Prosecutor Keenan. The role is played by this young and handsome red-haired youth, and the tip of his pencil dictates to the orchestra of the Tribunal as if it were the baton.

The court was in session for three days just to complete the reading of the indictment, the entry of pleas, the hearing of preliminary motions and the dispensing of procedural matters. A recess was taken to allow the defense an organization period before the actual presentation of evidence.

At this point, the defense began to understand the complexity of the task that lay ahead. The charter of the IMTFE, as established by proclamation of the supreme commander on January 19, 1946, and amended on April 26, 1946, provided for the just and prompt trial and punishment of the major war criminals in the Far East. Among other things, it stated that each accused "shall have the right to be represented by counsel of his own selection, subject to the disapproval of such counsel at any time by the Tribunal." Each accused had to designate in writing which attorney he wished to retain.

Captain Coleman attempted to present an application to obtain more time during the two-week delay between indictment and arraignment, but Sir William Webb denied him a hearing on the grounds he had not been retained in writing by any of the accused. Therefore, he had no standing in court. As soon as the other American counsel recognized this as a harbinger of things to come, they immediately raced to Sugamo Prison and had the accused "sign them up" on a temporary retainer basis. The next day, Captain Coleman did the same thing and was retained as joint counsel to several of the defendants so that the Tribunal would hear him. This process paralleled the procedures in the courts at home. The court had to know whether a defendant had selected a particular lawyer to serve as counsel.

Technically, the Tribunal was following the correct procedure, but it did not seem fair to place the attorneys under such time pressures with all the other problems they faced. The constant argument was, "What difference would one or two weeks make in the overall scheme of things?" This was going to be a long trial, so why create so much pressure from day one?

Justice William Webb

No one knew where they stood. The captain protested against this legal fiction of a client-attorney relationship, which he felt could not be satisfactorily explained to either the Japanese counsel or the accused, and which did not guarantee recognition of the legal standing of the Defense Division. He felt the charter should be amended to place the defense on a level comparable to that of the prosecution; thus making his appointment as chief counsel legally valid.

This did not make sense to some of the attorneys, as there was no way to compare the prosecution's job to that of the defense. The prosecutors could all unite in doing their job, which was to present evidence and obtain convictions. The defense's job was to advocate the innocence of the individual client represented by the client's attorney. This made a unified approach impossible, since each defendant's activities were those of that individual defendant. Each lawyer had to separate his client and his client's activities from those of the other defendants. It seemed as if each defense counsel was willing to suggest that some other defendants might have acted badly, but not the client he was representing.

The Tribunal vetoed the request for Captain Coleman to function as chief defense counsel because it would violate the fundamental right of every accused person to have counsel of his own choice. On May 13, the order establishing the Defense Division and announcing the appointment of a chief defense counsel was rescinded. It was then recommended, that the defense be established as a separate staff section under the supreme commander. That tactic did not work either.

The defense attorneys quickly developed "defense complexes." They felt like stepchildren, lost in technicalities and feeling unwanted. In these particular circumstances, the reluctance of the Tribunal to grant defense counsel "real credentials" was understandable. The Tribunal did not want to be connected with either prosecution or defense because they were the judges appointed to try the case.

Justices of the Military Tribunal

General MacArthur refused to claim the defense attorneys to be part of his command as he was the reviewing authority and had to remain completely neutral. The end result was an attachment to the Legal Section of the Supreme Commander for the Allied Powers for purposes of administration only. Captain Coleman was designated to represent the defense attorneys in all matters pertaining to their administration. "Administration only" meant exactly that and provided no answer to the captain's contention that some central authority was necessary for the defense staff to function as a solid unit.

The defense attorneys

On May 17th, the much-awaited group of defense attorneys arrived from the States only to be immediately caught up in a round of meetings. These dealt more with organizational and procedural matters than with the legal motions that had to be presented when court reconvened. As personalities clashed and factions developed, no assignments of client to attorney were undertaken. One group wanted to have a nominal head take the lead and direct the energies of the others. On the opposite side were those who favored the present arrangement, which resembled the "Keystone Cops" of early movie days. Everyone was a general and there were no privates. Throughout this chaos, correspondence flowed fast and furiously between our office, the general secretary, the Legal Section, and General MacArthur.

Amidst this litany of assorted troubles, the court reopened on the morning of June 3, 1946, with a slow parade of judges to their seats in a pseudo dignity that lacked only a funeral-march accompaniment. Fierce klieg lights burned continuously overhead so that even with the darkest of sunglasses, headaches and eyestrain ensued day after day.

Although the weather was still moderate and pleasant, the heat generated by the lights was almost unbearable. Adding to the physical discomfort was the tremendous obstacle of the language barrier, which hindered the orderly presentation of the proceedings. (It was infinitely worse than at Nuremberg, for contemporaneous translation in Japanese was impossible.) The language officers often took five minutes of earnest debate to translate a phrase from English to Japanese. This problem plagued all parties concerned throughout the trial.

Accurate translation was vital to a fair trial. A familiar expression became "Observe the red light." As a sentence was delivered in English, the red light flashed, which meant an immediate halt for translation whether or not the sentence was completed.

The first day's proceedings saw the introduction to the court of American counsel, the presentation of preliminary motions and the reading of the prosecution's opening statement. In the weeks preceding this, separate and distinct from the personnel battles that had raged, was the human side of the joint endeavors of the Japanese and American meetings with the defendants in a quest to understand what this trial was all about.

At that time, the names of the twenty-eight defendants (with the exception of General Tojo) and the roles they had played in governing

Japan were all unfamiliar to me. However, I was determined to acquire any and all available knowledge. Perhaps I was unconsciously seeking to justify my role as a legal secretary for the defense. My relationship with the accused intensified as the trial continued.

We all quickly developed strong loyalties to our clients. Even at this early stage, defense attorneys began to vigorously defend their clients' actions and take issue with anyone who did not share their belief in their particular client's innocence. By asking questions and indulging my natural curiosity, I soon discovered plenty of information about the accused and their crimes.

I had heard about the Japanese atrocities in China. Thus, it was no surprise to learn that one of the defendants was Kenji Doihara. He had been commander-in-chief of the Japanese Fifth Army in Manchuria (1938-40). I had no idea how many armies the Japanese had, but I knew they had fought in China for many years.

General Doihara was always stern looking and a loner. In the book The Other Nuremberg by Arnold Brackman, General Doihara was described:

> *From his early days as a military officer, he was a master of intrigue, terrorism, and clandestine operations. Doihara was also deeply involved in the Army's drug trafficking in Manchuria. Later he ran brutal POW and Internee camps in Malaya, Sumatra, Java, and Borneo.*

His attorneys would have an immense amount of work to do in preparing his defense; since the crimes of which he was accused had taken place in more than one country, more than one judge would be very attentive to the testimony presented by the prossecurors.

I knew the Japanese emperor was an object of reverence and worship by his subjects. Although the leader of his country, he was not one of those sitting in the dock. But the man known as his advisor, Koichi Kido, was a bureaucrat with a title that seemed familiar from the operetta, *The Mikado*. He was the Lord Keeper of the Privy Seal.

Kido was mentioned frequently. The Japanese had burned so many official documents it seemed there was no way to reconstruct the history of the many years the indictment spanned, except for one jewel among the rubble. The 5,000-page Kido diary was the source of most of the information upon which the prosecution relied. The diary was meticulously kept by Marquis Kido from 1930-45 and had 5,920 entries-a prosecutor's dream, containing names, dates, and locations of almost every political decision.

Kido voluntarily offered the diary to the prosecutors shortly after his arrest. There was no statement explaining why he did this, but some speculation was that he believed it would prove that the country had been in the grip of the militarists over whose actions the emperor had no control. Who knows? Surely at this time, none of the American defense attorneys had a clue.

The frailest defendant and the most kindly in appearance was Mamoru Shigemitsu, the foreign minister from 1943 to 1945. He was the Japanese man seen pictured signing the surrender documents on the U.S.S. Missouri. He was attired in a top hat and formal suit, struggling to navigate on one leg. (Some years before, he lost a leg in a bombing incident in Shanghai.)

Shigemitsu did not appear threatening, nor did Shigenori Togo. He, too, was another career diplomat who had held posts as ambassador to Germany and ambassador to Russia. He had a German wife. Later in the trial, we learned of his importance in the negotiations preceding the attack on Pearl Harbor.

In addition, there were Generals Muto and Sato. Sato had been chief of the War Ministry from 1942 to 1944 and Muto had held the same position from 1939 to 1942. General Muto had been a commander in the field in the Dutch East-Indies and the Philippines. Both men had a certain vigor to them and seemed quite approachable. As I came to know them, I liked them to the point that they were some of my favorite clients.

The Japanese Navy had three defendants: Osami Nagano, Takasumi Oka, and Shigetaro Shimada. All three had been admirals and chiefs of the Navy General Staff at different times. I came to know these men when later on I worked for John Brannon, the American attorney defending these Japanese Navy admirals.

I was puzzled at the indictment of so many military men. I had not thought this was a trial to find out who had committed atrocities. I did not know then how much power the military men had with the various cabinets that rose and fell. Our clients were some of those military men.

There was one career diplomat—Koki Hirota—who seemed out of place. Once he had David Smith as his American lawyer, it was difficult to know why he had been indicted in the first place. Smith stood up for Hirota and fought with the court so voraciously that Smith was eventually barred from appearing.

The defendant who seemed the most arrogant was Hiroshi Oshima, who had been ambassador to Germany. Picturing him sitting down with Hitler, I instantly disliked him.

Ambassador Hirota

A few of the defendants seemed very old. Others seemed to have a ferocious appearance, or maybe that was in my imagination, having heard of the samurai warriors of old. I wanted to picture them once more as commanders, chiefs, and generals. How different they must have looked when physically fit and wearing their uniforms or their best diplomatic suits! In the courtroom, dressed in cast-off clothing or uniforms that sagged on their wasted bodies, they did not look particularly formidable. In fact, the majority of these defendants appeared rather docile.

The American attorney, George Blewett from Philadelphia, was first assigned to defend General Tojo. Returning from an interview with the general, he said that Tojo may have been a "wrong guy" from our point of view, but nevertheless he was a tremendously impressive person. Blewett's opinion was unanimously shared. Anyone who spent time with Tojo could see that he was a person of unusual accomplishments and a physical presence that commanded respect.

Seated as he was in the center of the prisoner's dock, Tojo's poise and self-confidence drew great attention during the preliminary court sessions, even up to the very end. He was always alert, focusing with intense concentration and constantly writing notes.

The courtroom with Kiyose at the mike

Court convened each morning at 9:30. The accused were brought to the War Ministry Building an hour earlier to allow time for conferences with their attorneys. One of my responsibilities was to report to the holding room at the War Ministry Building to ascertain if the men wished to see their attorneys before the first session. This daily procedure that had been broached at a meeting of the defense attorneys suggested that my doing this would save the attorneys a lot of time.

When the time came to put names with the pictures and convey to these clients that I was there to help them, fortune smiled on me. The military police were charged with guarding the accused and their chief was Colonel Aubrey Kenworthy, a career Army officer who had been on duty in the Philippines. He had been, in fact, present at the surrender of General Yamashita. I had seen the colonel in the courtroom. He looked

47

stern and stood very straight. However, looks can be deceiving. He had been with the prisoners since they were first housed at Sugamo Prison, and he seemed to know each of the men by name.

When I walked into the room, he immediately asked how he could help me. I told him I was there to find out which of the men wanted to confer with their attorneys, to see whether they needed anything and, if they did, what all I could do for them without breaking any rules. Somehow the atmosphere in the holding room was relaxed; these men were not going anywhere, so why make life difficult? Many times I walked in and they were playing the Japanese board game "Go."

Becoming friends with Colonel Kenworthy was meaningful to me because he was such a decent human being with a huge heart. I was careful not to barge into the holding room, always waiting for the colonel to welcome me. I learned so much from him on my visits and in the dining room where I was allowed to have lunch. We almost always sat together. I had fun because he loved to gossip about all the little intrigues going on in the War Ministry Building. He knew which female was dating which soldier, which judge was cranky, or which one loved the party scene. He always made some mention of a family member's visit to the accused.

Colonel Kenworthy (center) with Meyer Levin (left) and Teichi Suzuki (right)

**From left to right: Hirota, Togo, Tojo, and Sato. The accused ate lunch
with large spoons so they could not hurt themselves.**

I came to know each of these clients on a personal basis.
Typically, they rushed to me the minute I walked into their room and
hurriedly said, "bengoshi hoshii. (I want my lawyer.)" At that time I
could not speak a word of Japanese, but one of the accused who knew
English was always there to help me out. It was most difficult when I
could not make myself understood. I knew I needed to learn enough
Japanese to solve this problem.

The attorneys did not want anyone to feel they were not always
available. Many times when I went looking for an attorney whose client
wanted a meeting, I could not find him. That meant apologizing and
reassuring the client. But, before the day was over, they met.

As I learned enough Japanese to understand what I was being
asked, communication became less of an issue. I remember finally feeling so good when I could be of real service, not just to the clients, but
to their Japanese attorneys.

After a few weeks, I knew each prisoner by name, face, and
personality. As the first American female they associated with on the
defense panel, I was the recipient of many courtesies and acts of kindness from the defendants, their families, and their Japanese lawyers.

At first it was exciting to be face to face with these infamous men (on whom so much attention was being focused), but after a while it was simply part of my job.

The day following the arraignment of the defendants, Okawa (the civilian propagandist who was famous as the "Tojo head-slapper") was committed to an institution for examination by Japanese and American psychiatrists. And on June 27, Yosuke Matsuoka, the American-educated statesman who had engineered Japan's participation in the Tripartite Pact, died of tuberculosis. He had said, "Let them hang me if they want to, but I cannot stand the trial." He had appeared to be the most virulent hater of the Americans. Upon his death, all charges against him were dropped, which led us to jokingly say, "Well, we got one man off anyway." The original twenty-eight became twenty-six.

During the preliminary weeks of the trial, the defense busily engaged in research on Japanese history, religion, national policy, and analysis of the indictment as it pertained to the individual defendants. The indictment covered a period from 1928 to 1945, during which time many Japanese political cabinets had come and gone. Several of the defendants had not participated in the early years, yet they were being charged as members of a conspiracy covering the whole period, including the many years when they were not upon the scene. I wanted to learn more about the law of "conspiracy" to better understand the indictment.

The court recessed following the arraignment and before the taking of evidence. The Japanese counsel were familiar with the factual situation, but they had no idea what would or would not be acceptable to the Tribunal. A Japanese lawyer proposed to the Tribunal that Gandhi, the Pope, George Bernard Shaw, and other "spiritual leaders" should be consulted regarding the morality of the trial and interpretation of international law.

One of the American attorneys proposed a defense that would include aspects of the Shinto religion, the Meiji Restoration, Japan's emergence into Twentieth Century civilization, Admiral Perry and the opening of trade, the weapons of modern war in the hands of the followers of bushido, as well as the distinction between the German trials and that of the Japanese.

Unlike the Germans, the Japanese were ignorant of the way other nations conducted their legal cases. They did not realize the defense would focus more on an explanation of the crimes charged rather than a denial of wrongdoing.

There was a lot of discussion about General MacArthur's lack of jurisdiction and whether an American general had the authority to set up an eleven-nation court. There was talk of a suit to enjoin him and to have the American judge removed. One argument suggested that MacArthur had exceeded his authority in appointing the court, because not all the participating nations were party to the Potsdam Declaration, nor were they all signatories to the Surrender Agreement of September 2, 1945. Further, they were not under his military jurisdiction or command.

The Potsdam Declaration had been issued on July 26, 1945, at 7 p.m. At 9:30 p.m., it was radioed to Japan. The United States, China, and the United Kingdom signed the Declaration, which called for the unconditional surrender of Japan. The Soviet Union was not party to the Declaration, which did not matter, as this was a prelude to the ending of the war. I acquired a duplicate of the original Instrument of Surrender, which is reproduced here:

THE INSTRUMENT OF SURRENDER

We hereby undertake for the Emperor, the Japanese Government and their successors to carry out the provisions of the Potsdam Declaration in good faith and to issue whatever orders and take whatever action may be required by the Supreme Commander for the Allied Powers or by any other designated representative of the Allied Powers for the purpose of giving effect to that Declaration.

INSTRUMENT OF SURRENDER

We, acting by command of and in behalf of the Emperor of Japan, the Japanese Government and the Japanese Imperial General Headquarters, hereby accept the provisions set forth in the declaration issued by the heads of the Governments of the United States, China and Great Britain on 26 July 1945, at Potsdam, and subsequently adhered to by the Union of Soviet Socialist Republics, which four powers are hereafter referred to as the Allied Powers.

We hereby proclaim the unconditional surrender to the Allied Powers of the Japanese Imperial General Headquarters and of all Japanese armed forces and all armed forces under Japanese control wherever situated.

We hereby command all Japanese forces wherever situated and the Japanese people to cease hostilities forthwith, to preserve and save from damage all ships, aircraft, and military and civil property and to comply with all requirements which may be imposed by the Supreme Commander for the Allied Powers or by agencies of the Japanese Government at his direction.

We hereby command the Japanese Imperial General Headquarters to issue at once orders to the Commanders of all Japanese forces and all forces under Japanese control wherever situated to surrender unconditionally themselves and all forces under their control.

We hereby command all civil, military and naval officials to obey and enforce all proclamations, orders and directives deemed by the Supreme Commander for the Allied Powers to be proper to effectuate this surrender and issued by him or under his authority and we direct all such officials to remain at their posts and to continue to perform their non-combatant duties unless specifically relieved by him or under his authority.

We hereby undertake for the Emperor, the Japanese Government and their successors to carry out the provisions of the Potsdam Declaration in good faith, and to issue whatever orders and take whatever action may be required by the Supreme Commander for the Allied Powers or by any other designated representative of the Allied Powers for the purpose of giving effect to that Declaration.

We hereby command the Japanese Imperial Government and the Japanese Imperial General Headquarters at once to liberate all allied prisoners of war and civilian internees now under Japanese control and to provide for their protection, care, maintenance and immediate transportation to places as directed.

The authority of the Emperor and the Japanese Government to rule the state shall be subject to the Supreme Commander for the Allied Powers who will take such steps as he deems proper to effectuate these terms of surrender.

Instrument of Surrender (1 of 6)

PROCLAMATION

Accepting the terms set forth in Declaration issued
by the heads of the Governments of the United States, Great
Britain and China on July 26th, 1945 at Potsdam and subsequently adhered to by the Union of Soviet Socialist Republics,
We have commanded the Japanese Imperial Government and the
Japanese Imperial General Headquarters to sign on Our behalf
the Instrument of Surrender presented by the Supreme Commander
for the Allied Powers and to issue General Orders to the
Military and Naval Forces in accordance with the direction
of the Supreme Commander for the Allied Powers. We command
all Our people forthwith to cease hostilities, to lay down
their arms and faithfully to carry out all the provisions
of Instrument of Surrender and the General Orders issued by
the Japanese Imperial Government and the Japanese Imperial
General Headquarters hereunder.

This second day of the ninth month of the twentieth
year of Syowa.

Mamoru Shigemitsu
Minister for Foreign Affairs

Iwao Yamazaki
Minister for Home Affairs

Juichi Tsushima
Minister of Finance

Sadzu Shimomura
Minister of War

Mitsumasa Yonai
Minister of Navy

Chuzo Iwata
Minister of Justice

Tamon Maeda
Minister of Education

Kehzo Matsumura
Minister of Welfare

Kotaro Sengoku
Minister of Agriculture
and Forestry

Chikuhei Nakajima
Minister of Commerce
and Industry

Naoto Kobiyama
Minister of Transportation

Fumimaro Konoe
Minister without Portofolio

Takstora Ogata
Minister without Portofolio

Binshiro Obata
Minister without Portofolio

Seal of
the
Emperor

Signed: HIROHITO

Countersigned: Naruhiko-õ
Prime Minister

Instrument of Surrender (2 of 6)

53

Signed at TOKYO BAY, JAPAN at 09+4. J
on the SECOND day of SEPTEMBER , 1945.

重光葵

By Command and in behalf of the Emperor of Japan
and the Japanese Government.

梅津美治郎

By Command and in behalf of the Japanese
Imperial General Headquarters.

Accepted at TOKYO BAY, JAPAN at 0908 I
on the SECOND day of SEPTEMBER , 1945,
for the United States, Republic of China, United Kingdom and the
Union of Soviet Socialist Republics, and in the interests of the other
United Nations at war with Japan.

Supreme Commander for the Allied Powers.

United States Representative

Republic of China Representative

United Kingdom Representative

Union of Soviet Socialist Republics
Representative

Commonwealth of Australia Representative

Dominion of Canada Representative

Provisional Government of the French
Republic Representative

Kingdom of the Netherlands Representative

Dominion of New Zealand Representative

Instrument of Surrender (3 of 6)

Translation.

H I R O H I T O ,

By the Grace of Heaven, Emperor of Japan, seated on the Throne occupied by the same Dynasty changeless through ages eternal,

To all to whom these Presents shall come, Greeting!

We do hereby authorise Mamoru Shigemitsu, Zyosanmi, First Class of the Imperial Order of the Rising Sun to attach his signature by command and in behalf of Ourselves and Our Government unto the Instrument of Surrender which is required by the Supreme Commander for the Allied Powers to be signed.

In witness whereof, We have hereunto set Our signature and caused the Great Seal of the Empire to be affixed.

Given at Our Palace in Tōkyō, this first day of the ninth month of the twentieth year of Syōwa, being the two thousand six hundred and fifth year from the Accession of the Emperor Zinmu.

Seal of the Empire

Signed: H I R O H I T O.

Countersigned: Naruhiko-ō
                Prime Minister

Instrument of Surrender (4 of 6)

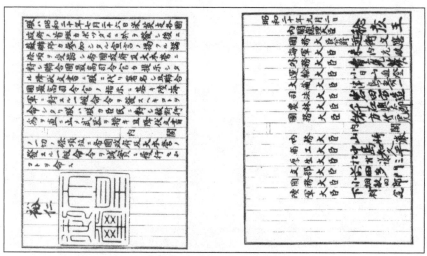

Instrument of Surrender (5 of 6)

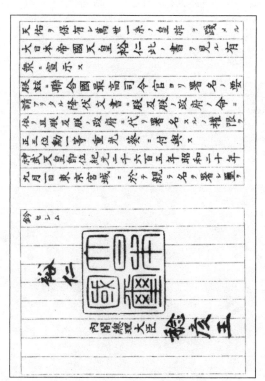

Instrument of Surrender (6 of 6)

Not being a lawyer, but armed with curiosity when attorneys spoke, I did a lot of listening. I was mostly curious to know about our clients and the American and Japanese attorneys.

My office was on the second floor near the rooms of the Japanese counsel. At the end of the corridor, the offices of the American attorneys had been hastily set up. Each attorney had to have his own office, if there was room. There was not always room. Sharing space was not to anyone's liking, but there were more important matters that took priority.

My office

The Japanese always entered my office, bowed, smiled and asked me questions. They never failed to compliment me on the slightest progress I displayed with my Japanese lessons, or to invite me to their homes for tea ceremonies or dinners to express their thanks and appreciation for my assistance. Sometimes I wondered if these people knew that the United States government was paying me to discharge certain duties. Their gratitude to me for simply doing my job led me to suspect that perhaps they thought that I worked for the defense because I was on their side.

I always tried to convey my appreciation in turn with appropriate sincerity and grace. I learned that the Japanese have respect for a person who fulfills their duties; I surely tried to fulfill mine.

I quickly saw that bowing was the correct way to greet a person in Japan. I took this custom seriously and learned to bow in the correct fashion. I appreciated the contrast with our shaking of hands. Bowing in return was an acceptance of a cultural tradition and a demonstration of an effort to adapt in basic ways to habits different from our own.

Ruth Benedict, the cultural anthologist who wrote a book on the patterns of Japanese culture called *The Chrysanthemum and the Sword* described the custom.

> *The wife bows to the husband, the child bows to his father, younger brothers bow to older brothers, and the sister bows to all her brothers of whatever age. It is no empty gesture. It means that the one who bows acknowledges the right of the other to have his way in things he might well prefer to manage himself; and the one who receives the bow acknowledges in his turn certain responsibilities incumbent upon his station.*

I was interested in many Japanese customs such as the tea ceremony, the flower arrangements, ikebana, the bonsai, tending of branches and trees, and the various seasonal ceremonies accompanying many of nature's rituals. I was moved by how my Japanese friends took time to educate me. The very least I could do in return was to demonstrate my appreciation by sharing their pride in these traditions.

To the newly arrived American attorneys, I became an old-timer to whom they often came with their troubles with Army "red tape." Everything was rationed and the men needed their "ration cards" for the Army Exchange (the PX). There were cards for eating, cards for identification, cards for living expenses, cards for Japanese money, and cards for obtaining clothes from the quartermaster, all of which I was supposed to miraculously produce.

I sincerely tried to increase my usefulness, continuing to learn from these attorneys as much as possible about the accused Japanese. The more knowledge I gained, the more useful I became to these men.

Almost within two or three weeks after their arrival, many of the defense lawyers were frequent visitors to Sugamo Prison. They returned with interesting tales about their clients. One day ten lawyers were in our office, each claiming his client was "a good boy in bad company" and "so-and-so" was the real culprit who had done such evil deeds and killed himself. He was to blame for everything.

These attorneys made it sound as if our clients were a group of angels, which led me to timidly ask, "Who started this war anyway?"

The unanimous answer was, "Well, my man didn't."

Amidst the interest and excitement, I was despondent that my boss, Captain Coleman, along with three of the civilian attorneys and two of the naval officers, had each filed resignations with the supreme commander. The major crisis revolved around divergent views on how the defense staff should be organized, administered and directed. I knew that this group, all of whom were the captain's friends, did not think the other lawyers were smart enough to mount an adequate defense. With no apparent solutions that could satisfy their moral and ethical dilemmas, these six men felt it better to resign before they undertook the obligation of defending one of the accused war criminals.

I do not think anyone from the defense, prosecution, or the Tribunal wanted to see them leave, but they could not be swayed from their decision. The newspaper reporters invaded the offices, but came out with little information; there was "no comment" from any of the men involved, no hard feelings, and nothing personal in their remarks. The only bright spot for me was Captain Coleman's suggestion that a farewell weekend be enjoyed by all of them and I was invited along.

Early Saturday morning, three jeeps holding seven of us headed for scenic Nikko, about ninety-two miles from Tokyo. After ten minutes on the bumpy and wretched Japanese roads, it felt more like 1,092 miles. However, we soon forgot our discomfort as we passed through the Japanese villages and the rice paddies that lined the way. It was a perfect picture of life as it might have been a thousand years ago.

The men had made reservations at a Japanese hotel located near the entrance to the shrine area. I was billeted at the Army Recreation Hotel up on the hill. My accommodations were set amidst glorious cryptomeria trees and overlooked a magnificent waterfall. Early the next day, we drove to Lake Chuzenji and went sightseeing. A 325-foot underground elevator took us to a perfect view of the Kegon Waterfall. The exquisite scenery soon made us forget the IMTFE back in Tokyo.

Kegon Waterfall

The next day we visited the famous 300-year-old Toshogu Shrine. Fifteen thousand men had worked for twelve years on this project. The carvings, gates, and statues had to be seen to be believed. In Japanese, the word "kekko" means "magnificent." One of their famous sayings is, "You can't say 'kekko' until you've seen Nikko." We all concurred with that saying as we journeyed back to Tokyo, merrily characterizing everything as "kekko."

A few days later the captain and his colleagues left, and I found myself looking for a new boss. He gave me an autographed picture that said, "With deep appreciation of your earnest and efficient work and loyal support during those trying weeks in Tokyo." I was happy I had done my job well enough to warrant the praise of such a fine person. I missed Captain Coleman and I was sad that this "dream" job had ended. Now what?

Note from Captain Coleman to Elaine

CHAPTER 4 ~FINALLY A DEFENSE TEAM

There were three Japanese lawyers seeking to represent the war criminal suspects, although they were not allowed to see any of them at Sugamo Prison unless they were indicted. They busied themselves battling the prosecution on general issues of international law, jurisdiction, and how the trial was to be conducted until such time as they acquired the status of counsel for one of the accused men.

These men were Dr. Ichiro Kiyose, Dr. Kenzo Takayanagi, and Dr. Somei Uzawa. Seeing them at work in their ill-fitting clothes and their mild demeanors, I found it hard to believe they were internationally recognized legal scholars. Dr. Kiyose had been a member of the Japanese Parliament; Dr. Uzawa was a professor and president of Meiji University; and Dr. Takayangi had studied at Harvard and was considered a superb lawyer.

All three lawyers were quoted in the Japanese press. Dr. Kiyose said General Tojo's case was considered defensible; it was not possible to hold one individual or a group of individuals responsible for a conflict as wide as the war just concluded.

I wrote to my mother: "*Dr. Kiyose is so tiny and frail I always want to mother him.*"

The Japanese attorneys were always so polite to me and thankful for any favor I could accomplish at their request. If you looked at our clients as they sat in the dock in the courtroom, they did not resemble in any way the kind of powerful or stern men who once led a nation.

As I began to have more regular contact with the prisoners, I found them to be almost deferential and, to my surprise, likable, even defendable, as Dr. Kiyose said. As lawyers joined the staff and began to have contact with their clients, they voiced similar sentiments. Despite the grueling war that had just ended, all of us found reasons for justifying the behavior of these former leaders.

My mother, close family, and friends back in the States could not understand my sympathy for the prisoners or the friendships I began to enjoy with their families.

When I wrote to my sister, I went out of my way to impress her with the informality of my contacts with these former leaders. In retrospect, I did not want my family to feel that I had been carried away by the positions these men once held in their government.

Had to interrupt this letter to take some Japanese attorneys down to see the defendants. They love me there because these men are all the time screaming, 'I've got to see my lawyer' or words to that effect, and I try to round up the lawyers and take them down there. Tojo and I exchanged the old greeting, "Ohayo gozaimasu" [Welcome, honorable early one] and he looked sharp today in his white suit. He's really a brilliant guy and impressive. Kuniake Koiso and I are practically buddy-buddy since his ever-loving wife sent me some white silk and we "knock each other out" with the old bow. He bows; I bow, etc. He was premier after Tojo. He's not very good looking—looks a little fierce, but he's nice. The one I don't like is Marquis Kido who's considered the No. 2 war criminal after General Tojo. It's a crazy world when you think about fighting these people for three years and hating them, and here I am knocking myself out for them. I hate to say this, but being around some of these people you get a different idea of the Japanese. They were a bunch of misguided fools and, while they deserve to be punished and hanged, you can see a little of their side if you can penetrate into their way of life.

I think the following reflects my loyalty to the defense attorneys and the prisoners while simultaneously trying to address my family's strong sentiments of disapproval for my work assignment.

Things are beginning to get exciting as things have broken up now. It's crazy to say this, but now that I'm with the defense I'm on our side, and it's all kind of silly because some of our clients are going to die before the trials end; some of the others will shoot themselves; but, I'll bet we get some acquittals. Another thing, everyone hates the prosecution, so it's really ironic that I end up on Tojo's side. Of course I hope they're all hanged, but I like our people so much I want them to put up a good fight and show up the jerky prosecution section.

I did not hope they would be hanged—just the opposite. I began to hope they would go free (except perhaps those clients who had been active in the horrors of the Philippines and China). I continued to feel the need to justify my loyalty to the defense without alienating my family. My brother-in-law had spent four years with the Army's Seventh Division from Attu to Okinawa. I was sure he thought I was either hypnotized or just plain crazy and had let all the notoriety go to my head. I wrote:

> *It's an honor to work with the defense instead of the prosecution as we were set up on directives from MacArthur and have a lot more to do with actually helping the Japanese people become democratic more than the prosecution. Personally, I wouldn't want to work for the prosecution as they don't have the caliber of people we have.*

Finally, I decided to say what I really felt.

> *You'll probably disown me for saying it, but I can't hate them. The Japanese are different from the Germans in that they fought a war of expansion and not so much ideology as the Germans...*

General Tojo was the best known of the accused war criminals and the most reviled by Americans. Although considered diabolical by the press, he had enormous personal presence and dignity. I sounded like a movie struck fan when I wrote:

> *...you really have to admire General Tojo because he sits up there in court like a real man and has a terrific amount of poise; nothing distracts him and he looks so darn smart.*

I was intrigued by General Tojo and mentioned him often when writing home, though I tried to justify my obsession by pretending to be aloof.

> *General Tojo was at the end of the [holding] room. He motioned to me and then came up to me and I asked him if he*

*wanted to see Dr. Kiyose, his attorney. He said, "Yes, please,"
and gave me the smile and the bow; he was pleasant enough. I
wasn't really excited at meeting Tojo but thought I should be;
but he's just Japanese and a darn smart one at that. Spoke to
Tojo again today for a minute as he wanted to see his lawyer
again, and he knows me now when I come into the room. I've
met most of the gang now but they're all just some more Japs
to me. By the time this is over, Tojo and I will probably be
buddies.*

I feel so ashamed that I constantly referred to these people as
"Japs." Although "Jap" was a term commonly used by Americans at
the time, I wish I had not used what is now considered a degrading
term to describe people I considered friends and colleagues.

The press had covered the failed attempt by General Tojo to
commit suicide. On September 11, 1945, American counter-intelligence
soldiers went to his home in the suburbs to take him into custody. He
identified himself at the window of his home and then disappeared. A
shot was heard. The soldiers found the general severely wounded. His
life was saved by American military doctors.

Many Japanese were critical of Tojo's failed suicide attempt.
When he knew he was going to live and be tried as a war criminal,
he assured those guarding him that he would not commit suicide. His
mission was to take full responsibility for the war and make certain
the emperor was completely shielded from blame of any kind for any
activities that led to war.

As the trial progressed, so did the rumors. One was that Chief
Prosecutor Joseph Keenan was resigning. He was not. Then the judge
from the U.S. resigned with hints that the defense might ask for a mis-
trial. They did not. Along with the rumors was old-fashioned gossip to
which very little attention was paid. I supposed that was not unusual
when one trial involved so many different people.

CHAPTER 5 ~ MEETING THE PEOPLE
AND THE PRINCE

Life went on, and those of us staffing the Occupation never had it so good. The Army furnished us with maids who did everything from polishing our shoes to cleaning our rooms and serving our food. Yet I never detected any resentment from these "so-called" former enemies. Rather, I took their friendliness as a sign that they understood we were defending their countrymen.

I had personal business cards made. They stated in Japanese where and for whom I worked. When I handed people my cards, they inevitably smiled and bowed, showing surprise as they read the identification on the card.

The more I knew of the Japanese, the more I understood that their attitude toward me and other Americans was that of a citizen displaying the conduct that was expected of a Japanese as proclaimed by the emperor at the time of the surrender. In a way, the Japanese citizen was fulfilling his duty, just as I was fulfilling mine.

ELAINE B. FISCHEL
International Military Tribunal for the Far East

Office-War Ministry Bldg.	Associated with :
Room 270	Wm. Logan Jr.
Phone 26-6885	Counsel for KIDO
Residence-Rm. 424	John G. Brannon
Kanda Kai Kan	Counsel for SHIMADA,
Phone 26-7264	OKA & SATO

My business card: English and Japanese.

I finally knew enough Japanese to explain about my work at the trial. I told those I met that I worked with the Japanese and American lawyers at Ichigaya, the site of the trial. Once I knew I could engage someone in conversation, I usually asked if they knew of my lawyer bosses, and I could tell by their reactions whether they were following the trial happenings. The exchange of cards always seemed to "break the ice" and lead to pleasant conversations.

The Kanda Kai Kan was filled to capacity with American women who worked for different agencies all over Tokyo. Each was assigned a maid. I learned that my own job did not account for the extraordinary kindness shown to me, though I do think my efforts to be polite and learn the language helped. I enjoyed knowing I could speak to Kazuko and Cheoko in their language. Kazuko, my waitress, took my coat, pulled out my chair, put my napkin in my lap and even made little presents for me. Cheoko, my maid, behaved in a similar manner, striving to do everything she could to please me. She kept my room "spic and span."

At no time did I experience rudeness or resentment from any of the workers who had been employed to take care of us. I even had a Japanese assistant, Hiroko, to do filing and legal research. We were repeatedly admonished not to "spoil" these girls, an admonishment I gladly ignored.

When I was able to come back to my billet before nighttime, I often took walks in the area. There was always something new and interesting to notice. There were so many buildings going up and constant renovation going on. The barren landscape grew brighter and brighter, bit by bit. Smiling and greeting people was sheer joy; there was never a time that I felt isolated or lonely.

In the course of my work, I met interesting and brilliant correspondents, such as Gohl Obeah, who was working for All-India Radio. Originally from Beshar in the Punjab, Obeah was Oxford-educated and very entertaining. He joked about how Tojo should not be tried for attempting to force on the United States what England had successfully practiced in India for nearly three hundred years.

Victor Boisen was covering the Occupation for *Liberty Magazine*. After Obeah's genial charm, I found Victor to be a morbid soul who seemed absorbed with his own thoughts, and who might have only smiled twice since arriving in Tokyo.

Two French correspondents admired my Ping-Pong skills. To my surprise, I seemed to fit in with them all, although I felt intimidated by the high level of intelligence among these reporters. However, my high level of skill at Ping-Pong intimidated them.

Meanwhile, I dated various officers who alternated between singing my praises and suggesting ways I could improve my looks. The higher proportion of males to females was a guarantee there would be no shortage of dates if I wanted to socialize.

I eventually developed a serious though short-lived attachment to Ensign Dave Hornstein, the main interpreter of our proceedings and, as described earlier, the so-called "star." He was highly intelligent and regarded by the Japanese press as "the ruler of the court," as no translation could proceed or conclude without his approval. Each time I was with him, it amazed me to see how the Japanese reacted to this flaming redheaded youth speaking their language so fluently.

One day Dave grabbed a jeep and we drove out of the main city. Wow, what a different sight! There were no tall buildings, no rubble, and almost no cars. The little village we entered had not been a bombing target, so it still existed in the traditional Japanese lifestyle. Along the main street there were tiny shops. Carts were loaded with produce, which meant there was no shortage of food in this little village.

Old car still being used

We joked about the "honey-bucket" carts that carried the night soil used for fertilizer. Several Japanese shops had souvenirs that were exact replicas of the carts. Of course, they did not carry along the smell, which indicated that a cart had recently been on the streets. When David spoke to the people, they smiled and invited us to have tea with them. As I absorbed the scenery of rural Japan, I realized that I was seeing how the countryside had looked for many centuries.

I wrote to my mother about seeing David in the courtroom directing all the translators, and how important he was for one so young. When I finally got to know him, I was surprised to find out that he knew about astronomy, history, music, and even sports, and that his mind embraced many aspects of life other than Japanese. This made him seem more human rather than simply a "star of the show."

We played Ping-Pong and I beat him something awful so we decided to go for a walk and went to the shopping district and the stores were closed; but he can read all the Japanese signs. Then we walked through the Imperial Palace grounds. He's so deep and interesting and is just fun to be with. You gain so much being with a person like that.

I sounded like a giddy schoolgirl when I talked about him. I told my mother that even though I was flattered by his attention and his declarations of how much he wanted to be with me, he was simply too young for me to be completely carried away. I knew, too, that he would soon leave the Tribunal when the translators were able to function without so much direction.

Our friendship did not end on the best of terms. When he became demanding of my leisure time, I told him I could not see him as much as he wanted. I wondered if there was something wrong with me—here I had been so thrilled and happy to have someone as outstanding as Dave care for me, yet I felt as if he were smothering me. I had been refusing other requests for dates for weeks and weeks, but finally my feelings for him just vanished. After he left, his presence and waving pencil were missed in court.

The trial went on without David, but ultimately with tremendous language problems that consumed inordinate amounts of time. The only ones who benefited were the court reporters. There were so many pauses for translation that they were not forced to record any of the proceedings at the speeds to which their work had accustomed them.

My first six months in Tokyo had been filled with constant socializing. I was surrounded with men in uniform and civilians. While the prosecution had occupied the courtroom of the Tribunal and presented its evidence, I did not yet have to work sixteen hours per day. I was able to work a regular day. This freed me to have some good, old-fashioned fun, and I found myself with a "full dance card."

The ease of everyday life added to the happiness I was feeling, almost as if it were a delicious fairy tale.

> I can't believe [this is] all true. Cheoko, my little Japanese girl, gave me 2 presentos—a pretty Japanese picture and a cute little box she made me. She sews buttons on for me and mends my pajamas and fixes my stockings. It's a tough life—but I'll take it.

My letters home were somewhat scattered. For three days I related stories about work and the Tribunal. For another three I wrote about dates with this man and that one, and what we did, and how my mother should not worry. She reminded me, "You don't go to bed with anyone unless you're married; you don't go out with married men; you don't believe everything someone tells you; and you are to always act like a lady and be independent."It must have been good advice because no one talked about me in a derogatory way. There were some girls who had bad reputations for being out to get all they could from the men they dated. There were even a few girls who were sent home pregnant. That was scary; I was never going to be one of them.

My friend Audrey Davis, with whom I made the flight to Tokyo, was beautiful with long, blond hair and the nicest personality. She was always meeting officers who invited her to one club or another. Audrey and I were walking down the street one day when an officer approached us and said, "Can you tell me where I could find two American girls to talk to?" Appreciating the original approach, we quickly made friends with the gentleman, Scotty, who was stationed at Camp Drake, which was headquarters for the 10th Cavalry Division. He invited us go horseback riding there anytime we wanted.

One Saturday, Scotty came to pick us up but Audrey was sick, so I went with him alone. He took me to the officer's stables where I met Cog, whose actual name was Campbell. Thanks to Cog, I learned the proper way to ride a horse. I was proud of my newly developing skill, and because of Cog, I was able to ride the horses at the Camp Drake stables often. I found Cog to be the best friend I could have had. He became very important to me. Meeting him was a high point in my life.

We went riding with Scotty's friend, Lt. Bruce Collon Campbell Clark the VIII, or Cog, for short. He's just a little bit out of this world—really high-class New York society from Tuxedo Park and is 6'4". [He is] really nice looking and had on the most beautiful dress cavalry riding habit. They got me a wonderful horse and instructed me for 2 hours as I'd never ridden English saddle, and these guys are experts, as they're cavalry officers. I had a great time, and all the G.I.s took pictures of me. It was swell. When we finished [we] went over to their club and [I] beat the guys at Ping-Pong and [then] sat around and talked.

I could not believe this elegant man truly cared about me. We came from two different worlds. His background was one of wealth and privilege in Virginia, and a future career as a lawyer. I was the secretary with dreams of becoming a lawyer and knew we would never have more than these few months to remember.

After meeting Cog, I planned my weekends so I could go back to Camp Drake. My letters always mentioned him.

> *Next Saturday, Cog is going to work me out in the ring for about three hours as he said that's the way to really learn. After we rode, there was a huge party and I danced and danced. I went home with Campbell, as he intrigues me. He's kind of belligerent and rugged, but he sure softened up on the way home. He told me I was the only girl he'd met here he liked—he really did give me a beautiful line but was a perfect gentleman so "all's well that ends well." Campbell isn't really handsome but there's something fascinating about him but, honestly, Mother, there are so many guys around asking for dates that you get so you don't know what's the score—what I mean is everyone of these guys treat you so nicely that you get overwhelmed and don't believe a word any of them tell you, which is really the best and most satisfactory way.*

I wrote to my mother about how lucky I was to have met Cog while reassuring her of my safety on horseback:

> *About the horses—I only go once a week and how I could possibly be hurt is beyond me as I ride inside the ring and Campbell is right there with me every minute. After all, I'm getting to be a good rider so don't you worry. Tojo's horse is very beautiful and all the horses at Camp Drake seem to have fared well during those war years…they surely look good.*

There were so many men in uniform; each one handsomer than the next. With the shortage of females, almost no one worried if they had a "date." I simply was not interested and was completely content to have met Cog, who was an extraordinarily gifted young man in so many areas. He seemed like my guardian angel. He always reminded me not to be carried away by the attention I was receiving and to keep my eye on the goal of law school once I left Japan.

Cog was such a good influence. I idolized him. He was so tall and handsome, such a beautiful rider, super intelligent and very kind and attentive to me. He talked for hours about the war, how it all happened, and his views of the Occupation. He was about ready to ship back home, and this meant my time with him was both happy and sad.

Knowing we were from two different worlds, there was only so much enrichment Cog could bring to my life. That he cared for me gave me a feeling that maybe I was more than just someone with whom he rode horses. I cherished these words he wrote to me:

> So I wanted very much to be with you Saturday night, as much as I have desired anything in quite some time. Please don't laugh because it's unfortunately true. You're a real person, Elaine; just don't get lost en route as so many of your category do. Whatever you do, never lose sight of the ultimate goal in your life—school. Even though I cannot help myself, I can lend a valuable hand to my friends. So, sincerely, when in doubt, when you need help, always remember one look in those smoky pools [eyes] and it's yours.

Elaine and Cog

73

Cog seldom complimented me except when my riding improved. He often told me that, even though I was not pretty, I did have lovely eyes. My feelings were not hurt at all. I was glad to know something about me appealed to him.

Elaine on horseback at Camp Drake

The more time I spent with Cog, the more I realized what a fine person he was. I wrote home that I had stayed the night at Camp Drake, which had no rooms for female visitors. I assured Mother that it was a long way from the men's quarters and no one even knew I was there.

> *I've known him 2 1/2 months and we've been out a lot, and he has absolutely no ideas about me at all and wouldn't try anything because we are just friends. When he kisses me, it's just a kiss and that's it. He's human of course but refuses to have "glands" with me. No matter how much he wants me, he'd never ask me; so everything is O.K. He told me Saturday night that he loved me very much, but he doesn't mean it that way; he really only likes me the way I like him. He'll never even kiss me more than 3 times during a date and even that's rare.*

Cog's departure was on an "any-day" basis, but he made sure to leave instructions that my riding lessons would continue. The day came when he did leave. I felt somewhat desolate to lose him after losing Captain Coleman as well. I expressed how I felt when he left:

> *I told you there wouldn't be any hurt, but I guess it wouldn't be natural if I didn't miss him a little; it just hit me this morning. Every morning for 6 weeks now we've spoken over the phone and the last 3 weeks I've seen him practically every night. He's the best thing that could have happened to me over here and I hope you can understand that in spite of my repeated statements there could never be anything serious between us. He's told me things you've told me about being aloof and independent and not worrying so much about hurting other people and I'm applying it now.*

My goal was not to be the most popular girl in the Occupation. But fortune smiled upon me again when I met Claude Wall, the United Airlines station manager. My friend Audrey and I enjoyed our roles as hostesses whenever Claude asked us to assist him in entertaining both military and civilians who we were told were important people. We were able to talk about what it was like to be workers in this Army of Occupation and give these guests a view of life to which they would ordinarily not be exposed. He hosted one party after another as part of his business marketing. Were it not for Claude, we could never have attended such parties.

> *Last night I went to this terrific sukiyaki party with about 12 of us in addition to the Japanese. Boy, it was fabulous! These people are some of the richest people in Japan and the house was lovely. Claude says the house we were in last night was a mere shack compared to the many estates they have all over Japan. The meal was delicious—all the sukiyaki you can eat and I love it. It's really deliciously good beef cooked right in front of you. Then all this Jap beer, which is good. Claude had his own drinks and champagne and everything. There were geisha girls to serve and then they danced afterwards. I [met] the whole family and made a big hit, because I told them I work for the Japanese. They bowed and thanked me. I'm a big shot because I know Tojo and the rest of the crew. These*

people invited me back to go to the estates. Then I met this fabulous character Miki Mio—(that's the wrong spelling)— but anyway, he is a terrific tennis fan—shows me pictures of himself touring with the Davis Cup Teams, and he's been all over the States to the swankiest places and what a character he was—speaks English, French, Spanish, Russian, and we were talking Spanish a lot. He's a pretty good-looking Japanese, but what a personality. We 'kicked' the geisha girls out and he and I were dancing, and then we had a Japanese conga line and it was something to see.

There were things available in Japan that could not be obtained in the U.S., such as stockings, that I shared with my mother. It is odd to look back and remember the shortages. It also seems strange to remember how badly I needed to feel her approval about my decision to work in Japan. I hoped that the care packages I sent home would sweeten her outlook towards me.

Claude obtained luxury goods like nylons for me in exchange for PX liquor. The shipment I describe below cost me a bottle of Seagram's VO.

Well, I sent the captain's chauffeur down this morning to send off your package, registered airmail. It contains 5 pair of rayon stockings that will be nice enough for work—one pair of silk chiffon which aren't very good, and one pair of new nylons that are gorgeous, so let me know if you receive them.

Claude Wall with United Airlines crew

With all the activity outside of my work, I was careful to conserve my energy so I could always do my best work each and every day. I wrote about a meeting I attended in which thirty men assigned to the defense were present. When I presented my summation of the meeting, the praise I received made me glow.

One of the attorneys, Michael Levin, said I was the best secretary he'd seen in an awfully long time. They even made a speech about me at their morning conference [and] about how I've done all the work practically singlehandedly. They refer to me as "the girl we can't do without."

My flexible, easy schedule was about to undergo a major change. As the prosecution busied itself putting on its case for the conviction of all the defendants, the Defense Section began to more intently prepare a response to the prosecution's evidence. Work was about to take over my life again. The complication was that I did not know who my boss would be, since Captain Coleman was no longer there.

Captain Coleman had spoken with Commander Harris and asked him to use his influence to get me the best assignment in the place. He said I was an excellent secretary and a hard worker. It turned out I would be working for two bosses; there were not enough secretaries for each defense attorney to have his own secretary. We did not have enough supplies to make us comfortable and we only had hopes that things would get better.

I was allowed to pick my new bosses. My first choice was William Logan, the attorney who was defending Marquis Koichi Kido, the Lord Keeper of the Privy Seal, the man closest to Emperor Hirohito. Mr. Logan had been a partner in the New York law firm of Hunt, Hill, & Betts, which had represented many Japanese companies before the war. I heard the talk about Marquis Kido's 5,000-page diary being used by the prosecution to develop its case against the Japanese leaders. I wondered what it looked like and could only guess that it must have taken up volumes. I did not know at the time how important Marquis Kido was, but I did know that when I met Bill Logan, I liked him a lot and felt he would be a wonderful boss.

My second choice was John Brannon, a former Naval officer. Perhaps for that reason, his clients were from the Japanese

Navy—Admiral Nagano, a leader and planner of the Pearl Harbor attack; Admiral Shimada, the Navy minister from 1941 to 1944; and Admiral Oka, who had been with the General and Military Affairs Bureau and the Navy Ministry.

I was in the peculiar position of actually being able to interview the men for whom I would be working. It was less an interview and more of simply getting to know each of them. I very much liked John Brannon. He seemed to be full of enthusiasm for the job ahead and had an air of confidence about him. He expressed his liking for the Japanese attorneys and felt sincerely sorry for them being caught up in the American system of justice. This meant he had compassion for those with whom he would be working. It was almost all I had to hear.

I learned Brannon was from Kansas City, Missouri, and that he had a brother who was also an attorney there. When I told him I wanted to be a lawyer, he said working for him would provide me lots of good experience.

Commander Harris made the assignment official. I looked forward to working with both William Logan and John Brannon and never regretted my choices.

Since most of the important documents pertaining to the years leading up to the war had been burned by the Japanese, they could not be used by the United States; but Marquis Kido had *voluntarily* turned over his diary to the prosecution. When I saw Kido in the holding room, I disliked him. Perhaps it was because he seemed so arrogant, as if he were the only defendant wanting to see his lawyer. His son was soon working with Mr. Logan. I liked the son and later felt ashamed for my initial bad attitude towards his father.

I heard that Admiral Shimada had been brought into the Tojo Cabinet (the cabinet that declared war against the United States) by General Tojo himself. The Declaration of War had to be unanimous and Shimada was known to be a Tojo admirer who would insure the vote. I did not know if this was true, but it certainly did not sound very good.

Mr. Brannon began spending hours with the admiral in order to unravel the puzzle. Brannon's first priority, however, soon became Admiral Osami Nagano, who was equivalent to Admiral Nimitz in rank and importance to the Japanese Navy, and very much involved with Pearl Harbor.

Had Admiral Yamamoto, the brilliant designer of the Pearl Harbor attack, not been ambushed and killed over Bougainville in 1943, he would have been our client.

As time went on, the admiral's aide, Captain Yasuji Watanabe, became friends with Brannon and was helpful to him in planning the Japanese Navy's defense. The United States had been most anxious to destroy Admiral Yamamoto for they knew he had been the "star" of the Imperial Fleet.

Fourteen-hour days became the norm for me. Logan was a morning person. He and I were in the office at 8 a.m. sharp. Brannon was a night person strolling in at 1 p.m. and working until 5 p.m. He would ask me to come to the Dai Ichi Hotel at night to continue the work he started at the office. A work schedule of 8 a.m. to 11 p.m. or midnight was not uncommon.

I must admit; the long hours were brutal. But Brannon never seemed to tire. I never ceased to be impressed and startled by his legal acumen. He was both concerned about working me too hard and, at the same time, never stopping until he reached the end of whatever preparation he felt was vitally necessary to properly defend his clients. He had genuine passion for the law and for the men who had entrusted their lives to him.

A highlight of my time at the Ministry Building was when I met Prince Takamatsu, brother of Emperor Hirohito. Accompanied by Captain Yasuji Watanabe, the prince came to meet with John Brannon. John wanted to ascertain Takamatsu's value as a potential defense witness.

On December 1, 1936, Yamamoto had become Navy vice-minister. Shortly after, Prince Takamatsu had joined the Navy Ministry as a staff officer of the Naval General Staff. He was a young lieutenant commander, a graduate of the Navy Staff College. There was a story that when he was to report for duty, elaborate plans were made to welcome him. When Yamamoto found out about this, he angrily told his subordinate that the prince was coming as a member of the Japanese Navy and expected to be treated as such. He was not coming as a royal personage, so there was no need for an elaborate welcoming party. Still, he was personally welcomed.

At the time of our meeting, Prince Takamatsu was forty-one years old. He had an older brother and a younger one. Members of the royal family were not raised by their parents. To call their upbringing "sheltered" would not describe how truly protected it was. They were never allowed outside of their prescribed environment and they were kept away from the public. The prince had a country villa with a tennis court where the emperor and he played tennis once in a great while.

When John Brannon told him that I played tournament tennis, the prince quickly became my friend. We did not have any problems communicating. He spoke just enough English and I spoke just enough Japanese to somehow enable us to speak with ease. He told me the Tokyo Tennis Club had been bombed and the courts were in terrible condition, but he very much wanted me to play there with Japan's national women's champion. He loved watching tennis. Throughout the time I was in Japan, I eventually played several matches, providing him with an occasional diversion from more troubling realities.

Elaine at Tokyo Tennis Club

Prince Takamatsu was always good humored, smiling much of the time and enjoying the informality that marked our meetings. We talked about the trial and the personalities involved. He told me he had been at the White House when Herbert Hoover was president. He and his wife had been received by Hoover. He said he liked the United States. I asked him to think about making another trip, especially one to California. I told him of the wonders of my state and how we could travel from the mountains to the sea in one hour.

Our times together were usually prearranged by Captain Watanabe or others. When His Highness picked me up at the Kanda Kai Kan, people stared. Once we were in his car, and off to whatever destination he had chosen, the atmosphere was totally relaxed. Technically, Occupation personnel were not supposed to eat outside their billets because any food being grown was for the Japanese who had come so close to starving. Being with the prince and being invited to the homes of the wealthy Japanese did not make me feel I was violating any protocol. Our friendship was genuine.

When I finally did return home to the U.S., he and I corresponded for many years and I always hoped he would visit so I could make good on my promises to show off the wonders of California.

There was never any romance between the prince and me. The only times we spent alone were when he was picking me up to go to an event that had been planned or taking me back to my billet. We were just two people who liked each other and had fun together. Once I thought of Wallis Simpson and her romance with the future king of England and stories of the prince and the commoner. I was happy that this royal personage chose to spend time with me. I cherished our friendship and how genuine it always felt to be with him.

Elaine and Prince Takamatsu

CHAPTER 6 ~ MEETING THE ENEMY AND HISTORY

As I grew more "settled in" for the duration of the trial, I had time to reflect on what was happening outside of Ichigaya. The realization came that I was a member of the Occupation living in a country that had fought a great war and was now being occupied. The most visible sign of the Occupation were the soldiers who seemed to be everywhere; they appeared to be totally at ease, comfortable, and happy. Allied military coaches were provided at the train stations so that Americans were not crushed by the Japanese travelers whose train service had been badly curtailed. I often felt sad being in an Occupation car that was almost empty of people while an adjoining car was packed to the limit with Japanese.

When I walked through the streets, I noticed the poverty of these people who were always standing in line for food or a train, and whose clothes seemed so ill-fitting. This was so unlike the Japanese I met at the War Ministry Building, who had decent clothing (even if shabby) and who had rice in their lunch buckets.

The bulk of the people I saw seemed to be adapting and adjusting to their status of being "the occupied." Street venders peddled their wares with crude signs and offers to make souvenirs on the spot. Oxcarts were on the streets next to trucks with charcoal burners for fuel. Japanese women wearing kimonos or baggy work clothes (mampei) walked alongside young girls in modern attire.

Jeeps were plentiful, though it never seemed as though the soldiers on the streets were patrolling them. Rather, they seemed out for a walk.

Every day was a new adventure when I left Ichigaya for my walks. There was never a boring moment. Many signs in English attempted to describe what street might be an actual route to somewhere. Each new day seemed to bring the Tokyo closer to being a city again instead of a bombed-out shell.

If one word could be used to describe Tokyo when I first arrived, the word would be "flat—very flat!" The city was totally bombed out except for the buildings in use by the Occupation. There must have been some buildings left outside the main streets we frequented (the Japanese people had to live somewhere), but I never saw them. I never even visited the homes of my waitress or maid.

Dai Ichi Building

Sometimes I walked to the Dai Ichi Building, headquarters for the Supreme Commander of the Allied Powers—SCAP. Along with the Japanese, I watched General MacArthur come down the front stairs of the building. He was always in his khaki uniform with his staff around him, looking as he did in the pictures in the Japanese papers. He was aloof, but not arrogant. I thought he was handsome.

Each time I saw him, his demeanor was the same. He never seemed to be looking around, just straight ahead. His carriage was military, yet non-threatening.

Again I reflected on the precision bombing that allowed this modern building (which had housed an insurance company) to survive and be ready for occupancy when MacArthur landed in Tokyo in August of 1945.

General MacArthur

Most of our news came from the Army newspaper, *The Stars and Stripes* and the English edition of the *Mainichi Shimbun*. The avowed purpose of this "American Emperor" was to promote a transition to genuine democracy. If you dug deeper, however, and talked to other Americans working in other places, you quickly learned there was censorship in what was being printed and disseminated to the Japanese. Not a word of criticism against the Occupation ever appeared.

I learned that ordinary Japanese citizens wrote directly to MacArthur expressing their thoughts and concerns about what was happening in their everyday life. Before the Americans came, the thought of a Japanese citizen writing to the emperor or to any of his ministers was unthinkable. The ordinary Japanese could not even look directly at the emperor for fear of being blinded by his radiance.

What feelings they must have had to write to General MacArthur without asking for permission to do so! I felt so lucky to have the opportunity to learn all these things and to have contact with people who did not work at the trial (i.e. waitresses, maids, and shopkeepers, who were trying to start businesses again in the midst of flat, devastated streets where wheat was growing in the cracks)

Devastation

My coworkers and I were handed a booklet emanating from the Office of the Supreme Commander. It began with a twinkle, saying:

WELCOME TO GHQ
OHAYO GOZAIMASU (Welcome Honorable early one).
You are now in Japan, in the land of the cherry blossoms and "Excuse please."

I was amazed at how much helpful information the booklet had and how pertinent it was to our situation as occupiers of the land of a former enemy. It covered every question an American might have; it described in detail what behavior was expected of us and how our actions could contribute to the success of this endeavor. What pleased me so much were the words "Japan is truly beautiful." I felt I had a kindred spirit in the author of the booklet who knew as I did that the scenery could take your breath away. Yes, there are other places in this world that can take your breath away, but Japan is one country that can take away your breath and then give it back to you with awe.

The ideals of peace and democracy clearly appealed to the Japanese. What better showplace for "democracy in action" than the presence of the American lawyers at the International Military Tribunal for the Far East?

I noted that the booklet was written in March of 1946, when the troops would not have been in Tokyo very long. Whoever collaborated on distributing this document to personnel, both civilian and military, covered so many aspects of the Occupation that I was even more proud to be one of those to whom the booklet spoke.

YOU IN TOKYO

WELCOME TO GHQ

Ohayo, gozaimasu! (Welcome, honorable early one!) You are now in Tokyo, the capital city of Japan; in the land of cherry blossoms and "Excuse, please." You are an employee of General Headquarters, Supreme Commander for the Allied Powers, and a member of the occupation forces.

As an employee of GHQ, SCAP, your services have been eagerly sought and you are most welcome. You will carry part of the burden of the vast amount of work that is necessary to the mission of the occupation.

ASSIGNMENT

In GHQ, you will be assigned to the staff section in which your services are most needed, and for which your past training has best fitted you. You will probably work in down-town Tokyo in one of Japan's most modern buildings. The offices of the Supreme Commander and many sections of GHQ are located in the Dai Ichi Building, a beautiful, well equipped building which faces the park surrounding the Imperial Palace. Other

buildings housing GHQ are in the immediate vicinity. You may find yourself working in the Finance Building, the largest building in Japan, or in the Radio Tokyo Building from which Tokyo Rose broadcast. Perhaps in the American Club, or in the Teikoku Building in which the Office of Civilian Personnel is located. From the Office of Civilian Personnel you will be

1

billeted, assigned to duty, and provided with any necessary
employee services for the duration of your stay.

FACILITIES

The civilian employee is provided the same type
accommodations as the military so far as billeting, messing,
transportation, P.X., Q.M. sales stores, recreation and all
other facilities are concerned.

Each billet has its own mess. Fresh fruits, vegetables,
and meats are provided and all messes are considered good.

Everything possible will be done to provide comfortable
living quarters for you and, in spite of the vast devastation,
sufficient billets have been found to house all persons on
official duty with the occupying forces. Other buildings are
rapidly being repaired.

Large, heated buses transport all personnel from their
billets to their duty stations and all official occupation
personnel may ride without cost on the public transportation
systems.

RECREATION

The civilian employee in Japan has the same recreational
facilities as military personnel. You may choose the kind you
like from a variety of entertain-
ments. There are movies every
night, and a GI variety show once
or twice a week. There are
organized sightseeing excursions
and a vast number of places where
one may go with one's own group
to visit famous cities, shrines,
museums, scenic wonders, etc.
One may listen to the Japanese
Symphony or watch performances of
famous Japanese ballets and
theatrical groups.

Japan is truly beautiful;
no one can deny that there are many places of unsurpassed charm
that are well worth seeing.

The Office of Civilian Personnel or the Japan Travel
Bureau, with offices in the Dai Ichi Building, the Imperial Hotel,

2

and at many other locations, will assist you in arranging trips
of interest.

SEE TOKYO

Tokyo, the largest city in Japan, as well as the
capital city, is situated at the head of Tokyo Bay, on the
Pacific side, and about midway between the northern and south-
western extremities of Honshu Island.

In 1940, the estimated population of the city was over
7,000,000. It covers
an area of about 213
square miles. Almost
all sections of the
city are penetrated
by trams, electric
railways or motor-
buses. A trip on the
electric railways
affords glimpses of
the activities and
life of the city which
are usually of absorb-
ing interest to new-
comers.

There are also many shrines, parks, museums and other
places of interest to visit in Tokyo, even though the city was
virtually leveled by the B-29 fire raids.

BE CAUTIOUS

Wherever one goes in Japan one is cautioned not to
eat uncooked vegetables or fruit and to drink no water that has
not been boiled or properly chlorinated. It is wisest when away

from your army mess to take rations and a canteen with you. Do
not eat in public restaurants unless they have been approved
by the army. Current directives place all public civilian
restaurants, cafes, cabarets, eating and drinking places of all
types serving food from Japanese sources out of bounds to all
Allied Occupation Forces personnel.

3

OFF LIMITS

Your personal safety is of great concern to this headquarters.

means you, too!

Civilian personnel working with the army are subject to military restrictions.

YOUR EMPLOYMENT AGREEMENT

You should be thoroughly cognizant with your employment agreement. If there are terms which you do not understand, the Office of Civilian Personnel will be glad to discuss them with you.

COUNSELING

The Employee Relations Branch of the Office of Civilian Personnel provides counseling service. You are welcome there at any time to discuss on-the-job or personal problems. Every effort will be made to find a mutually satisfactory settlement of any grievance.

INJURY OR ILLNESS

Any military dispensary or hospital is available to you in case of injury or illness. If you become ill or are injured on duty report to the nearest dispensary, the location of which you will be informed when you go on duty. If you are injured or become ill on the streets or in a public place contact the nearest MP who has been instructed to take you to a military dispensary or hospital.

If you need medical attention while in quarters, contact the office of the custodian. The person on duty will call for medical attention for you or you, yourself, may call a physician.

Unless you are advised otherwise, the facilities of the Officers' Dispensary, located on the second floor of the Dai Ichi Building are available to you.

When absent from duty because of illness it must be reported to your superior in order that you may be properly carried on the time reports.

Required immunization for contagious diseases will be taken.

4

If injured or killed in line of duty you are subject
to the provisions of the United States Employees' Compensation
Act of 7 September 1916, and amendments thereto. Any injury,
no matter how slight, should be reported to your superior
immediately in order that proper forms can be filed. Failure
to report an injury within 48 hours, as required by law, may
result in loss of compensation.

HOURS OF WORK

Office hours
in General Headquarters
are from eight to five,
with one hour for lunch.

TOUR OF DUTY

The present tour of duty is eight hours per day, six
days per week. Your day off will be established by the section
for which you are working.

RATES OF PAY

You will be paid at the rates provided in the Federal
Employees Pay Act.

LEGAL HOLIDAYS

Legal holidays
will be declared as
they arise and as
working conditions permit.

ANNUAL AND SICK LEAVE

Annual and sick leave will be accumulated in accordance
with your employment agreement and Civilian Personnel Regulation
of the Office of the Secretary of War.

INCOME TAX AND ALLOTMENTS

Specific information concerning income tax and allotments will be furnished employees by the Office of Civilian
Personnel upon request.

5

91

DON'T TALK!

The success of the occupation may depend upon what you DON'T say. Be careful, don't discuss classified information concerning your work with anyone outside your own office. Civilian employees are subject to army regulations concerning dissemination of information.

IDENTIFICATION

If you do not have WD AGO Form 65, "Identification Card", you will be issued a temporary card until such time as one can be procured for you. You will also be issued P.X. and mess passes.

CLOTHING REGULATIONS

Employees recruited from outside the theatre will wear civilian clothes both on and off duty.

Employees recruited from within the theatre may wear the military uniform less all distinctive insignia as to rank and with special permission in each case.

Articles of the uniform will not be worn mixed with civilian dress.

You may ask at the Office of Civilian Personnel for a copy of the Civilian Personnel Clothing Regulations.

CIVILIAN AWARDS

Provisions have been made to recognize your faithful meritorious and exceptional service with an appropriate award in accordance with War Department standards.

PASSPORTS

You cannot travel outside Japan unless you have a passport. Before one can be issued you must have a certified or photostatic copy of your birth certificate. Passports cannot be issued from army discharges. Send for a copy of your birth certificate. The Office of Civilian Personnel will assist you in securing your passport. It is suggested that you attend to this matter as soon as possible in case of an emergency leave.

6

YOU MAY LEARN

You may learn the Japanese language from highly skilled instructors; lessons twice weekly.

Noted Japanese will instruct you in the arts of the tea ceremony, Japanese wood carving and block prints.

There are lectures on Japan and the customs of the Japanese people given for your particular benefit by a noted lecturer.

CHURCHES

There are beautiful churches of all denominations in Tokyo, any one of which you may attend. Also, there are Protestant and Catholic services held every Sunday in the Dai Ichi Building, The Finance Building, Army Hall, 42nd General Hospital and at other locations occupied by the Army.

APO NUMBER

Your address will be:

Miss Mary Smith,
Office of Civilian Personnel,
GHQ, SCAP, APO 500,
c/o Postmaster, San Francisco

When you are assigned to a permanent section, the Office of Civilian Personnel should be changed for the designation of that Section, such as Economic and Scientific Section (ESS).

REPORTING FOR DUTY

You are requested to report to the Office of Civilian Personnel, second floor, Teikoku Building, within twenty-four hours after your assignment of billet for your initial interview. If for any reason you are unable to do so, please advise the Employee Relations Branch, telephone AFPAC Exchange 2-3214, in order that you will not be placed in a leave without pay status.

7

Transportation from your billet to the Teikoku Building is provided almost continuously during the day. The custodian of your building may be contacted, or you may phone AFPAC Exchange 2-3214 for emergency transportation needed.

AGAIN

You are welcome here and it is the intent of this Headquarters that you be made as comfortable and your tour of duty be as pleasant and as profitable as possible. Continuous effort will be made to offer you the best possible in the way of facilities.

8

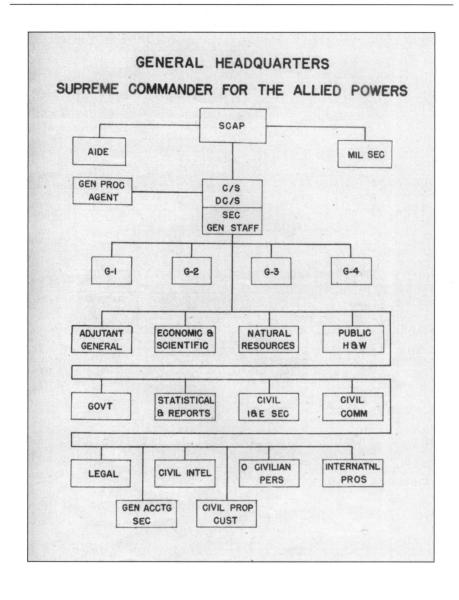

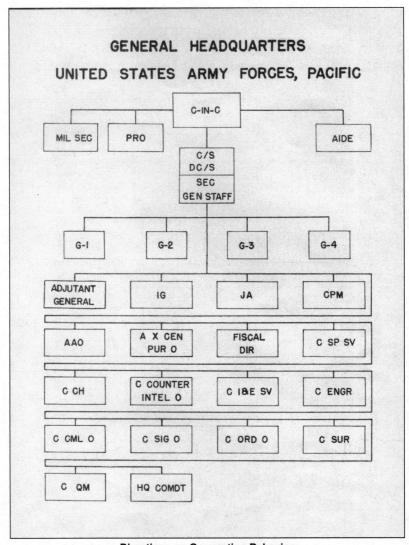

Directions on Occupation Behavior

The letters I wrote to my mother while in Japan were often written in haste; there never seemed to be time to think about my correspondence skills. I simply wanted my mother (and anyone else to whom I wrote) to know something about what was happening at this historic trial and how I felt about almost everyone I encountered. I also wanted to describe Japan, which constantly heightened the pleasure

I felt at being able to see so much (i.e., the well-known scenic spots, the villages, parks, shrines, and the Japanese people living their lives under these harsh conditions)

The Three Monkeys at Nikko

My letters from the early months contain many descriptions of the prisoners and their families. Some of my contacts with them were not just about arranging to meet with their lawyers, but also included requests to see the doctor or get books and papers. I tried to explain to my mother the protocol of how and where the prisoners were kept and to further justify my frequent contact with General Tojo.

About meeting Tojo—you misunderstood and thought I went out to Sugamo Prison where the defendants are held. They hold all the potential Japanese war criminals at Sugamo, which is about 8 miles outside of Tokyo, and I've never been there. Tojo and the other 26 (there were 28 to start but Matsuoka died the other day, and Okawa is still listed as a defendant but he's in the hospital because he is insane more than somewhat) are all being tried out here at the War Ministry Bldg. They come out every day court is in session. They get here about an hour before court starts and are held in about 4 rooms, which are guarded by MPs and wired in. There are 4 rooms partitioned off so the lawyers can consult with the defendants before court starts and also during recesses. I started going down there with the Japanese lawyers, as an American has to accompany them into the room. Then Col. Kenworthy started calling me every morning to come down and get a list from the defendants who wanted to see their lawyers. So, I go down by myself and walk into the big room where the 26 of them sit. When they see me come in, those who want to see their attorneys come up to me. I write down their names and that of their Japanese counsel. I know most of the defendants now by name so I just ask who their attorney is if I don't already know. The minute I walk into the room they come right up to me and that's how Tojo and I got together. I see him every day and I've spoken to him 3 times, but just about whether or not he wants to see Dr. Kiyose [his lawyer].

I also had to explain to my mother the Japanese customs of hospitality and generosity to visitors after I told her about the gifts, meals, and invitations to their homes.

About voicing your opinion about these Japanese parties, I'm glad you did so. I can straighten you out on that. From a legal point of view there's nothing a bit wrong, because everybody goes to parties like that. Capt. Coleman was invited to a lot of them by these ex-generals in the Jap Army, Cmdr. Harris goes all the time, so it's perfectly O.K. and legitimate. There are no FBI agents around. You only have to worry about them if you're out black-marketing on a big scale and that of course would never occur to me. Also, about accepting a kimono. I think the guy was lying, but it's the national custom to give "presentos" over here and that's all it is. Just like the Japanese lawyer giving me the powder box and Koiso giving me the silk. One of the other defendant's wives gave one of the secretaries here a fan. I'm really entitled to mix with them because I work with and for them, but I can understand your concern.

Most defendants who are incarcerated are probably eager to meet with those chosen to represent them. Colonel Kenworthy and I worked together to give the defendants reassurance that their needs would be addressed.

Colonel Kenworthy always greeted me with a hug when I walked in. I told him he would make General Muto jealous, as he had promised to give me his boots before the trial was over. The colonel told me that the defendants asked for me if I did not show up each day.

I continued to try to articulate my feelings towards the Japanese prisoners. Some of my mother's letters reminded me that Shelby Cullison, one of my sister's closest friends, had died on the Bataan death march.

About remembering the deeds of the Japanese—I can never forget them and I'm always talking in their favor so I imagine you—and I can't blame you—must think I'm a Jap lover and do forget. I've told you that you never know what they're thinking. I don't forgive them or condone them. All I do, or try to do, is understand why; and that's why I talk as I do. I can understand a little—their approach to things is entirely different. From their standpoint, they all have a legitimate excuse—that is, the big wheels on trial -- the public thinks in terms of revenge for atrocities and while in the long run the war leaders must take the responsibility, they didn't commit the actual atrocities, they are responsible for the planning, all right, but I understand why, and that's all. I'm not a "gook lover" believe me, and I can't forget all the boys I knew who were killed either, and the way we knew the Japs acted in the war. I guess I'm trying too hard to understand why they are like they are, and when I find out I'll try to tell you. I want you to know I'm not a Jap lover and I'm only conveying surface impressions and if Tojo is nice to speak to and visit, I'll say Tojo is a nice guy.

I wanted to know more and more about how the Japanese thought they could conquer the Far East. Japan seemed to be a small country that had not entered the modern world until the late 1800s.

Working with Japanese who had served in diplomatic posts in Europe and Russia made me realize that Americans did not have a monopoly on brains. The Japanese had a first-class Navy modeled along British tradition, and an Army modeled on what they saw in Germany. For some reason they admired the Germans, but feared the Russians. How confusing it must have been for their leaders who wanted to expand to accommodate a growing population!

The worst attribute I could sense was the need to conquer and subjugate other people. That did not seem right at all.

There were no history books to help me in my quest to understand this aspect of the culture. Most of my knowledge came from listening and scanning documents. There was not always time to do that. I thought of the old proverb, "Curiosity killed the cat, but satisfaction brought him back." I was determined to learn and achieve a better understanding.

I tried to send most of my salary home each month, using various items I received through rationing to barter for goods and cash. Inflation was rampant and so was the black market.

These Japanese all have plenty of yen, but it doesn't mean much to them as they can't buy stuff and actually it probably takes 70 yen to make one American dollar. But for occupation forces, we only get 15 yen to 1 dollar, so the system here is peculiar. That's why black-marketing goes over big. The Japanese have so much money but they want merchandise. For instance, a G.I. buys a carton of cigarettes for 9 yen and a Japanese buys it for 200 yen. Last week the price went up to 300 yen. At 15 yen to a dollar, it is 20 dollars for a carton of cigarettes. That sounds like a lot of money and a lot of yen. If you can go into an Army PX and buy some pajamas for 300 yen, you're really making a terrific deal and these G.I.s will buy anything they see because they have to have an outlet for this black-market yen. If they buy at the PX, they're doing O.K. because if you buy a kimono from a Japanese, you're paying say 1000 yen. These G.I.s are terrific operators and can sell anything, and they all have loads of yen. You're only allowed one carton of cigarettes a week as you have a ration card, but they're big dealers. The military tried to control black-marketing by issuing their own version of yen. Next week, though, this all goes out as Conversion Day is coming. On that day you change all your present issue yen to Army yen, and that's the only kind that will be good in the PXs.

Brannon, one of my new bosses, had an impressive mind and such chiseled good looks that the Japanese press took to calling him "The Beautiful One." No one could deny that he was a very handsome man. I must have failed to show him how much those good looks did not register with me.

Elaine and John Brannon

I've learned a lot since coming here. It's your teaching and the old Cog helping me see through people. Brannon says how come I'm not a bit impressed with him—other girls are. He's cute about it and not conceited—he just laughs at the world. Then he'll pull a different line like—"You don't like me at all, do you?" I'm supposed to get excited and say, "Sure." As a matter of fact I find him very amusing, but I told him all he does is play little games and that he's got little girls running around in his brain. That stopped him. But he called up Sunday for a date and I said no. I rarely date him as it's a waste of time more than once in 2 weeks maybe.

While I was writing and feeling these things, I had no idea that Brannon was to become the most important man in my entire life.

With a bottle of scotch or bourbon by his side, he worked long hours writing legal briefs and expected me to work with him. I would meet him at the Dai Ichi Hotel where he stayed, usually have dinner with him and then go with him to his room where he started dictating.

He was easy to take dictation from, as his voice and diction were so clear. Everything he was saying was so interesting that I did not seem to mind until the next day when I had to transcribe it all—and it had to be perfect, since he hated errors—and, at the same time, Logan dictated for at least an hour and then ran to court. I went a little crazy worrying about whose work to get out first. But I managed it somehow. I also wanted to keep writing to my mother. That too got done.

> First I'll cover yesterday's activities, as it was sort of interesting. I worked till about 1:30 p.m. and then went out to Sugamo Prison with Mr. Brannon, one of my bosses. It was my first visit to the prison and he needed to interrogate his client, Admiral Nagano, and I took the statement. Admiral Nagano is quite a charming man with a definite sense of humor. He's the guy who is "Mr. Pearl Harbor"— he was Commander in Chief of the Fleet (probably the equivalent of American Admiral King) and gave the word to attack Pearl. I guess he's in this mess pretty deep, but he impressed me as being a strictly Navy man and not involved in the military expansionist clique in Japan. It seems more or less as if he was just carrying out orders as he wasn't involved in the politics that went on here. After the interrogation was over I made a few jokes with him and Mr. Brannon asked him to give me his autograph. But he wouldn't do it—said he wanted my name written out for him on a separate piece of paper and that he'd work up a real nice "present" for me. Maybe he'll give me a scroll or something. It was interesting all right and I've seen pictures of the admiral in his heyday. Seeing him out there at the prison and how he appears in court is quite a difference. He's in civilian clothes that are miles too big for him since he's lost a lot of weight. He really is a [jokester] and usually sleeps through the court proceedings—seems indifferent to it all, almost as if it is beneath him. (July 17)

I asked Captain Watanabe about Admiral Nagano. He told me he had been a delegate to the Second London Disarmament Naval Conference in 1934. Japan withdrew from that meeting. When he returned to Japan, he asked Admiral Yamamoto to be his vice minister.

Though Yamamoto was the better known of the two, Admiral Nagano was actually his senior. Captain Watanabe said Yamamoto's love was naval aeronautics and he could stay as head of the department if he took the post Admiral Nagano offered him.

While the defense counsel was still listening to the prosecution evidence, I wanted to know more than anything why and how the war started. Part of my job was to set up files for the testimony of witnesses, dates of the various cabinets, names of the different prime ministers, names of the important Army and Navy men, and a catch-all file called "historical events."

All of the defendants were charged with being a part of a conspiracy. That charge led Brannon to prepare the important legal brief that denied there was a conspiracy. It was vital to know what events influenced the rise of the military. Defending the Japanese Navy meant showing that the admirals were not a part of the military cliques that came and went.

One of the attorneys found a quote from U.S. Secretary of State Henry Simpson written in his diary in 1931: "Trouble has flared up in Manchuria. The Japanese, apparently their military elements, have suddenly made a coup." That coup was followed by thirteen years of the military cliques controlling foreign policy. At the trial, the prosecution introduced evidence that the incident of which Henry Simpson had spoken had been started by Army officers who wanted to conquer Manchuria, and in so doing proved they did not have to listen to any of the moderates in the foreign office in Tokyo.

Those militarists took over Manchuria by the end of 1931. In 1937, the Japanese Army invaded China. The atrocities there were sickening. In 1941, the Japanese Army occupied French Indochina, present-day Vietnam. The French could not defend their possession as the country had fallen to the Nazis.

Before that, in 1940, following the fall of France, Japan seized North Vietnam to firm up its hold on South China. Japan's domination of that portion of the world came to be known as the Greater East Asia Co-Prosperity Sphere.

How could the defense counsel effectively rebut the evidence and defend their clients? General Tojo seemed to be the leader of the pack, believing Japan had a destiny to rule the world. How could one say he was not a planner of "aggressive war?" He had been chief of staff of the Kwantung Army in China and then vice minister of war when he returned to Tokyo. He became minister of war when Japan allied with Germany.

America, Great Britain, and the Netherlands had not allowed Japan to import any more oil from the Dutch East Indies. Secretary of State Cordell Hull demanded that Japan withdraw from the Chinese mainland and Indochina. Japan would not withdraw; it chose to go to war. In October of 1941, Hideki Tojo became premier of Japan. This warrior was not going to be told what to do. War was around the corner.

My bosses were not representing General Tojo. Still, as attorneys for the "number two" accused war criminal, Marquis Kido, and for the Japanese Navy, there was so much they had to learn to put together a defense. They sincerely felt their clients were not guilty of the charges specified in the indictment. Brannon and Logan were busy analyzing the evidence, and they were ready when the defense had its turn.

CHAPTER 7~ THE SOCIAL WHIRL

One day, two officers from the Marine Corps stationed at Yokosuka Naval Base invited Audrey and me to visit them at their base about an hour away. We were more than eager for a chance to ride the Japanese trains and see some of the countryside. We selected a day and off we went. It was so much fun and we were so proud of ourselves navigating our way outside of Tokyo.

Tennis had always been a big part of my life. In Tokyo, tennis helped me gain entry to different social circles that I might have not otherwise been a part of. I sometimes reflected on the fact that here I was—a secretary—welcomed into the friendship of the brother of the emperor. How had that happened? Many times I thought that, were it not for the fact that I played tennis well, Prince Takamatsu and I might not have become such good friends. How many American females in the Occupation were friends with a prince?

When I first met Brannon and told him I played tennis and could probably beat him, he did not believe me, until we actually did play in Hibiya Park and I beat him. From then on, he always sang my praises as a player and was happy that my skills brought me closer to Prince Takamatsu.

Tennis at the Tokyo Tennis club

Meanwhile, the defense was beginning to feel a little optimistic about our chances for some acquittals of our clients. The defense attorneys did not think the prosecution put on a good case, but there was no way to predict what the judges were thinking or what kind of a case the defense would present. I knew the time was coming when the lawyers would be working long, long hours to be prepared to outshine the prosecution.

My friend, Daphne Spratt, received an invitation to visit Kyoto, the former capital of Japan. She invited me to go with her. It was a memorable trip. The hotel where I stayed was beyond lovely, with open rooms set among trees, little waterfalls, and Japanese bridges. The food was fresh. I especially remember having celery and plums; and the vegetables were delicious.

Like millions before me, I found Kyoto a magical place, a sanctuary of loveliness, especially after the bombed-out ruins of Tokyo. There were many Americans sightseeing because most knew that Kyoto had been spared from bombing. It seemed almost a necessity to visit the many shrines and temples and to try to get a feeling for what this city was all about.

Kyoto

You should see this hotel—it's out of this world. It's built on a hill surrounding a ravine or something. It has 6 floors to it but even if you're 6 floors above the ground on one side of the building -- if you walk around to another side the 6th floor will open up on to a terrace and a garden and actually be the ground floor. And on that side of the building the 2nd and 3rd floors will be above the 6th floor. The dining room was just gorgeous -- a large room with 2 smaller rooms seemingly set in a forest of trees and little streams of waterfalls and Japanese bridges so perfect it all seemed like a make-believe sort of picture. What a dinner, too—luscious steak, fresh celery and plums, good vegetables, and chocolate sundaes. They call this Miyako Hotel the plush-lined foxhole and the senior officers really have it made.

The next morning I played tennis at 7:15 with the hotel pro who is from Spain and a foreign national. It so happens he's beaten the Army champ from Kyoto and everybody; but I was lucky and beat him. It was a cement court and I was playing well. [Daphne and I] visited a large shrine on top of a hill from whence we could see the whole city; it was very nice. We [toured] the palace, then visited the lacquer and cloisonné factories and the Yamanaka Art Gallery, then drove all over the local area.

Incidentally, when I [come] back to Kyoto, I'm going to

take lots and lots of money as they have the most beautiful stuff down there. All I bought this trip were 3 exquisite pieces of Satsuma ware for Ruth's home. Satsuma is a kind of porcelain. Don't tell Ruth; I just want her to enjoy this stuff, but all I bought was a cigarette box for a table, a small candy bowl, and a dinner-size plate. These 3 items cost me $45. So you can imagine that they are plenty lovely. My next trip I'm going to try and get you a dinner set. I'll send you some books about Kyoto, too, as I can't remember what all I saw. Kyoto has more 'chicken' colonels than most any place I've seen. I had a really nice time and saw a lot.

Kyōto seen from the Yasaka Pagoda. Kyōto is a city of temples and shrines, of brocades and traditional dancing girls, which attest to her old glory and splendor.

KYOTO

Ginkakuji, or Silver Pavilion located at the foot of pine-clad Mt. Higashi-yama, dates back to the time of the Ashikaga Shogunate in the 15th century. Its unusual garden, designed by Sōami (d. 1525), is one of 216 the most noted sites in Kyōto.

Kiyomizu-dera Temple, standing on a cliff, commands a panorama of the city and its neighborhood. In autumn the temple is encircled by glowing maple leaves.

Maruyama Park is famous for its knarled cherry-tree over 400 years old. When in bloom, the entire tree is illuminated at night, and attracts thousands of people. 217

110

Kyōto is a city of cherry blossom in the spring. The garden of the Heian Shrine located in Okazaki Park is a mass of white and pink during this festive season.

Heian Shrine built in 1895 is beautiful at any season of the year. This is a winter scene showing one of the covered passage-ways which connect the buildings. 219

111

This trip to Kyoto came toward the end of July. At that time, the dependents had not yet arrived in Japan, so the military men seemed anxious for female companionship, and did whatever they could to make the visit enjoyable. There were dances at the hotels with other women present.

I always wondered where the military men worked. I felt both insulated and isolated at Ichigaya. However, I was truly experiencing the best of both worlds as my work let me know the Japanese in a way that few other Occupation personnel would ever know them. This accounted for my believing my experiences might be somewhat unique.

The defense personnel began to be entertained in the homes of Japanese families. Some were connected with the trials; some were family members of the accused. Others offered us hospitality out of kindness and appreciation for what we were doing on behalf of their fellow countrymen. The visits were always memorable for the beautiful gifts we were given and for the occasional extreme measures our hosts took to ensure that we were comfortable. It was a surprise to me that some of these Japanese had such lavish grounds. I had thought land was at a premium; so expensive homes might be lavish, but never with large and beautiful gardens.

Sunday, Daphne took me to visit some Japanese she knew. They were really nice people—plenty nice. We spent the afternoon and Mrs. Wakabayashi gave me two beautiful real pearls as a "presentos." I'm going to see about getting something made up for you that you'd like. I've got a good idea, but I won't tell you until I have it made. I don't know when I could get it to you, so I won't mention it again. But the pearls are gorgeous and perfectly matched. Then they gave me a lovely sandalwood fan and a piece of silk. We ate dinner there and took a lot of pictures and met this Buddhist priest who wants to take us to his temple. Mr. Wakabayashi is a friend of most of the defendants so I took them all greetings from him. It was really very pleasant. This next weekend I'm going to Marquis Kido's summer villa for the weekend with Daphne and Mr. Logan. The Kido's son is "going crazy." I told him I didn't want to sleep at the house because I don't like the Japanese beds; so Dr. Hozumi, Kido's attorney, told me young Kido has been trying to find a Western-style bed for me so I'll come for the whole weekend. It should be nice and a good rest.

Occasionally I asked myself why these people were so extraordinarily nice to us. The invitations we received varied — often including participation in a uniquely Japanese type of event, such as lectures on wood-block prints, classes in the formal tea ceremony, or visits to a Kabuki theater or a pottery factory rising out of the rubble. The food was always so good and not scarce at all.

Dinner Japanese-style

In reading the Pulitzer Prize winning book, Hirohito and *The Making of Modern Japan,* by Herbert Bix in 2000, I was astonished to learn that all of this hospitality was not an accident. Bix wrote:

Members of the Imperial Family, particularly Prince Takamatsu and palace aides such as Matsudaira (Kido's secretary and advisor to the emperor) invited the American attorneys to cocktail parties, receptions, and Imperial "duck hunts" with the aim of favor, nurturing collaborators and gaining information. Hirohito personally sanctioned increases in palace spending precisely for such entertainments. His

113

officials cooperated in the interrogations and gave depositions because they wanted to pin responsibility for aggression on a handful of military cliques.

Duck hunting

Though I believed what I read, I did not think it applied to me and the friendships I continued to make during my stay. I never thought I was that important. I prefer, of course, to think I was sincerely liked! Who knows?

The invitations from the Japanese were the most memorable, but not the only ones I received. On my trips to Kyoto, I played so much Ping-Pong and tennis that I became a little bit famous as the girl who could beat all comers. This led to city trips in Army staff cars so I was sure to see all the famous shrines and gardens. A trip to the top of Mt. Hie for the second time and seeing Lake Biwa again were wonderful excursions.

Back in Tokyo, I was invited to so many dances and parties that I wondered if this social whirl was really happening to me. The time came when an evening at home was something for which I yearned.

Before I knew it, my work assignments grew and the social life faded away.

CHAPTER 8 ~ THE LAST CHINESE EMPEROR AND MORE LETTERS HOME

The prosecution was putting on the evidence it needed to present the Pearl Harbor phase of the trial. This was of deep concern to Brannon for it involved his naval clients. The Kido diary was the most important piece of evidence upon which the prosecution was relying (that enormous 5,000-page manuscript authored by Logan's client, Marquis Kido). This kept Brannon constantly at work. The defense lawyers were not only dedicated to their clients, but other lawyers also came to them with their problems and to gain information on the history leading to the war.

Though Brannon was not easy to work for, he made up for his incessant demands with his continual concern about my health and welfare. He also had so many endearing qualities as a man. No one could have been more solicitous of my well being than he was. His personal life had not been a happy one. He was in the process of dissolving his marriage when he went into the Navy, and I did not know a lot about what that meant. He showed me the legal papers so I knew he was being truthful; I did not have to worry about being seen with a married man.

Brannon had a true interest in learning. He insisted I expand my Japanese vocabulary via learning two new words each day, and that I understand the events that led the Japanese to war and keep up with the Tribunal developments. Last, but not least, he asked me to improve my tennis to the point where I could beat *anyone* who came along.

In the midst of my two bosses' long work hours, there came a break. The trial was to have a celebrity witness in the person of Henry Pu Yi—the last emperor of China, immortalized in the eponymous film by Italian director Bernard Bertolini, *The Last Emperor*. On August 1, 1946, he made his appearance.

Emperor Pu Yi

I did not know why the emperor was called as a witness, although I did learn that by the 1930s the Japanese had conceived a plan to take over Manchuria and start a war without officially declaring one. The Japanese had created an incident by blowing up the tracks of a railway they owned in southern Manchuria and blaming it on the Chinese. Using the attempted blow-up as an excuse, they seized Manchuria, changed its name to Manchukuo and placed Pu Yi, the last in the line of emperors of China, on the throne as its ruler. Pu Yi was known to have collaborated with the Japanese, who tried to have him regarded as an "independent" ruler of Manchukuo. He was not independent at all; he was a "puppet" of the Japanese. Because there was so much publicity and fuss being made about him, I wrote home:

> *Just finished lunch and didn't take my full hour so will try to get this letter off. I'm going to try to run into court today as Henry Pu Yi, the "puppet" emperor of Manchuria, is on the stand and I'd like to get a look at him.*

Perhaps the knowledge that China would no longer be ruled by royalty made the opportunity to see a royal personage such a big event. His appearance was actually more relevant to the attorneys defending

General Doihara, who had been so prominent in the Japanese activities that had gone on in China for more than ten years.

As for Henry himself, there was nothing spectacular about his testimony. He looked so uncomfortable the whole time he was in the spotlight; I could not help but feel sorry for him. So much for publicity.

I continued to be invited to parties, giving me the opportunity to meet unusual people and see a way of life in Tokyo that was astonishingly opulent considering how poor the city itself appeared as it dug itself out of the rubble.

Last night I went to a party with Mr. Pong. If I didn't make it clear who Mr. Pong is, this is it. When Lt. Haynes was here (he was one of the group that left with Capt. Coleman) he kept asking me out and I never did go; and he told me about Mr. Pong and asked me to go to parties at his house, and I never did. Evidently when he left, he gave Pong instructions to invite me to a party. Pong had been around several times and I always refused, but finally he got me on a free night, so I accepted and I went last night. What a surprise that was. The party was at the home of Mr. and Mrs. Kow who are the head of the Chinese Association in Japan. It's kind of like a protection league or something. Anyway you should have seen this house. First of all, it's absolutely modernistic in design (something like those new modernistic homes in the movies.) It was on a hill and done in white with black pillars. The rooms are small but millions of rooms, beautiful wood on the floor and gorgeous paintings, beautiful dining room overlooking a garden, and then there's a sunken ballroom and a stand for a band. They really had a feast with all sorts of Chinese food and fresh fruit for dessert—peaches and apples and cherries.

Whenever there was a break from work, I tried to go back to Camp Drake to ride horses. I found a new riding instructor in Bobby Merrit, a jockey and the principal rider of Tojo's horse. To thank him for his lessons, I arranged for him to meet General Tojo. I had discovered that Tojo was concerned about the well being of his horses.

My friend, Daphne Spratt, who stayed in Japan after the trial was concluded, was featured in a *Stars and Stripes* article in which she talked of General Tojo's concern for his horses. The interview spoke of the former leader in such human terms. Daphne's observations could have been my own. We both loved Japan.

Mrs. Faison Recounts Memories Of 2½-Year Historical Event

By A2C Bob Eckel

TACHIKAWA AB — Mrs. Paul (Daphne) Faison, recently awarded a 20-year Civil Service pin, began her Civil Service career on an historical note in 1946. She was one of 12 American court reporters at the International Military Tribunal for the Far East, which convened in Tokyo.

Of the 25 high-ranking Japanese officials on trial the most famous was Hideki Tojo, Japan's war leader and prime minister.

Mrs. Faison came to Japan at the beginning of the trial in April 1946. After 21 years she is still working as a court reporter in Japan, presently employed in the 6100th Support Wing Staff Judge Advocates' office.

As she prepared to travel to her hometown in Marion, S.C. on leave July 21, Mrs. Faison's thoughts turned back to her first days in Japan and the Tojo trial.

"Tojo was on the witness stand only eight days of the two-and-one-half year trial," she said.

"When he was on the witness stand I was sitting within five feet of him. I liked him, he made an excellent witness.

"He was very quiet and intelligent looking. I think his quietness impressed me the most about him. During the entire trial, he listened carefully and made notes."

When he was on the witness stand, he actually knew the trial and the facts better than the prosecutor. At one point the prosecutor stormed out of the room, he was so angry, Mrs. Faison related.

The American press reported that Japan may have lost the war, but that Tojo had won on the witness stand.

When the verdict was returned after the long trial, seven defendants, including Tojo, were sentenced to be hanged. When the judge read the sentence, Tojo removed his earphones faced the court and bowed very deeply to show his respect — he remained silent the whole time, Mrs. Faison said.

The seven took the sentence nobly; however, one man was so shaken that he had great difficulty removing his earphones to stand up. It was so touching that several of the court reporters started to cry.

"We all felt a great sense of loss after the trial, not only for the lives of the men, but because we had all become so involved in the entire proceedings," Mrs. Faison said.

"I'll never forget that day — Nov. 14, 1948. When the trial was over, someone pulled the electrical cord on the clock, stopping it on the last minute of the trial."

Of the original 12 court reporters only eight were left. One had died, the others had departed for personal reasons. The complete transcript of the trial, which was the responsibility of the court reporters, numbered more than 50,000 typewritten pages.

"I have a complete copy in my home in North Carolina," said Mrs. Faison. "When I get time I am going to have it bound and present it to the legal library in my hometown."

Shortly after the trial Mrs. Faison returned to the United States.

"That lasted only three months," she said, "Japan had become a part of me — I had to come back.

"This is a beautiful country, but it is the Japanese people who make it as wonderful as it is here."

Mrs. Faison lives with her husband, Paul, a retired lawyer she met at the military tribunal in 1946.

Reflecting on the trial and Tojo, she remembers a Saturday when she and a friend made a trip to a Tokyo riding stable where Tojo's horse was being kept.

"It was a beautiful horse, you could tell it was a thoroughbred," she said.

An Army private was taking care of the horse. The private had written Tojo, telling him that he would see the horse got the best of care and the proper exercise.

Tojo had written back, thanking him for the letter and confessing that up to that point he had been worried about the animal's well-being.

"That's the kind of person Tojo was," Mrs. Faison remarked. "With all his problems, which included being on trial for his life, he still had time to acknowledge the letter and be concerned about his horse."

Hideki Tojo was hanged Dec. 23, 1948 in Tokyo, less than two months after he was convicted on nine counts of war crimes.

Tojo's concern for his horse

I hoped my letter home would give my mother a chance to see a pleasant interlude among the legal happenings:

Had a nice experience today. I told you this Bobby Merrit is a swell little kid and is really instructing me on this horseback riding deal. I did want to do something to repay him and didn't know quite what to do about it. I bought him an officer's shirt at the PX for just $2, which is nothing as the instruction he gives me is worth at least $5 an hour; and any officer could have gotten that for him. I had invited him to come out to the trials and today he dropped by all dolled up; he's a typical jockey—real tough looking—all 5 feet tall of him. Well, he has Tojo's horse out there and rides him all the time, so I told him I'd take him in to meet Tojo, and he thought I was kidding. I went to see Colonel Kenworthy, who's this real tough MP Colonel, but he likes me and he said sure thing. Nobody is allowed in the prisoner's room during court intermission, but he let Bobby and me in. I took Bobby right into the room where all our clients are held. I don't like to take advantage and tag along because I can go in there any time, so I just peeked in and the colonel brought Tojo up to Bobby, and Bobby was standing there telling him all about his horse. Tojo was really happy to hear about him and thanked Bobby and told him to take good care of the horse.

It remained important to me that my mother and family, who were Stateside and still quite bitter and angry about the war, understand my feelings about the Japanese defendants. I was constantly trying to explain to them what it was like to work closely with these men.

DURING A RECESS IN THE TRIAL, Tojo and Mrs. Paul Faison, then Miss Daphne Spratt, pose for a picture. When asked to pose for this picture, Tojo gladly agreed. He later autographed the print.

Daphne Faison with General Tojo

Also from what I wrote about the Japanese, don't get the idea I think they're innocent, because I don't. And I don't love them all or anything like it. Maybe it's because I work for the defense that I even think they're nice, but you say to hang them all. I read that part to Mr. Logan and he said you better think other ways about Marquis Kido. He said no matter what I'd write to you, I couldn't explain what it's like over here. I told him about Shelby and how you worshipped him, and he says he doesn't blame you for feeling as you do, but that this situation is different. I don't forget that either, Mother, or all the B-29 boys I knew; but it is different.

Over time, I became fond of Tojo. His name comes up again and again in my letters. I even made special arrangements to have my photo taken with him.

Tojo is nice to talk to. I went in this morning to show him the picture and he liked it. He got out his pen to sign it without my even asking.

Elaine with Tojo

121

We always kid about Kenworthy—(the strict MP colonel who was in charge of prisoner security) Tojo calls him his "papasan" and I say he's not my "papasan" but my "koibito" (sweetheart). Tojo and I manage to exchange little jokes and we're always laughing when we talk, and he's okay. Wonder how I'll feel when they decide to hang him. When I went in today—in the detention room—to see him, General Sato and Admiral Oka were there, down in his end of the room. Sato is really funny. He's almost the wolf-type and I guess he went to some trouble to find out my name. One day when I walked into the press section of the court room (I rarely go to court) Sato saw me and gave a little bow and a smile; so today he said, 'You—Miss Elaine—I watched you in the press section and you come to court.' Then Admiral Oka had to get in the act and give me the old 'one-two-three.' He's a wicked-looking character as he has the perpetual expression of the Samurai warrior. They're the ones responsible for this big damn mess. I guess my trouble is I can't align in my mind a picture of these guys committing atrocities. Then I think in terms of them being responsible for military and political acts like so many other nations that have done the same damn thing on a political scale. Why, if the English were on trial for what's going on in Palestine, you couldn't go in there and spit at an English defendant. What I'm trying to convey is that—when I saw the actual criminals down at Yokohama, I would have gladly killed any one of those Japs. But some of our clients guided political policy and weren't soldiers—and how many other statesmen are responsible for just as much evil, and that means nations that are our allies? Maybe I can't convey what I mean and I, for one, am more anxious than anyone to see that justice is done; yet, I feel it's necessary to excuse my attitude. Just because I'm on defense (as you say) is no reason for me to bother with these people. Yet, you develop a certain amount of loyalty to their case even if not to the individual defendants. Damn it, though—some of them are nice to talk to and I don't feel criminal in saying that—maybe I should. I'd like your opinions.

I wanted to know more about Hideki Tojo. He had been chief of staff of the Kwantung Army in Manchuria. From there, through the years, he had advanced to the position of premier of Japan by 1941. In 1944, he was removed from power by the "elder statesmen of Japan," who were the behind-the-scenes power brokers. Toward the end of the war, even he did not think Japan would win, but he was afraid of the peace terms the Americans might impose.

The Japanese fought in Singapore, the Dutch East Indies, Malaya, and the Philippines. In those places, there were reports back to the Japanese from the international observers of the horrible conditions under which prisoners were forced to live. There was no way they could be expected to stay alive as they were marched through the jungles and starved. There was evidence General Tojo knew about these matters and did nothing.

As the trial progressed and General Tojo testified on some of these matters, he explained that Japanese commanders in the field almost had a free hand in the performance of their mission. This did not sound like much of an explanation.

Tojo always preached the necessity of hard work. He visited barracks, industrial plants, and markets, always on his white horse portraying the hero doing all he could for his country. But *torture is torture*. How do you live with it? I surely did not know what was going on in the minds of the defendants who heard the evidence of their misdeeds.

Mt. Fuji

123

CHAPTER 9 ~ MEMORIES AND TENNIS ANYONE?

My tennis and Ping-Pong abilities allowed me into a world of rank and "important" people. I was often asked to come to the Canadian Embassy. They had a great tennis court that was not touched by the bombing, and lots of people were anxious to play on it. I was careful to be respectful of the high rank held by my "playmates." It was a delicate balance between the games we played and the attendance at dinners at the embassy. For a little while they were tennis partners or opponents; but most of the time they were brigadier generals or major generals.

One of the men I met was not a soldier. His name was Herbert Norman—the head of the Canadian Legation. I was amazed and impressed by how much he knew especially about Japan and the subject matter of the trials. I really liked him, more than any man I had dated since Cog left. He was always wonderfully attentive to me, called me either to accompany him to a social event or to just be alone with him and talk. He had the nicest face, spoke beautifully and was so courtly that I found myself "swooning" over him. I wrote home about my newfound friends at the Canadian Embassy and about Dr. Norman.

> He admired my tennis or something; then another time I played doubles against him and this Canadian Capt. Boland, who had taken me over there in the first place. My partner was an English Capt., Rex Davies who I didn't like at all when I played singles against him and beat him, but who I now like very much. You have to understand the British. Well, the new man's name is Dr. Herbert Norman and from now on I'll call him Herb. Anyway after the doubles, he insisted on my staying for dinner over there at the legation and, gee, it was nice. For one thing I got to take a bath and it was my second bath in Tokyo; I was sitting there grinning like a chessy cat; after showers, a good Stateside tub is a treat [along with] king-sized bath towels. Then we had a nice dinner—me and 12 other guys. I guess I was kind of the queen—2 brigadier generals, 2 full British colonels—one of them is Col. Wild, who's here as a

*witness as he was in the Jap prison camps. For him I'd go over
to the prosecution. Is he ever a dream walking—talks beautifully and looks even better with the bluest eyes I ever did see.
He thought I had a nice backhand—wish he'd like something
else about me. (Probably has a wife and 6 kids, though.) There
were other people there—all VIPs, but they don't really faze
me. Well, Herb talked to me a lot and, in spite of his youth,
he's the most important guy there and he sits at the head of
the table, and Brig. Quillaim was on one side of me and I was
at Herb's right—the honored guest so to speak. We talked a
lot about the Old Testament and he's kind of scholarly but real
sweet. [He's] 6' tall—blonde, blue eyes, wears glasses and is
really nice looking, if not scholarly looking. Anyway I had the
date with Capt. Boland but Herb insisted on taking me home
and going along. [He] has a new 1946 Ford. Well the next day
Herb called me 3 times and I knew he kind of liked me. I played
tennis with him yesterday and beat him 6-2. We had a gallery
again and they all like my tennis and are so darn complimen-
tary. (Incidentally, I'm playing much better now.) Well, Herb
took me home and we had dinner and then went back to the
Legation. It's real pretty out there and nice and cool. I try to
make him feel more like a regular guy because he's written 3
books and has this real big job. Heck, he's like anyone else,
as far as I can see—he plays nice tennis, too; so I told him I
didn't think he was so historical or scholarly because he was
real human. He of course ate that up. The poor guy was really
in a bad way—he kept wanting to put his arms around me all
the time and he's supposed to be the dignified historian—Dr.
Norman. He kept saying he hoped I wouldn't hold it against
him, and he didn't know what had come over him or how he
could grow so fond of me in such a short time. Well, anyway,
it was nice and he's real eager to see me all the time; but I'll
see. He wants to bring me books and talk to me about history,
so at least he wants to help my personality, but he's probably
like all the other men in this world.*

I certainly sounded smitten by Dr. Norman. What a bitter blow
it was when I learned he was married! The only consolation was that

I had not fallen too hard for him—only enough to be terribly disappointed when the realization came that any more socializing with this man was out.

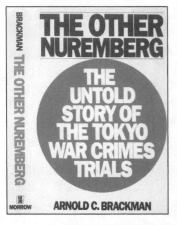

Life works in mysterious ways. Arnold Brackman, a *United Press* staff correspondent, wrote a remarkable book in 1987 called *The Other Nuremberg: the Untold Story of the Japanese War Crimes Trials*. It was the eeriest feeling to read in his book that Herbert Norman had been the chief of the Research and Analysis Section of SCAP's Counter Intelligence Corps while an employee of the KGB! It was he who had persuaded General MacArthur to arrest Marquis Kido as a "Class-A" war criminal. He described Kido as the emperor's principal agent and confidant. I know I told Herb that I was working on Kido's case, and I even brought Logan to the Canadian Embassy.

Dr. Norman described Kido as "an energetic, bustling man with an excellent mind, orderly rather than brilliant, quick, and perceptive." He stressed to the SCAP officials that it was Kido who recommended to the emperor that Tojo be appointed premier in 1941. He probably hoped that the emperor himself would be arrested and tried as a war criminal. That was not to be. It was amazing to learn how important Herbert Norman was in the days leading up to the arrest of so many who found themselves in the dock. Many years later, he committed suicide by jumping off of a building in Cairo, Egypt.

APRIL 26, 1957   25 CENTS

U.S.News
& World Report
The United States News ④   World Report ⑫

WHAT'S BEHIND THE POSTAL "MESS"?

THE
STRANGE CASE
OF
MR. NORMAN

Story of What Preceded the Suicide
Of Canada's Ambassador to Egypt

U.S. News and *World Report*, **April 26, 1957, features Herbert Norman's suicide.**

U. S. News & World Report

THE
STRANGE CASE
OF
MR. NORMAN

E. Herbert Norman, Canadian Ambassador to Egypt, committed suicide April 4 by jumping off a high building in Cairo.

Canadian officials and newspapers blamed the suicide on revelations made last March in hearings before the U. S. Senate's Internal Security Subcommittee.

Those hearings produced testimony linking Mr. Norman with Communism.

Editorials in U. S., Canadian and British newspapers denounced the Subcommittee for making public that testimony. Controversy developed as to whether secret information supplied this country by Canada had been improperly released to the public.

Canada threatened to stop sharing its security secrets with the United States.

As the controversy grew, there were demands to know more about what really happened. Questions were asked in Canada's Parliament and in the U. S. Senate. Additional information began coming to light.

Lester B. Pearson, Canada's Foreign Minister, under sharp questioning in Commons, admitted that the American Subcommittee's action involved no disclosure of secret information supplied by Canada.

Then came a change. Some Canadians began to criticize Mr. Pearson. One member of Parliament charged: "If Mr. Norman was hounded to his death," Canada's Government "must bear a large part of the blame."

Mr. Norman had been in Canada's diplomatic service for many years. Born in Japan, he was a recognized expert on Far Eastern affairs. He was Canada's Minister to Japan from 1946 to 1950, Representative in the United Nations in 1951, then was Chief of the Far Eastern Division of Canada's Department of External Affairs and High Commissioner in New Zealand before going to Cairo in 1956.

Was Mr. Norman really a Communist? Where does the blame lie in his strange case?

Presented here is the record: testimony about Mr. Norman in the Senate Subcommittee hearings, official statements and debates in Canada's House of Commons and the U. S. Senate. You get, in what follows, both sides of this dispute.

Herbert Norman's suicide article (page 1 of 3)

U.S. News & World Report

STORY OF WHAT PRECEDED THE SUICIDE OF CANADA'S AMBASSADOR TO EGYPT

How Data on Mr. Norman First Came Out

The strange case of E. Herbert Norman first came to American attention in 1951. The Senate Internal Security Subcommittee at that time was investigating the Institute of Pacific Relations. In its report on that investigation the Subcommittee described the IPR as "a vehicle used by the Communists to orientate American Far Eastern policies toward Communist objectives."

On Aug. 7, 1951, Dr. Karl August Wittfögel was testifying before the Subcommittee, under interrogation by the Subcommittee's counsel, Robert Morris, and its director of research, Benjamin Mandel. Following are excerpts from the transcript of the hearing:

Dr. Wittfogel: I am professor of Chinese history at the University of Washington and director of the Chinese-history project sponsored by this university together with Columbia University, where the project is located. . . . I joined the Communist Party in 1920 and was a fee-paying member of the Communist Party until the winter of 1932 or the beginning of 1933, when Hitler came to power. I had disagreed with the party.

* * *

Mr. Morris: Dr. Wittfogel, after you left the organized Communist Party, did you remain, psychologically speaking, within the Communist periphery?

Dr. Wittfogel: Yes. If you emphasize both the psychology of the matter and the periphery, namely, the borderline situation; but in form, indeed, yes.

Mr. Morris: In other words, even though you were no longer an organized member of the Communist Party, you were hailed and welcomed by members of that party; is that right?

Dr. Wittfogel: That is correct.

* * *

Mr. Morris: Did they discuss the American Friends of Chinese People and the publication, "China Today," as if that were a Communist organization and a Communist publication?

Dr. Wittfogel: You didn't have to discuss it with me. I had seen too many of these organizations. It was very obviously an organization which was run in the way in which

Mr. Munzenberg, the greatest German Communist organizer, at that time, ran all these outfits. It was, so to speak, one of those. There was nothing particularly exciting about it for somebody who had seen that for about a dozen years.

Mr. Morris: Did Moses Finkelstein in the summer of 1938 run a summer camp or a summer study session?

Dr. Wittfogel: Not that summer. He later became a very active organizer of some academic-front organizations, of which you know, and which had many prominent persons of the campus and, I think, of some other campuses in them. He was a very skillful man that way. He had sometimes, it seems, study groups assembled in his house.

Mr. Morris: Was he a Communist?

Dr. Wittfogel: Yes.

Mr. Morris: Did he tell you he was a Communist?

Dr. Wittfogel: Sure.

Mr. Morris: Was this study group that he ran a Communist study group?

Dr. Wittfogel: Well, it was a discussion among a group of friends, of people who belonged to his political creed. There was no problem about that.

* * *

Mr. Morris: . . . Who were some of the other students at this study group?

Dr. Wittfogel: There was a talented and pleasant young man who was studying in the Japanese department at Columbia. His name is Herbert Norman.

Mr. Morris: Was he a member of this study group?

Dr. Wittfogel: Yes.

Mr. Morris: To your knowledge, did he know it was a Communist study group?

Dr. Wittfogel: Yes, it was obvious.

Mr. Morris: To you?

Dr. Wittfogel: I think it was obvious in general.

Mr. Morris: Was it obvious therefore that he was a Communist?

Dr. Wittfogel: Yes.

Mr. Morris: Mr. Mandel, I wonder if you would introduce

121

Herbert Norman's suicide article (page 2 of 3)

. . . Norman "supported U. S. and U. N. interventions" in Korea

worrying me, but I am afraid that even in this letter I cannot bring myself to tell you the true reasons that impel me to commit suicide.

"I have decided to die near your home. I know this may cause you some trouble and I am sorry, but you are my best friend."

DIFFERING REPORTS ON 1940 CASE AGAINST NORMAN

Two more developments in the strange case of Mr. Norman were noted in the press on April 19.

In Ottawa, Canada's Minister of Justice, Stuart Garson, said that the Royal Canadian Mounted Police received a report in February, 1940, from a secret agent in Toronto that a "Prof. Herbert Norman" was a member of the Communist Party.

However, the Minister said, there was "no positive identification" of the "Professor Norman" and "a cursory check" showed numerous points in the information "to be in error." The "Professor Norman" cited, for example, was said to be connected with McMaster University, Hamilton, Ont., but

attending Harvard at the time. Yet no such Norman was found connected with McMaster.

As a result, Mr. Garson said, "the matter was not followed up further" until October, 1950, when a report was made repeating the information collected in 1940. Then, according to Mr. Garson, a further investigation was made, and, in December, 1950, Canadian authorities "arrived at the decision that the information given is one of either mistaken identity or unfounded rumor by an unidentified source."

Later the Senate Subcommittee, in August, 1951, took testimony from Dr. Karl A. Wittfogel, a professor at the University of Washington, who declared that it was obvious to him that Mr. Norman was a Communist in 1938.

Last week, on April 19, a New York "Times" dispatch from Ottawa said:

"In Toronto, meanwhile, a former Communist identified himself as the agent who informed [the Mounted Police] against Mr. Norman in 1940. Pat Walsh, secretary of a group known as the Pan-American Anti-Communist League, declared that the first police report was correct, and that the second amended version that cleared Mr. Norman followed as a result of the direct intervention by Mr. Pearson."

NORMAN THE DIPLOMAT—A NEWSMAN'S SIZE-UP

As a Regional Editor for "U. S. News & World Report," Joseph Fromm knew Mr. Norman as a news source both in Tokyo and in Cairo. The following recollection of his acquaintance with Mr. Norman was cabled by Mr. Fromm on April 19, 1957, from London, where he is now stationed.

What one remembers most vividly about Mr. Norman was the extraordinary scope of his scholarly interests. He was regarded as an authority on Japanese language and Japanese history. Mr. Norman spoke, wrote and read Japanese as fluently as English, and several years ago wrote a book in Japanese on an obscure aspect of Japanese history. When I called on Mr. Norman at his office in Japan while he was chief of the Canadian diplomatic mission, I usually found him surrounded by a clutter of old Japanese books.

The range of his scholarship outside his special field of Japan constantly surprised Mr. Norman's acquaintances. One night at dinner he sat next to an Italian Cabinet minister and carried on a lively discussion ranging over Italian literature, music, art and history of Italian political parties.

In Cairo, diplomats commented on the extent of Mr. Norman's reading of Arab history and politics before he took up the post as Ambassador to Egypt and Minister to Lebanon. After his first meeting with Mr. Norman, a British diplomat with years of experience in the Middle East said: "He's been here less than a month and seems to have done more reading about this area than I've done in 10 years."

Although he was soft-spoken and slow to show anger, I recall Mr. Norman's arguing heatedly on occasion. During the Korean war, for instance, he supported U. S. and United Nations intervention against the Communists, but argued hotly against the U. N. advance to the Yalu River, on the ground it would lead to Chinese Communist intervention.

In Cairo, when I saw him last September, he acknowledged that President Nasser threatened Western interests but argued vehemently against use of force by Britain and France at a time when Anglo-French intervention was threatened. He maintained this would unify the Arab world behind Nasser and against the West, and would discredit Britain among Asians. He contended that, while Arab nationalism might not

be a constructive or progressive force, it was a fact of the political life in the Middle East that had to be faced.

Norman argued that generations of foreign domination—Ottoman Turk, British and French—had warped Arab behavior and outlook, and that this had to be taken into account in dealing with the Arabs today. The Russians, he contended, were seizing the initiative in the Middle East by exploiting this situation.

Mr. Norman was uninhibited in his professional associations. Besides the usual run of ambassadors and government officials commonly contacted by diplomats, he saw extreme right-wing militarists and ultranationalists and left-wing intellectuals while working in Japan. Occasionally he would wander into an obscure Japanese bar to drink beer or sake and argue about the current Kabuki—Japanese drama—performance. He seemed to feel as much at home in a Japanese setting of that sort as in Western surroundings.

On first meeting, Mr. Norman appeared to be shy, but among people he knew he was gregarious and showed a lively sense of humor. Typical was a performance one night when he regaled a party of diplomats with a long, colorful dissertation on the scandals of Japanese royal-court life several hundred years ago.

Even with closest friends, though, Mr. Norman seldom discussed his personal or family affairs. He commanded an almost fanatic loyalty among his subordinates, took an active interest in their personal problems but rarely shared his own personal problems.

When I saw him in Cairo after his appointment as Ambassador, he was gay and enthusiastic about his new job.

Some people who knew him well had a feeling that Mr. Norman's many years in Japan as son of a missionary and later as student and then as Government official—and the fact that he had been steeped in Oriental culture and customs—had subtly influenced his thinking and outlook. There was something peculiarly Oriental about the manner of his suicide.

Judging from press reports here, it was all done with the same studied deliberation associated with a Japanese general's hara-kiri.

[END]

Herbert Norman's suicide article (page 3 of 3)

130

For me to sit down to dinner at an embassy and be the only female among a dozen men was exhilarating. I attributed some of the attention I received in these extraordinary encounters to the fact there were so few females among the Occupation personnel. I did not do a lot of analyzing, though, as it was all too enjoyable and very "heady." I thoroughly enjoyed myself and found everyone to be nice and "down to earth."

Tokyo had a charmed quality during the months prior to full Occupation. I suppose, in some ways, it felt free of constraints. The Japanese were so welcoming. For those of us who were in the first wave of arriving Americans, there were lots of opportunities to celebrate. We were young and had survived the war. A difficult job lay ahead, yet we were not overwhelmed with work; it felt like we had been invited to a special party put on just for us.

I always wondered if other Americans working for the U.S. government had as much exposure to the Japanese as we did by working at the trial and working for the Japanese side. I kept writing home, and each letter preserved for me a part of my experience. My persistence in using the term "Japs" in my letters home became part of an intentional effort to assure my mother I was not carried away by the parties, the people, or the country itself:

Last night the Japs threw a big party for us and I had a good time in a way, but I danced my head off. It was at a beautiful casino and they had two bands, a lot of Jap girl hostesses, all the Jap defense counsel, and loads of liquor and tempura. Tempura is fried shrimp, which I don't eat. I don't drink liquor and had only a glass of Jap beer, which is good; so there wasn't anything else to do but dance, and [wow] I danced and danced. It was a panic, because [all] Jap lawyers wanted me to dance with them. I started off with Mr. Noritomi, who's a sweet little guy; and I do mean little. He giggles all the time like a child and comes to about here on me so for 2 cents I'd have picked him up and carried him, but I figure you have to be a good sport about it. Then some of the Jap office boys asked me to dance and all I could smell was the yak grease on their hair. I [also] danced with all the Americans. Not to appear conceited, [but] it's almost funny, because everyone I dance with tells me

I'm the best dancer they've danced with in Tokyo. This Dick Tullis, who used to work in our section, asked me to dance and he's terrific. I had never danced with him before and we took about 20 steps and he just stopped and said "My God, you're wonderful!" I just like to dance and they say I'm terrific; so I guess I do dance O.K. They had two bands as I said, and one of these Jap bands was terrific. First they had this kind of Hawaiian dance band on and then they changed and got this other band up with a lot of brass in it and the music started and their first dance was the "Dark Town Strutter's Ball" and Sho Onadera ([a] Nisei language man) was sitting with me and asked me if I jitterbugged; so I said Yes. The minute he heard the band he said let's go. There wasn't anyone on the big floor as the music was hot and this 2nd band's first number, but I figured what the hell. So I took off my shoes and Sho and I took off and we were really jitterbugging. It was a lot of fun but they wore me out. I had to dance with every one and his brother. After the dance I had to get a ride for Mr. Logan and Daphne and [as] it was impossible to get transportation.

Other special memories are of the Kido family. Despite my trepidation about staying with them at their beachside home, I did visit them with my friend Daphne and Mr. Logan. Daphne had been admitted to the Bar in her home state of North Carolina, but she had never practiced law. We had become immediate friends when we met at the train station in Los Angeles as we were both going to our Japan assignments.

Being with the Kido family gave me more insight into how the prisoners' families were coping with the financial and social reversal that had befallen them since Japan's defeat and the war's end. I even came to like Marquis Kido and wondered why I was so against him when I first heard about him. Then again, I was against all the Japanese before I came to know them.

The Kido Family

William Logan with Kido grandchild

Mr. Logan, Daphne, and I went away Sat. afternoon at 1:30 to Zuchi, which is right on the bay, and is the Pacific Ocean. We were guests of the Kido Family as Mr. Logan is defense attorney for Marquis Kido, who was Lord Keeper of the Privy Seal. It took us about 2 hours to get there and we took 2 little girls with us in the car. It really is a gorgeous place they have, just half a block from the ocean—A beautiful 2-story house mostly Japanese-style with about 2 American rooms. These people are strictly the high-class stuff and as nice a family as ever I've seen. Mr. Logan works as hard as anyone because he really believes his client is innocent. After being with the family and hearing them talk against the Army rule and the Germans, you surely tend to sympathize with them. The great-grandmother was there and the wife of Marquis Kido and the 2 sons—one who was married and the other with his fiancée; then the daughter (who is simply gorgeous) and her husband who is 6' tall, which is plenty tall for a Jap, and they are the handsomest couple. Then the husband of the sister who died from typhus during the war was there with their little boy. It was really nice, and we 3 Americans, of course, were the honored guests. All the women cooked for us and prepared these lovely meals. I went swimming in the ocean and sunbathed, and slept there every night. It was very pleasant indeed. These people showed us their albums taken before the war and they really knew how to live—golf, tennis, skiing, and swimming; it's kind of sad to think about the old man sweating it out in Sugamo Prison. What impresses me most is a family like this, who were the highest in the Japanese society, now being subjected to financial and social reverses; yet they're as nice and pleasant as can be and don't seem to be living in the past—the Japanese seem to accept things and actually adjust themselves very well.

To know the enemy can make all the difference in the world. I learned this when I met a girl who had worked at the Nuremberg trials. In my constant defense of the Japanese to my family, I was starting to hone my future skills as an attorney. My relatives could not imagine how I could enjoy friendships with the Japanese people that they considered villainous murderers. It was even more difficult when I realized that I felt towards the Germans as my family did toward the Japanese, and I was just as appalled as my family when I heard someone defend the Germans. Yet here I was defending the Japanese.

> *...you say you don't want to sound like butting in, but you wouldn't bother with those Japs. This is the third time you mentioned something like that. In one letter you said have I forgotten about Shelby being killed and all that. The reason I mention this is about the third time is not because I am angry in any way or anything like that, and I certainly don't think you're butting in; but it worries me a lot and I naturally imagine you think it's terrible. I'm only sorry I can't better explain the situation over here. I don't blame you at all for speaking the way you do and I wouldn't blame Bill for not ever speaking to me after I write about going to a party and dancing with the Japs. That must sound awful to you and then I go for a weekend at a Japanese home. I just wish I could sit down and talk to you about it so I could explain everything and not worry you in the least about my thought concepts or my conduct. For you to say what you did is the most natural thing in the world. Some girl just came over from the Nuremberg trials and she told me Goering had such an interesting personality and was so individual and nice. She had been in on his interrogations. When she said that, I just about blew my top and said, 'Why, how can you say that?' I couldn't imagine him having any personality, feeling the way I do about the Germans. Yet, here I am saying the exact same things to you and writing them, which is even worse. Like Tojo is a nice guy, and I'm presently wearing the blouse that General Koiso gave me, or rather that I had made up from the silk Gen. Koiso gave me. Then I write that Marquis Kido's family is as nice a family as ever I have met or seen—now what must you think? That's what worries me. Words fail me to make you understand. Mr. Logan, my boss, believes absolutely in the innocence of his client Marquis Kido. Many of the defense lawyers feel as sincere as he does about their clients. Mr. Shigemitsu, who was ambassador to China, is charming and intelligent and has a nice face. Maybe the reason I can say they are nice is that, like so many other people,*

I came over here after seeing the U.S. cartoons expecting to see 26 monkeys sitting in court and being on trial, and yet there are 26 men up there each with individual personalities and faces. That's probably surprise No. 1. Then, too, when you speak to them and learn their background, you find they are intelligent. They're gracious and they show it—these men occupied high positions in the government and you can't help but feel they are misguided fools. Even the worst ones on trial have valid defenses. There are some of the 26 who sanctioned atrocities even if they didn't perform them themselves. That doesn't excuse them and I know it; whereas when I saw the Japs on trial in Yokohama—the class-B criminals (who were the lieutenants and sergeants at the prison camps) that committed atrocities, and I heard those trials and the charges against them, I hated the Japanese as much as you hate all of them. If I told you that when I go in and see Tojo I just want to take him and spit on him, I'd be lying; but at the same time, I don't forget he signed the order saying it was O.K. to behead the Doolittle flyers. I'm not blind or impressed by the glamour, but there's a difference in being close to the situation that I can't explain in writing so that you wouldn't worry or misunderstand. Maybe when I come home I'll be able to really talk to you about it, but I'm not a Jap lover.

It was December 6th, 1947, almost six years since the attack on Pearl Harbor. I wrote a long letter to my mother. I wanted to tell her so much and did not know where to start and where to stop.

Well, our case is well along the way. We presented all our witnesses and Admiral Shimada is now testifying in the courtroom. He certainly makes a nice looking appearance in the witness box and he gives real sharp answers. The prosecution is cross-examining him and we are very much afraid that they have enough stuff to hang him. They started yesterday but the admiral did O.K. so far. I wish I could explain the intrigue that goes on and what the setup politically is in this trial. There are lots and lots of repercussions. One angle is that the emperor hasn't been indicted as a war criminal and

136

he's the nominal ruler of Japan. Well, the prosecution here evidently has orders from MacArthur to leave the emperor out of this thing and make sure it comes out that the emperor is innocent. However we get the impression that the judges might be thinking Hirohito is the No. 1 war criminal. Now none of these defendants will say anything about the emperor so you have a queer picture alright. Well, some day maybe I can say more. Anyway I'd like to see the admiral not hang since we've worked pretty hard on his case. It's a funny feeling to know his life is in your hands. John is terrifically brilliant—you can't imagine so. I guess it has been quite wonderful training to work for him, but he's eccentric and at times it's been quite difficult. When it's all over, he gives me all the credit, so there are compensations.

My letter went on to tell how I discussed with my boss not mentioning a certain admiral who was anti-Tojo and could have hurt Admiral Shimada. Brannon was concerned that the prosecution would call that man as a rebuttal witness and it would hurt our case. I more or less talked him into taking a chance and remaining silent. It turned out the prosecution did not even know about him. Brannon told the Japanese lawyers about my part in that strategy.

He makes the Japanese treat me as a complete equal. Of course I don't really do anything except be patient as he is temperamental, and with Logan to contend with, you could go crazy. I don't pay attention to either one of them. I just try to do my job and I'm not half the secretary I was when I worked for Major Frost, but I don't really care. I'm frankly a bit tired of this whole trial.

That was not true; so many times I felt myself right in the middle of something historic. How many secretaries were treated as well as I was by two truly wonderful human beings as Logan and Brannon? They were not just my bosses; they were my friends.

John Brannon, Admiral Shimada, and Colonel Kenworthy

CHAPTER 10 ~ SPECULATIONS AND REALITY

My mother wrote to me asking about Colonel Kenworthy since I mentioned him so many times. I answered her questions by telling her how well he treated the defendants; that he gave them candy and his entire cigarette ration, and he treated them with respect and kindness. He had been in the Philippines when General Yamashita was tried and executed and he told me he was heartbroken. Perhaps I was trying to say that, if he liked the defendants, there was nothing wrong in my liking them, too.

Following the war, my mother lived alone, renting a room from a family. She had worked for the Air Force over the years at different bases throughout the U.S. and had no real home. I felt pressure to return and try to find the two of us a permanent place to live. Her brother lived in Buenos Aires and she was considering leaving the States to live with him down there. When I was approaching six months in Japan and filled with guilt over her lack of a settled domestic situation, I began to speculate about when the trials would be over and I could return to the States. In hindsight, I had a completely unrealistic sense of how long the trial would drag on.

> *Don't plan on me being home in February as then you'll set a date in your mind and I will too, and I'm not sure. The trials may end then and may go on to April so I'll probably stay 'till they end as long as this Yokohoma deal fell thru, but it won't be too long. I've been here almost 5 months and that went quickly and I hope the next months do, too. I think South America would be a swell trip for you and I could meet you there.*

To my dismay, I kept losing my riding teachers. First my beloved Cog, who introduced me to the pleasures of horseback riding; then the little jockey Bobby Merritt who rode Tojo's horse.

> *Bobby came over last night to say goodbye. He's leaving for the*

States. Ain't that a bitter blow?—first Cog and then Bobby; but Bobby is going to fix it up so I can keep riding. He knows some fellow over at 2nd Cavalry Brigade, which is right in Tokyo, who can help me so I'll get some more riding in.

Despite my attempts to reassure my mother that I was not being swept away by my affection for the Japanese, in spite of the two pictures I had taken with Tojo, my visits to the homes of the prisoners' families, and my constant socializing with the Japanese people, the opposite was true; I liked the Japanese people enormously and I found the countryside amazing.

The trials are going on but I haven't been to court since the first week and haven't even been going to visit the prisoners. I must go in tomorrow though and thank Admiral Nagano for his autograph—he's awfully sweet; but that doesn't mean a thing because he is "Mr. Pearl Harbor" and planned the whole thing. Mr. Brannon is his attorney and I keep telling Brannon to settle down and work because we can't let the admiral swing. It's a funny situation and there's only a handful of the 26 that represent our preconceived notion of what a Jap is; but it isn't fooling me one bit because they'd undoubtedly do it all over again. Whatever you say about the Japs, this Japan is a beautiful country, so what's fair is fair. The scenery outside of Tokyo is out of this world. As I told you once, it doesn't take your breath away like the waterfall in Yosemite or the Grand Canyon but it is just plain lovely, and this Hie Mountain in Kyoto is a gorgeous spot. Sunday I'll get my first visit to the beach, as we'll go to Kamakura, and perhaps Hayama if it isn't too far. Someday I'll have to get up to Mt. Fuji and that country. What holds me back more than anything is riding on Saturdays, as now we don't work Saturdays. But I think I'll do my traveling now before autumn sets in as I can ride all autumn and into the winter if I'm here. I don't know who to go away with though. Audrey is laid up and Daphne hasn't much ambition, but I went to Kyoto myself and can go other places alone and have as good a time and the scenery interests me anyway.

In the middle of September, Ambassador Nomura, who had been at the White House when Pearl Harbor was bombed, came to the War Ministry Building to be interrogated by John Brannon. Three of the official court reporters wanted to report the meeting, but John insisted that I be the one. The Japanese photographers took pictures and there I was in the Japanese newspaper with my stenotype, recording the event for our use at the trial. Ambassador Nomura was never charged with being a war criminal and seemed to be respected by everyone.

Ambassador Nomura (with glasses)

I went to the Canadian Legation often to play tennis with various generals. They made me feel so much at home that I invited Brannon and Logan to come out one afternoon. They watched me play tennis and then I saw them deep in discussions with Sir Arthur Comyns Carr, the British prosecutor. Those discussions were very heated.

They thanked me afterwards for giving them the chance to meet with the other side on such an informal basis. It did not hurt my feelings either to have Logan, who was a golfer, compliment me on my tennis. Working for him did not include the uncertainty of the mood swings that were common with Brannon. Logan worked constantly and could lose his temper, but he was so kind and loving when he was with any of the Kido family members.

The person I liked the best was Brigadier General Nolan, who was the Canadian prosecutor. We played a lot of doubles. There was always time for me to listen to him talk about his family. He seemed somewhat protective of me and always exposed the officers who tried to become overly friendly with me by saying such things as, "Did you tell Ms. Fischel you were married?" or "Did you tell Ms. Fischel your wife was coming over with your children?" He was a genuinely nice person and a very good tennis player.

In one of my letters home I explained that Marquis Kido was closer to the emperor than almost any other official. His position seemed to be that of an agent for the emperor. There was some talk that if he were to be found guilty, then the emperor should be found guilty as well. As I said, that was not going to happen; the prosecution never gave even a hint of the emperor's complicity in the war.

...when I know about the atrocities I want to hang them all because they are horrible, and there's no question about their guilt. This is a civilized world and they are wrong and we're right from anyone's standpoint, but each one of the Japanese on trial acted the way he did because he felt he was right and it's just that we are the victors and so we use our standards.

As the days and weeks went by, I seemed to be spending my work and non-work time with John Brannon, who by this time had become "Johnny" to me. I made arrangements for him and Logan to go with me and a friend, Rose Zaretsky, to Fuji View Hotel for Labor Day weekend. Perseverance paid off in getting reservations for this popular retreat.

You wouldn't believe what kind of a place this is. It's at the bottom of Mt. Fuji and you step out of the front of the hotel and there's Fuji. It's Western style and is beautiful—on the other side is Lake Kamaguchi. You come right to it when you step out the back of the hotel. They have tennis courts, badminton courts, archery range, sailboat and rowboats and a swimming beach, then you have game rooms, inside bars and lounges —and movies are shown at night. The food is wonderful up here. On Sunday I ordered breakfast in bed for Logan and

Brannon. The setting is much like Lake Tahoe or Arrowhead and you have all this greenness, which is wonderful. A place like Fuji View in the States would cost at least $20 a day and wouldn't be as nice.

Clouds cling to the top of Mt. Fuji.

My feelings for John were growing by leaps and bounds.

We took a walk at night and I feel I got to know him, and I honestly like him. I guess I told you he was a wise guy. I had the idea he was playing around and laughing at everyone, but I know better now and I like him so much. The next day we went row boating and I dove off the boat and swam in the lake. It was super swell. Then we played tennis and Ping-Pong and watched the Japanese archery exhibit.

We spent a weekend in Kyoto filled with touring the shrines and gardens, playing tennis, strolling along the streets and practicing our Japanese. I loved being with this man. It was that simple. At these times I did not think of what an almost impossible boss he was. All I could see was a sensitive human being enjoying a culture of which he knew so little, but was determined to understand.

I wanted my mother to know that my spending so much time with him was not something bad.

Johnny doesn't shut me off from other people and honestly, Mother, he's so good to me; it's not even funny. He takes care of me like I was his own little girl and he laughs about it because I'm so big and husky and yet he watches me all the time. He makes me put on my sweater after tennis and checks to see if I've gotten all my shots and then, knowing I don't eat pork, he wants me to get vitamins from the doctor. About the phone call, he was so excited about talking to his dad and brother that he wanted to give me the money to call you right then and there. He's not the easiest person in the world to get along with, but we do have nice times together. He tries so hard for us to keep doing things that will help us so we won't get serious. He's never kidded me at all.

John went out of his way to get me a raise. He exposed me to so much that would have otherwise passed me by. We did not just go to a Japanese play—we spent some hours learning what the Japanese plays were meant to be and the messages they conveyed to their audience. I could not just go to the synagogue—I had to know how the prayers evolved and how the traditions developed. Brannon kept encouraging me to go beyond "just learning something new" to a deeper place of reasoning and understanding.

He was so kind and generous with his praise of my work; our Japanese lawyers seemed to consider me more of an assistant than simply a secretary. But that was not true either, as they would see me taking dictation and typing furiously in order to produce lengthy documents for both Brannon and Bill Logan. I did know that Brannon always wanted to place me in the spotlight, be it in the office or on the tennis court. I could not have found a better friend in the whole world. He and Mr. Logan wrote a wonderful letter about my work, which I proudly sent to my mother.

5 August 1947

MEMORANDUM

To: Mr. E. R. Harris - Administrative and Legal Liaison
         Officer, Defense Section, Legal Section, SCAP

From: Wm. Logan Jr., John G. Brannon

Mr. Nelson advises that you desire us to state in writing our
reasons for rating Miss Fischel as "Excellent" in regard to her
employment here.

We feel, not only by comparison with the rest of the stenographers
employed in the Defense Section here but also by comparison with
any of the stenographers and assistants we have been associated
with in private practice, that she is by far the most outstanding.
Even you well know her qualifications and abilities and I am
certain that this writing, except for formalities sake, is un-
necessary.

She, among other things, is able to not only take ordinary dictation but to report depositions and conferences with high speed
accuracy. She further is diligent and industrious to the point
of working many hours overtime when there is no provision for
compensation.

We have learned her judgment is on par with that of the attorneys
here and consequently have relegated to her for decision many
matters which ordinarily would be within the scope of the lawyer.

Therefore, while serving as a classified Legal Stenographer,
she is in effect much more than that. We do not hesitate to say
that her association with us has been that of an assistant in
legal matters which, supplemented by her graduation from college
and study at law school, well qualifies her for the trust imposed.

We trust this brief note, while totally inadequate, will somewhat express our feelings in the matter and satisfy Civilian
Personnel that she is entitled to a rating of Excellent and
above.

                                    WM. LOGAN Jr.

                                    JOHN G. BRANNON

Letter of Commendation

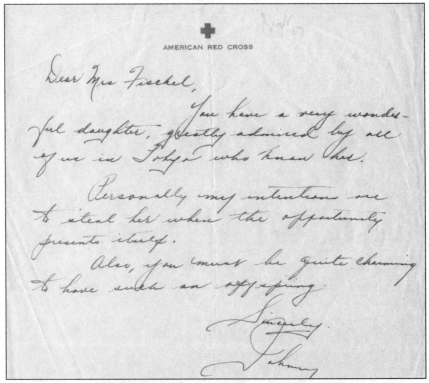

Personal note from John Brannon to Elaine's mother

The end of September was marked by the saddest event. Colonel Wild, who had been a prisoner of the Japanese in Singapore, came to the trial to testify against those who had held him captive. He was a wonderful witness for the prosecution. He was a close friend of Rex Davis, the assistant Canadian prosecutor and one of "my" tennis-playing Canadians. Both were on their way back to Singapore when their plane crashed and they were killed, along with a prominent journalist.

It was ironic that the colonel had survived his brutal imprisonment in Singapore only to be killed in a plane crash. There was a tribute to these men at the trial so their deaths would not go unnoticed. The only defense counsel who knew these two men were Bill Logan and John Brannon. That was because I had invited them to the Canadian Legation when I went there to play. They joined in the tribute on behalf of the defense.

Colonel William Wild

In October, the Jewish high holidays came. I was able to attend services at a make-do synagogue that had been created by one of the chaplains. There were lots of enlisted men in attendance and the services were lovely. After the traditional fast was over, Brannon was waiting for me with Dick De Martino, the trial historian, and Mr. Okuyama, the Japanese lawyer with whom he worked. We drove to the home of the Sogi's (Mrs. Sogi was Admiral Nagano's sister). Mrs. Nagano was there and I wrote home to describe the event.

> *Mrs. Nagano is a lovely little Japanese lady. The 3 daughters*
> *of the Sogis were present along with 2 ex-Japanese admirals.*
> *It may sound odd but food is so scarce among the Japanese*
> *that Johnny paid for the party so they could purchase the food*
> *from the black market, and they prepared it. This party cost*
> *Johnny 200 yen, or over $100, and he gave it in my honor so*
> *I was the guest of honor and I looked it. Incidentally Admiral*
> *Nagano had the same rank in Japan as MacArthur—he had*
> *those old 5 stars and these people are really classy. Well, we*

started out with the real formal Japanese tea ceremony, which was a good way to break my fast. Then we went upstairs to the room where the meal is served. Well, I've never in my life seen such a beautifully set artistic table. It's fantastic and beyond description; all the food was fish and there were 5 huge platters (gorgeous china) with the different fish on each and all really fancy. There'd be a whole fish with flowers coming out of the mouth and leaves all around. Then fish sliced and stuffed with rice.

Each time I was able to be with the Japanese people, I loved the experience. To see the different families in their homes made me realize how fortunate I was to be working at the trials. The opportunity I had to mingle with the Japanese was not one shared by other employees.

The trials were entering the "Russian Phase." The presence of Russians at the trial was subject to criticism and speculation as they tried to justify their own actions in going to war against the Japanese. After all, the Russians had been allies of the Japanese until six days before hostilities ceased. So, many people wondered why they were one of the eleven prosecuting nations.

The Russian phase of the trial is on now and I might run into court and see what's going on. It's generally conceded that no one is going to pay too much attention to it, and it's slightly fouled up, but the French phase was worse. The prosecution is still presenting its case and it now looks as if they won't be through till the 1st of the year and then the defense will take over. So the trials probably won't end before May or June. The defendants are a little nervous these days what with the news of some of their friends about to get it in the neck in Nuremberg. Then the Russians have the stage, and poor Tojo has diarrhea, or whatever the heck it is. I've got a lot of work to do but will have it easy again after today. I spent the first three days of this week fixing up Johnny's office. There were hundreds of documents to go through, files to set up and a couple of interrogations to report. In the meantime I let Logan's stuff lay around, so I have to bring it all up-to-date and then I'll relax.

The Russians had signed a non-aggression pact with Japan in 1941, which was to end in 1946. The Russians had honored that pact. The Soviet government had not helped Britain or the United States in their war against Japan. Japan had not helped Germany, her ally in the battle with the Russians. It was said the arrangement worked, as long as Japan allowed her Manchurian border with Russia to be neutral, and as long as Russia was busy with Germany. Then Russia announced that the non-aggression pact with Japan would not be renewed.

The conference at Yalta in 1945, which President Roosevelt attended, was probably when the Russians decided to enter the war against Japan. More compelling was that on August 8th, 1945, when the Soviet Union declared war on Japan, Japan was facing defeat. Okinawa had been lost in June and on August 6th the first atomic bomb had been dropped on Hiroshima. Germany had been defeated and Japan was the only power that, supposedly, wanted to continue the war.

The allied forces actually approached the Soviets and asked them to join in and wage war against Japan. We did not understand at the time why the Soviets declared war just six days before the expected end of World War II. Perhaps this was the answer but it was not possible to avoid a sense of irony. There was evidence that hundreds of thousands of prisoners were taken by the Soviets in Manchuria and in China. Murders in large numbers followed. Yet the Soviets were sitting in judgment of the Japanese. Why? I did not know.

My visits to the actual courtroom were infrequent. There was too much work to do in the office. I was surprised to receive a copy of an article in the *Sydney Sunday Telegraph* dated August 25, 1946, describing an early trial scene.

"Sunday Telegraph," (Sydney)
August 25, 1946

ALLIES GIVE JAPS GLAMOR TRIAL ... ALL-STAR
CAST

From RICHARD HUGHES

TOKYO, Sat.--The International Military Tribunal
trying Japanese war criminals in Tokio is a glittering,
impressive, and distinctive show, staged with a star
cast and absolutely no regard whatever for expense.

The setting is a large theatre, brilliantly lighted,
admirably aircooled, with 11 judges and 26 war criminals
facing one another in the middle of the front stalls.

The world's Press fills the back stalls, and officers'
wives, distinguished guests, and foreign observers recline
on the stage.

Packing the dress circle are goggle-eyed Japanese
onlookers, for whose enlightenment and entertainment
this colossal, stupendous production of dread of Western
justice has been specially staged.

Certainly, the war criminals could be livelier,
more animated, more ruthless-looking.

Sullen Kingoro Hashimoto, the evil genius of the
Black Dragon Society, does look the part, with his
brutal mouth, sly slit-eyes, and batwing ears.

But the little shrivelled Doihara, the architect
of Japanese diplomatic bribery and corruption in China,
looks like a friendly monkey.

The notorious Army Minister Oka, leaning back
with his eyes closed, recalls a well-fed politician,
slumbering placidly through a Canberra all-nighter.

War Premier Tojo, who is the worst insurance risk
in the dock, is disarmingly benign, as he peers through
his spectacles at witnesses, writes incessantly, and
bows unfailingly to his wife in the gallery, before he
leaves the dock.

In the main, the black-robed judges are also a
disappointing, colorless lot, except for Sir William

Text for article in Australian newspaper, the *Sydney Sunday Telegraph* **(page 1 of 3)**

2.

Webb, the Australian President of the Tribunal, who is, without doubt or compare, the leading man of the production.

His fleshy nose, black eyebrows, silver hair, heavy jowls, flushed cheeks, choleric personality, and rasping voice dominate the court.

"You are not helping the Court . . . sit down . . . objection overruled . . . I have warned you before . . . sit down, objection overruled."

His harsh, querulous accents whistle and crack about the wretched heads of defense attorneys like a tireless stockwhip.

Hollywood could have cast Sir William Webb as the President of the Tribunal, and Hashimoto as the ideal Japanese war criminal.

It is difficult at first to follow the procedure of the Court, because each question, each answer, and each blistering observation by Sir William Webb must be translated, sentence by sentence, into Japanese and Chinese (if you want Russian or French you must clip on earphones and tune in to those translations).

A red light flashes in front of witness, counsel, or judge, if his rhetoric begins to exceed the amperage capacity of the straining and desperate translators.

First, Prosecutor Keenan asks a witness whether he saw Japanese soldiers murder 10,000 Chinese at Tientsin.

Then he pauses, and the microphones splutter the same question in Japanese.

There is another pause, and microphones repeat the question in more sonorous Chinese.

The witness replies in English that he doesn't understand the question. A red light flashes in front of him, and the Japanese and Chinese translations of "don't understand" echo through the court.

The witness laboriously begins to answer. The Japanese counsel challenges the translation. The shorthand transcript is read aloud by a blonde stenographer whose crossed legs immediately distract the Court's attention.

Sir William Webb breaks into the discussion, his jowls quivering like a furious bloodhound. He warns

Text for article in Australian newspaper, the *Sydney Sunday Telegraph* **(page 2 of 3)**

3.

both defense counsel: "I will not tolerate this
deliberate flouting of the Tribunal."

The ferocity of his rebuke is emphasised by the
technical necessity of pausing after each sentence for
the double translation into Chinese and Japanese.

Prosecutor Keenan returns with bland triumph to
his original question. The impassive accused hearken
politely.

This week's star witness at the Tribunal has been
the illustrious Mr. Henry Pu-Yi, last of the Manchu
Emperors of China and puppet Emperor of Manchukuo under
the Japanese.

He is a poor, little, lying craven with a cow-lick,
hugh spectacles, and a nervous tic over his right eye.

The defense counsel becomes brusque with Pu-Yi.

Henry Pu-Yi tells a Phillips Oppenheim story of
the murder of his wife "who loved me deeply," by the
Japanese in his Imperial Palace in Manchukuo.

It is all part of the utter lack of reality in
this court that Pu-Yi's personal, colorful story of
the mysterious death of his wife makes a more profound
impression than the incredible, colorless details of
the mass murder of millions of Chinese, and the deliberate planning for war in the Pacific.

Text for article in Australian newspaper, the *Sydney Sunday Telegraph* **(page 3 of 3)**

Time seemed to fly. It was November of 1946. There was a tremendous housing shortage in the States and my mother could not find
a place to call home. She decided to go to Buenos Aires, Argentina. I felt
terrible that I was not there for her, but I was not ready to leave Japan
yet. Here I was involved in a historic trial, but at the same time, my life
of parties, plenty of food and nylons, maids to take care of our rooms,
and waitresses serving our meals was one of relative luxury compared
to my mother's daily struggles to find housing. I hoped by sharing the
wonderful things I was experiencing in Japan, I could take her mind off
her own problems and somehow justify my absence.

*Last night was the night of the cocktail party to which Navy
Captain Dunning and his wife invited me, and to which I invited Juanita (a friend from Los Angeles) after asking Captain
Dunning. I got home from work and dressed and hitched a
ride in a sedan car to Juanita's billet and talked these 2 G.I.s*

into driving us up to the GHQ Officer's Club—the Mitsui Club. I wore the black dress with the petit point that I got from Mina, and Juanita had on a nice black outfit and looked very nice. The club is beautiful and they had a big reception room there. Captain Dunning was at the door to greet us; he's a wonderful person. He's a Navy captain, which is a big brass, but he's real human and he'll wink at me and say I have to get out and circulate with the big brass, and things like that. He's 6'6" and he's the one who is the tennis partner of the British general. I played against him with Dr. Norman. The party was in honor of Mrs. Griffin and the daughter who just arrived in Japan. Well, I was introduced to Vice Admiral Griffin who's the highest-ranking naval officer in Japan; he's terribly distinguished looking. He fell all over me because he heard so much about me; I was the tennis player they heard was so wonderful. They served beautiful hors d'oeuvres and terrific service and cocktails, and Juanita started drinking. Anyway, whoever saw me or was introduced made a big fuss over me. Captain Dunning watched over us and I saw brass all over the place. The French general, who's head of the French mission, was there and I was introduced to Judge McDougall—the Canadian judge. He, too, made a big fuss over me. Capt. Dunning watched over us and as I said I saw brass all over the place. Norman formally introduced us to Sir William Webb who is the president of the IMTFE and the power here—he's the judge of this court—that is the head judge. On the bench he's a devil, but at parties he's terrific and as charming as they make them. When he found out I worked for Logan and Brannon, I had it made. He said he just loved Mr. Logan, and Mr. Brannon was the handsomest man in the court and spoke so beautifully. He was full of compliments and was very nice to us. Then we were introduced to the big shot Russian General Devereyenko who is the USSR representative on the Allied Council for Japan. He doesn't speak English but said he knew me; he saw me reporting the meeting at the Allied Council and started to make imitating motions about me and the stenotype. Anyway his aide said Juanita and I would get an invitation to the Russian reception Thursday to which 5 of

153

our defense lawyers were invited. When I see it, I'll believe it; but I would like to go to a Russian party just once. Then towards the end of the evening Norman introduced us to Major Freidinger who is aide to Major General Chase, the commanding general of the 1st Cavalry division. He's the guy I wanted to meet because this major has been riding my horse, Rabbit, when I've been out at Camp Drake the last few weeks. So I was mad because I like Rabbit; I started kidding him. Juanita told him she'd like to go to a dance out there at the Cavalry. Two minutes later this 2-star general and his wife come over and said, Hurry up and get your coats. A few minutes later I was sitting in the back of the sedan between Mrs. Chase and the general, and Juanita was with the major in the front. Fifteen minutes later we were in their house for a lovely evening and Mrs. Chase is the most charming nice woman. I was a perfect lady and spoke up and told them some stories about Tojo and it was very, very pleasant. Anyway, General Chase is one of the "biggest shots" in Japan as he commands the 1st Cav, which is the occupying division. We met everyone at the party and I guess we kind of "wowed" [them].

CHAPTER 11 ~ BUILDING A DEFENSE AND ADDING FRIENDS

I kept reminding myself that there would be life after the trials. I would then go back to being just another person trying to make her way in the world, the same world, but with a new perspective.

The parties and celebrations were wonderful; however, they did not and could not interfere with our working harder than ever. I had thought I was a good secretary until I tried to please John Brannon. Despite our friendship outside the office, as a boss he was impossible to satisfy. His demands for perfection forced me to perform at the top of my professional game. He proudly informed me that he had driven away more secretaries than he could count. If he found a mistake on one page, I had all I could do to keep him from shredding the pages that followed. I had so much respect for him that I was not going to let him defeat me.

When he met with Japanese associates, I came along with my stenotype to take notes. This machine shorthand was not that popular except in the courtroom where the reporters were all stenotypists. The exception was my friend Daphne, who still recorded the proceedings in shorthand.

We often found, however, that the Japanese idea of a business meeting was purely social and usually involved sharing a meal. Mr. Okuyama, Brannon's associate counsel, was usually present at these meetings. He had the best sense of humor and always seemed to be having a good time. Sometimes I wondered how much work he was doing, but I never questioned his dedication to his clients. Knowing Brannon respected him was enough for me.

The most memorable person I met was Juji Enomoto, a long time counselor to the Japanese Navy. He had been with Admiral Yamamoto at the London Disarmament Conference in 1930. His position was that of secretary in the Navy Minister Secretariat. Mr. Enomoto had a vast knowledge about the history of the Japanese Navy. It amazed me to watch him recall specific conferences, treaties, and statistics about battleships, carriers, landing craft, and even aeronautics.

Brannon greatly admired Admiral Yamamoto—it was difficult not to, being in the company as he was by his aide, Captain Watanabe, who had been with him in so many memorable Naval battles. He also accompanied Prince Takamatsu on many occasions, seeking to learn more about the Navy's activities to help in the defense he would present. He came to know how and why Admiral Yamamoto was a bonafide hero to the Japanese people, even before Pearl Harbor.

Mr. Enomato told a story about how Admiral Yamamoto taught him to play poker. They played all night on a transcontinental train ride from Seattle to New York. When the train reached Chicago, Admiral Yamamoto went to Evanston to watch a football game between Iowa and Northwestern. Afterwards, more card playing followed as the train continued on to New York.

George Mizota, the best interpreter in all of Japan, was often present at these meetings. We learned that he had gone to America with his parents when he was nine years old. He was in the United States for twenty years and graduated from law school at Stanford University in Palo Alto, California. He did not remain in the U.S. after his college years; he returned to Japan and traveled extensively with various Japanese missions to Europe, and then back to the United States. All that time, he was an employee of the Japanese Navy.

George Mizota

What a pleasure it was to be around Mr. Mizota! His language skills were creative and descriptive and he told us fascinating stories about Admiral Yamamoto.

In the book *The Reluctant Admiral*, the Japanese author Hiroyuki Agawa tells a story that in 1937 Admiral Yamamoto asked George Mizota to go to Shanghai. He felt Mizota's presence was necessary to avoid any incidents similar to what happened when Japanese naval forces bombed the "Panay," an American gunboat. With trouble constantly brewing in China, Yamamoto wanted someone on the scene to explain the Japanese position. Mizota agreed to go, subject to Admiral Yamamoto consenting to two conditions:

> *...first, if any problem did arise, I would be dealing in the negotiations with high ranking officials. I couldn't talk with them on equal terms if I was staying in some seedy little inn. So I'd like you to put me in a decent hotel. Second, I don't like sitting in front of a desk trying to look busy when there's nothing to do. I want permission to do as I please at such times.*

Admiral Yamamoto got the message—to do as Mizota pleased meant playing golf. Of course, he agreed.

Elaine "teeing off"

157

George Mizota could not have been happier when he discovered that Brannon had been on a golf team in his college days. They were so anxious to play...and play they did. Fortunate for me, they played plenty of golf and I was able to spend the day at a beautiful golf course along with John, George, Mr. Enomoto, and his daughter. Once we were away from Ichigaya, we enjoyed many stories from the Japanese men. The Tribunal and its problems faded away. But not for long; there was just too much to do.

John Brannon and his "caddies"

Captain Watanabe soon became a top favorite; possibly because he was one of the first Japanese Brannon believed could help him with his defense of the Japanese Navy. Aside from that, he was happy to be working with Mr. Okuyama and Brannon. He was reliable and prided himself on always being available for the needs of the lawyers.

Captain Watanabe was the one who had brought Admiral Yamamoto's remains back to Japan from Bouganville in the South Pacific where he had been ambushed by American flyers. Admiral Yamamoto, although known as the architect of the Pearl Harbor attack, had been the most vocal in his warnings that war against the United States was not right. He fought those in power, urging them not to go to war. However, he finally agreed. He had hoped that a successful attack would permit Japan to negotiate for peace on favorable terms.

An American girl seated at the table with Japanese men was not customary. They knew it was proper to serve me first, but they had a hard time remembering that. However, the Japanese felt it important to adhere to proper etiquette in order to "save face." That custom did not matter to me, but I was embarrassed to see them struggling.

These meetings usually occurred on Fridays; I referred to them as the "Friday Night Navy meetings." At one meeting, Captain Watanabe suggested taking Brannon and me to visit the tomb of Admiral Yamamoto. A few days later we went. The visit was solemn because it was raining, but the captain took photographs anyway. I suggested to him that the pictures may not come out because of the rain. He said, "No, the spirit of Admiral Yamamoto will make them come out." Sure enough, they did.

The Japanese Navy men liked Brannon, even idolized him, while probably considering him a martyr for his relentless campaign to save Admiral Nagano. In the courtroom, Nagano did not seem to pay attention to the proceedings and amused himself by writing poetry.

Yamamoto's aide, Capt. Yasuji Watanabe at Yamamoto's tomb

We learned it had been Admiral Nagano who had accepted the Anti-Comintern Pact with Germany, which was what the Army had wanted. Our impression was that he had not really wanted to be a party to it. He had no liking for the Germans, nor did he particularly want to be allied with them. Yet, he did consent to the Pact. That was the wrong thing for him to have done, knowing that the Navy was so against involvement with Germany and the European scene.

We knew of Nagano's closeness to Admiral Yamamoto and of certain time periods when they had become estranged. For the most part though, they'd had a good relationship. Both men were vocal in their opposition to war with the United States. The part Nagano played in fostering Japan's Pact with Germany would certainly be used against him. Clearly, the Pact originated with the Army; therefore it appeared that Nagano must have favored what the Army was doing. Why had he seemingly favored Japan signing that Pact? Was he unable to resist the pressure of the Militarists? That would become a hurdle Brannon would have to surmount to make his defense effective.

Friday night's Navy meetings were always interesting. I was embarrassed at my inability to use chopsticks with any type of grace, although I kept improving. I was not used to eating raw fish, and skipped the zushi courses. Besides, the zushi was always prepared so prettily that I simply wanted to look at it. We usually ate steak and sukiyaki at these dinners; and the sake flowed freely while we were entertained by geishas.

I did not really know what a geisha was at that time. Later I learned that in the 17th century an actual "geisha system" was created that included rules on how a geisha should dress and wear her hair, when she could leave the geisha quarters, and how many years of arduous training she had to undertake to become a performing artist. The geisha was recognized as skilled in the art of singing, dance, and conversation. She was not a prostitute as some in the West presumed.

During the period of the Meiji Restoration (1868-1917), Japan became a modern country, more like the Western world. The emperor was restored to power and the shoguns no longer ruled. In those years, the men who built the new Japan liked to hold their political meetings in what were called "waiting houses," where they were attended by geishas.

In modern Japan as well, businessmen did not have homes or apartments large enough for their guests; therefore, it made sense to meet in restaurants, where the presence of geishas made the guests feel at ease. The geisha was meant to be an agreeable companion, since Japanese wives did not attend such affairs.

When I was included in dinner at a Japanese restaurant, the time came when a geisha opened the sliding door and began to sing, dance, pour tea, help serve the food and speak to us. Usually two or three geishas were present. Their performances seemed stylized and formal. They were beautiful to watch; their kimonos were decorated with colorful, intricate patterns. The most famous geisha houses were still located in Kyoto and these were often visited by Japanese returning to prosperity and by Americans who sought to learn the tale of the *geisha*.

Brannon and I attended Kabuki plays together and watch Abbott and Costello at the Ernie Pyle Theater, a movie house for Occupation personnel.

Ernie Pyle Theater in Tokyo

I always tried to make life as comfortable as possible for my two bosses, John and Bill. I cultivated a knack for knowing the right people who could help when help was needed. When there were not enough jeeps, I became friendly with people in the motor pool so that my bosses were never left stranded by the transportation shortage. I had no qualms asking for special treatment for these two hard-working men.

The prosecution was rushing through their case and our office was overwhelmed with court documents. I helped Brannon prepare for his cross-examination of the prosecution witnesses. He wrote a series of questions, had me read the other side's statements, and then asked me to make sure he had not overlooked any important points. Participating in his preparation allowed me to become more confident that I could become a lawyer.

After Goering's suicide in Nuremberg in the fall, security was tightened around our clients, and even the attorneys had to speak through protective screens. Despite his reputation for fierceness and propriety, Colonel Kenworthy, always in charge of prisoner security, was kind to the prisoners. When Tojo had some teeth removed, the colonel brought him soft-boiled eggs and milk toast. I made sure to tell my mother about this as part of my unending efforts to help her understand my affection for our clients and the Japanese people.

Each of the American defense attorneys became so attached to his particular clients; the thought of seeing them hanged was unbearable. Tojo's lawyer, George Blewett from Philadelphia, liked Tojo more as time passed and expressed it to me when we met. Everyone thought General Tojo was remarkable, brilliant, sharp, and forthright. He appeared happy to take the blame for everything that had happened, refusing to involve the emperor in any way. Nor would he put the blame on any of his codefendants.

With a few exceptions, most of the other prisoners impressed me as having some of the same traits, particularly the sense of "duty." I began to think that in condemning many of these leaders, we might be judging Oriental people by Occidental standards.

As victors, Americans were convinced that our way of life was right. There were vital economic and financial interests, however, that had led the Japanese to attack us. These issues would never be addressed by the trial. Considering the size of the country and the total population expansion into other countries made sense to the military cliques.

Brannon and I had an instructive meeting with Captain Watanabe in which the captain explained Japanese military strategy and planning. I found it fascinating, especially his account of events leading to the Battle of Midway. Up to that point, the Japanese had accomplished everything they had set out to do; that battle was the turning point.

Listening to Captain Watanabe, it became crystal clear that Admiral Yamamoto was a man that men could follow, respect, and even love. The admiral was often quoted as having said, "We will dictate peace terms in the White House." Later I was shown the letter from where those words were lifted and found he had not said that at all. America had its propaganda, too. What he really said was, "If you were to go to war against America, to win that war would mean having to dictate terms of peace in the White House and Japan was not equipped to do that."

On one of our visits to see Admiral Nagano in prison, we found him dressed in pants and a woolen undershirt, but without a coat or adequate protection against the severe cold. Yet this high-ranking former officer smiled and bowed, happy to see us. Brannon had developed a great affection for him.

By now, most of the prisoners in this group of Class-A war criminals were quite elderly. Why were they being deprived of an extra blanket at night? Concerned that they would become ill, the defense brought this issue to the Tribunal's attention. Nagano caught cold and was not even allowed a handkerchief. We gave him some paper to wipe his nose. A characteristic shared by all the prisoners was that they seemed old, tired, and malnourished.

We felt so badly to see how little comfort was provided for these men. They had no other clothes than the suits they wore to court.

Mrs. Nagano gave Brannon a picture of the admiral in his prime with his gorgeous uniform and medals. He had a round, fat face in contrast to his current thin, drawn face. Still, he joked with Brannon. When Brannon said something about the admiral being cold, Nagano replied, "We are old men; and it's cold at night." I worried that, if conditions did not improve, these men could all become sick and die.

Brannon's position was that Admiral Nagano had been against the war, but at the last minute, under pressure from the cabinet and military advisors, he changed his mind and ordered the attack on Pearl Harbor.

Brannon asked Nagano why he had not resigned rather than issue an order that was so contrary to his beliefs. Nagano replied, "A warrior can't quit. A politician can, but a warrior cannot." Before we left, Brannon put his arm around Nagano, paying tribute to his classiness. We already knew that Nagano did not have much chance of acquittal.

Okuyama, Nagano, Elaine, and John Brannon

At the end of the month, Admiral Richardson, the former commander in chief of the U.S. Fleet, and a full admiral, began to testify for the prosecution. Brannon prepared a detailed cross-examination, but was exhausted and stressed by the whole ordeal. Admiral Richardson was a tough witness, requiring all of Brannon's skills to effectively cross-examine him.

The reporters praised Brannon's smoothness and his restraint in not turning the public against him, which could easily have happened if he annihilated Admiral Richardson. Brannon was the youngest man to appear before the court. Sir William Webb had a reputation for cutting sarcasm and jumping on every attorney who raised his ire, be they prosecution or defense. Yet Brannon managed to pick apart Admiral Richardson's statement in a slow, deliberate way, and he knew enough to quit when he was still ahead.

Joe Keenan, who served as the chief prosecutor said, "John had given the finest performance that's been witnessed in this courtroom by either defense or prosecution." Everyone praised his delivery, vocabulary, and mental ability in his Tokyo debut.

As he so often did, Brannon went out of his way to say kind things about my help in preparing for this particular witness. He stated that knowing I was there and that I too cared so desperately about saving Admiral Nagano, had boosted his morale and given him the strength to perform well.

Material available to the attorneys in the form of the Congressional Pearl Harbor report suggested that the Pearl Harbor attack was not a surprise to those in charge. Striving to place Admiral Nagano in the most favorable light might bring disgrace to Brannon's own country. For the first time, I thought about the irony of this former Navy officer having to do his best to discredit the actions of his own country. What a difficult situation! Brannon was caught in the middle of loyalty to his homeland and loyalty to his client's defense.

In December of 1946 the weather must have been fair because I played tennis with Judge Roling, the Tribunal Judge from the Netherlands. I beat him, but he did not seem to mind too much. Even though I was excited to be with this important person; I was not about to let him beat me.

The trial entered the Philippines phase. I was sickened by the accounts of Japanese atrocities. I was left confused. How could these horrible atrocities have taken place? It was impossible to reconcile that kind of conduct with the polite and gracious manner of the Japanese I knew.

While I was not working on General Akira Muto's case, I often saw him in the holding room. We developed a friendship that probably arose because he never seemed unhappy or morose. On the contrary, whenever he saw me he spoke to me. One day he tried to explain the Japanese game of "Go," which the defendants played during their lunch hour. He promised me his "Go" set, and later had it delivered to me.

Then I heard testimony about the troops under General Muto's command, who were implicated in the "Rape of Manila" and the "Rape of Nanking." Even worse, the general had charge of the prisoners of war camps in Sumatra where native populations were forced into slave labor. The Philippine population had suffered at the beginning of the war when MacArthur had to leave, and Corregidor fell. The Bataan Death March had followed. At the end, when Japan knew she was going to lose the war, the soldiers went on their fiercest rampages and caused further devastation.

Only a miracle could save any defendant so linked with the murderous conduct of the Army. I also wondered at my own reaction; how could I believe this General Muto was not evil?

After the Philippine phase finished, my workload shifted more to Bill Logan and his client. This meant I had to be more available for him than for Brannon. As already mentioned, my routine was to go to the Dai Ichi Hotel at night to take dictation from Brannon and be back at the office at 8 a.m. to be ready for Logan.

Since Logan represented Marquis Kido, his 5,000-page diary was front and center stage at almost every phase of the prosecution's presentation. This was not the time to put on the defense of Marquis Kido, but to listen and learn from the diary entries. The workload was heavy. Thankfully, Logan was aware of this.

Six different interpreters translated the document. The fact that corrections were always submitted after hours of transcription almost drove me crazy and, of course, there was always a deadline to be met. Still wanting to impress my bosses, I worked hard to meet every deadline. Showing their appreciation at Christmas, Brannon gave me a silver loving cup engraved with the Kanji characters for victory, and Logan gave me a nice watercolor painting for my room.

Elaine and John Brannon with interpreters

Kido's diary contained thousands of detailed writings that covered a period from January of 1930 to December of 1945. During this period, Marquis Kido held various positions. He had started out as secretary to the Lord Keeper of the Privy Seal, then went on to become minister of Education, minister of Welfare, and minister of Home Affairs. When those posts ended, he became Lord Keeper of the Privy Seal from 1940 to 1945. He was considered the emperor's principal agent. Logan would try to discredit the diary's characterization of his client when the time came.

There were other sources of information as the prosecutors had interrogated many Japanese who had been placed in prisons before the selection of the original twenty-eight defendants. Another diary of an important Japanese had surfaced, but nothing rose to the importance of the detailed accounts set out in the Kido diary.

Speculation continued as to why Marquis Kido told the prosecution about the diary. He presumed that the history he had recorded effectively demonstrated that the military was in charge; surely they were the ones to be prosecuted—and not the emperor.

It was going to be interesting to see what Logan would say when his time came. As mentioned earlier, the irony was that Herbert Norman, who I had admired and who had been somewhat enamored of me, was the man who insisted to General MacArthur that Marquis Kido be arrested. Had he not been arrested, the Kido diary might not have seen the light of day. There was no way in the world then that I could have imagined "Herb" as a high-ranking KGB agent.

Living in Japan included frequent earthquakes. While I was living in Tokyo, a serious earthquake in the Wakayama prefecture barely affected the city; it was already so damaged by the war that there was little left to fall down anyhow. I grew accustomed to the gentle swaying of the building during the frequent minor earthquakes. I had lived through the 1933 earthquake in Long Beach, California, and nothing in Japan topped that.

In early January, 1947, Admiral Nagano died of tuberculosis, pneumonia, and arteriosclerosis at the U.S. Army Hospital. He was sixty-eight. Brannon and I were the only non-Japanese present at his memorial service. In keeping with Japanese custom, we knelt before the altar and clapped our hands twice to call Nagano's spirit to us, bowed from our seated position and rose. We followed the gestures of the other attendees, trying not to call attention to ourselves.

Upstairs, former rear and vice admirals of the Imperial Japanese Navy, elaborately attired in striped pants and cutaway coats, mourned Nagano. They seemed surprised to see us, but welcomed us to a table where we ate and drank with them. The food was beautifully arranged and plentiful. A young boy entered the room on his knees and was introduced to us as Nagano's son. He bowed and said in English, "Thank you very much for the defense of my father." Nagano's son repeated his thanks to me and then, terribly nervous and shaky, poured sake for Brannon and me.

I wish I had known more about the Japanese customs of mourning the dead. Though, in many ways it was like our own services where people gather after the funeral to eat, drink and talk of the deceased. Seeing so many high-ranking naval officers made me wonder what the future held for them. Some were not that old and could have had years of service before them; but there was no longer a Japanese Navy, and there would not be one again.

Brannon announced to the court that Admiral Nagano died. He said he wanted to make public a letter written by the admiral wherein he said how sorry he was that the United States had not been advised of the coming attack on Pearl Harbor by at least a few minutes. International law proclaimed that the correct thing to do was inform the enemy ahead of a strike, even if the time of the warning was short.

Admiral Nagano's letter explained that what had happened was a mistake, one for which he assumed complete responsibility. He further wanted it known that he had originally opposed the alliance with Germany, had wanted Japan to withdraw from China, and had not wanted Japan to war against the United States. That same information would have been presented as evidence in his defense.

Later, when General Sato wrote his memoirs, he described how badly Admiral Nagano had been treated at Sugamo. When a window in his cell broke, he covered it from the cold with newspaper, but a guard removed it. General Sato suggested that this was the reason Nagano caught pneumonia. We recalled the day Nagano had not even had paper to wipe his nose when we saw him.

John Brannon announcing death of Admiral Nagano

I wrote to my mother that I might be home by June, but there was really no way to predict when the trial would end. But I was receiving a valuable education that no money could buy.

It was startling to me to learn about how isolated the nation of Japan had been until the Meiji Era. Rapid progress at that point had led to the creation of a vast Army and Navy with the most efficient machinery. The progress was admirable, if only the country had not been led astray by its leaders.

I developed a case of what was known as "service nerves." Everything about the Army irritated me, and I became very agitated. In addition to being deluged with work, I was always cold. There was no heat in our offices, yet the offices of the judges and prosecution were toasty warm. My room at the billet was equally frigid and I prayed for winter's end.

After wrangling with various Army personnel, I was fed up with bureaucracy and submitted a formal letter demanding payment for all my overtime hours. I was able to save money because so many of the necessities of life were paid for by the Occupation. I should have submitted that request earlier. I was happy when my request was honored.

Mr. Logan continued building his case to defend Marquis Kido. The Kido diary was a mixture of glowing personal encounters and official occurrences. The great value was in the record of names, dates, and locations for every important political development, including the rise and fall of the various cabinets that came to rule the Empire. Kido's defense was that he had acted merely as the man between the emperor and the government officials. He had not planned the war or participated in the field; he was not a soldier.

The prosecution introduced evidence that Kido had been ecstatic over the success of the Pearl Harbor attack. To counter that fact, it was argued that Japan only went to war when negotiations failed, but that did not make Kido a criminal. His somewhat famous response was: "Is the price of criminal immunity the corruption of patriotism?"

No one anticipated that Marquis Kido would testify for a full week. He wanted to make it clear that he and the emperor were not aligned with the militarists and that nothing the militarists did was right or approved of by the emperor, including the war plans seeking to conquer French Indochina and the Netherlands East Indies. The alliance with Germany was just plain wrong. He went so far as to say he welcomed the atomic bombing of Hiroshima because it resulted in the saving of millions of Japanese lives and thousands American soldiers who would not have to face a Japan prepared to fight until the end. He almost took personal credit for this benefit of the bomb.

In my opinion, Kido was a nosey, high-class squealer. As Lord Keeper of the Privy Seal, Kido formalized in writing and attached the royal seal to the instructions the emperor gave state ministers.

I spent hours on affidavits for Logan pertaining to this case. While Kido was regarded as the number-two war criminal, both Logan and Brannon felt he was not as important as the prosecution thought he was. The "big-shot" defendants, some of whom were former ministers of state, told Logan that Kido didn't do much more than open the door when they visited the emperor. When the emperor gave instructions,

Kido reduced them to writing and placed the seal on the formal document he had prepared.

I tried hard to like him, but I remembered the times I saw him in the interrogation room; he always demanded immediate attention. In contrast, Generals Muto and Sato exuded a bit of charm and grace, and probably had been a lot more active than "poor" Marquis Kido in formulating and carrying out some of the charges in the indictment.

In the middle of February 1947, I was asked to play a tennis match against Ms. Kama, who was considered Japan's "Number One Player." His Imperial Highness, Prince Takamatsu, appeared at the Tokyo Tennis Club for this match. Brannon wrote my mother that my playing the Japanese champion with the prince present was like fighting the war again on the tennis court. The court was too wet for us to play on the scheduled day, so we agreed to postpone the match.

When we finally did play, she beat me 7-5, 6-2. I was out of condition putting in overtime on the Kido case. I felt I could have done better had I been practicing and not semi-exhausted. She probably was a better player, though. Her sister had been the Japanese champion before her, and she had her own tennis court at home.

I wrote home to my sister at the end of February with a request to send me a dozen Singer sewing-machine needles—six for working on silk and six for men's suits. I explained that Prince Takamatsu was the one who asked for these things when I played Ms. Kama at the Tokyo Tennis Club:

> *I had her 4-0 and 5-3, but just pooped out as I was that out of condition and so winded. I sure sounded like a steam engine. Then too, I didn't have my own racket and had very little sleep the day before. Also this girl has her own court and does nothing but play, so I really did O.K.—except it's better to win.*
>
> *Well if you two don't get mad I must tell you more about Takamatsu Nomiya Denka, and the only way I can impress you is to ask you to forget for the moment that Japan is a defeated nation and that this guy is like God around here, and was received by Hoover in the White House, and given the key to N.Y., and all that. Also, he is the democratic spirit of Japan today. He is nicer than you can imagine, and he and I are having some long talks. Everyone jumps when he moves and*

gives those long deep bows. There were about 15 people [in the stands] and I am the only white person but tennis crowds are tennis crowds, and we are a cozy group of sportsmen. They take many pictures. I was so tired after playing I didn't play mixed doubles so the Denka and I were spectators. He started moving the chair for me to sit in and the chairman of the club brought up a blanket to cover my legs. Takamatsu fixed the above-mentioned blanket for me. We talked and sat together somewhat apart from the commoners; [others were] Mrs. Oura—a Baronness, Matsudaira—a Marquis, and there I am—Mrs. Fischel's daughter. I probably [talked] the Denka's "royal ear off a little;" but it is very nice. We have good times and he sure loves tennis. My jeep did not return to pick me up so the prince said he would take me home, which was O.K. with me. So we get in the car and [people] all line up outside the court and give with the bows and the sayonaras and off we go. As we go along the street I notice people look in the car. When they see the Denka their faces look more surprised than you can imagine. He takes me to my billet, we shake hands and I bow. If he asked me to get him those needles it means either he has no American lady friend or that he trusts me. Please, Bill [my brother-in-law], do not think I am impressed with this Japanese man because he is Hirohito's brother. This Takamatsu is a cultured, educated, and gracious man.

As all this was going on, I wrote my mother about Prince Takamatsu and his adventures in the U.S. when he met with President Hoover and was given the keys to New York City. During the Occupation, the prince was regarded as the voice of democracy for the New Japan. More important to me, though; he was just a nice guy. Whenever I had no transportation back to the Kanda Kai Kan, he always offered me a ride if he was there.

Brannon and Captain Watanabe arranged a special dinner with the prince. Being a female and an American, I had not expected an invitation, but the prince specifically requested my presence. We had a lovely evening and talked about the objectives of the Occupation, emphasizing the effort to introduce Japan to a new form of government.

The prince spoke at length about how much he wanted democracy to come to his country. There was no question about his sincerity.

Brannon spoke freely to the prince with his usual directness. He asked one of the women serving food to sing, but she was very shy. Brannon jokingly threatened to have the prince issue an "Imperial Order." The prince countered his joke by telling the woman he was requesting "democratically" that she sing for us.

When neither approach proved successful, the prince broke into song. When I heard him sing, I was happy he was a prince and not a crooner; he was not very good. His was, however, a great way to respond to our somewhat meaningful teasing about democracy!

Brannon and I taught the prince how to play gin rummy, and he picked it up quickly. I taught him some slang and, when he did not understand the word "ticklish," I demonstrated on his feet. Imagine me tickling the feet of this noble prince (second only to Hirohito in the royal line). I'm sure he did not expect his feet to be touched by an American girl. That would not have happened had he not been the gracious host that he was.

I met a remarkable gentleman who might well have prevented the war, General Ugaki. He was appointed premier in one of the cabinets way back when the Japanese Army created incidents in China to justify expansionist policies. Those incidents involved the murder of a Chinese warlord in Manchuria, which was the northernmost province the Army fanatics wanted to occupy. This was in the early 1930s, when a peace faction attempted to have General Ugaki form a new cabinet. The militarists uncovered the fact that in 1924 General Ugaki tried to reduce the size of the Army. With that information, there was no way they would permit him to become premier.

The cabinet fell when the Army refused to affirm the minister of War proposed by Ugaki. Had he been able to stay in office through the years that followed, there might never have been a war. He was known in Japan as the great peace advocate and his demeanor was that of a statesman. I found him charming and dignified. He cut a striking figure in a beautifully tailored kimono.

Exhausted from weeks of stress and long hours, Logan was sent away by an Army doctor to rest and recuperate. During his absence, I engaged a Japanese girl to reorganize his office. His office was constantly in a state of disarray. Despite my efforts to help him, he lost documents, left them in his room at the Dai Ichi or put them in the wrong file. The Japanese girl and I brought order out of chaos and were pleased with ourselves for doing so.

I sometimes used my influence with Colonel Kenworthy to get people in to see the prisoners. One of these was Mr. Tsuchiya, a millionaire. Privately, I referred to him as "Money Bags." He hosted great parties and I was willing to forgive his obsequious manners in return for his invitations to dinners and social outings. Did this make me seem shallow, only wanting to be part of the social scene? Well, I justified my attitude by saying there were not that many parties and it was a chance to interact with more Japanese people.

As the trial progressed, it became apparent the Japanese Foreign Office — the diplomats — would try to blame our clients for the war and its atrocities -- perhaps a natural conclusion for them to have reached. Someone had to be blamed.

Brannon and Logan interviewed several of these diplomats. While transcribing their interrogations, it was clear to me that defending our clients meant countering testimony offered by Japanese leaders who had not been indicted. They squarely blamed each and every defendant for the crimes with which they were charged. As badly as I missed Admiral Nagano, I thought it better that he died before he was convicted and hanged. I began to despair, thinking of Admiral Shimada's probable execution. Since the death of Nagano, Shimada succeeded to the role of our primary naval defendant. We also were charged with the defense of Admiral Oka. There was a bit of a break as we had to discover the order in which the defendants would tell their stories.

Beautiful cherry trees bloomed in March. I never encountered anyone who appreciated flowers as much as the Japanese. Flowers were part of their spiritual foundation and they seemed deeply obsessed with honoring them. The Sakura or cherry blossom was the national flower of Japan.

In 1931 the mayor of Tokyo presented the American people with a number of cherry saplings and grafts. The trees were planted along the basin of the Potomac River in Washington, D.C., extending a distance of six miles. By 1939, the trees were almost full grown and were much beloved for their spectacular blooms in five shades of pink. Cherry blossoms fall to the ground in full flower just a few days after they bloom rather than wither on the tree. That is why they are revered as a symbol of the fleeting nature of life. I wrote a letter/composition to my mother about the flowers.

25 March 1947

Dear Mother,

Sometimes it is refreshing just to talk about abstract things rather than family matters so, just like you were my English teacher, I am going to write you a little composition but based upon things that I have actually seen and know about.

SAKURA NO HANA

I don't think there exists anywhere in this whole wide world a group of people who appreciate flowers as much as the Japanese. Actually part of their spiritual foundation is based upon flowers. They go into it so deeply that it has become a science, not so much of growing them as the horticulturist would view it, but appreciating and arrangement of them in the house. There are certain definite ways in which flowers are to be placed on the table, on the floor and even in the vase.

Of all the flowers, perhaps the one liked the most is the national flower of the Sakura tree. Sakura, of course, means cherry but over here even the English speaking Japanese are apt to say the Sakura tree rather than the Cherry Tree. I suppose really we should refer to the Cherry Tree as the Sakura Tree too for this perhaps is the mother-land of the Cherry Blossom.

It was in 1931 that the Japanese mayor of Tokyo presented to the people of America and to the district of Columbia in Washington a number of cherry saplings and grafts. These were planted along the basin of the Potomac River extending over a distance of 6 miles. By 1919 the trees had attained almost their full growth and the people of Washington marvelled at the sacred beauty of the Cherry Blossom. The trees now have been planted and transplanted to various parts of Washington so that Washington, D. C. in the spring time has definitely the taste of Japan and owes it all to the gift from the Mayor of Tokyo.

Actually when you compare the beauty loving nature, the flower adoring minds of these people it is more than difficult to reconcile the vicious brutal war-like attitude possessed by them but a few years ago. It is one of the not humorous but oddly fantastic workings of the Oriental mind, not capable of comprehension by we Americans that must rest in this inconsistency of personality.

Mr. Brannon tells me repeatedly of the little waitress in the Dai Iti Hotel who will bring him a spray of peach blossoms or plum blossoms, carefully see that he waters them

daily so that they will live their maxium life and shed their
beauty as long as possible.

It is in the month of Shigatsu (April) that the Sakura
No Hana Sakimasu - The Cherry Blossoms Bloom. The contagious
fragrance of Mother Nature's beauty instills itself in the very
minds of the Japanese people and even I, today, as the fateful
month approaches, am able to see the Japanese in their dismal
surroundings of a battered and broken city step more lightly
and smile more gayly.

There are many kinds of Cherry Trees and Cherry Blossoms.
The kind that was sent to Washington was called the 5-colored
blossom - that is, 5 different shades of pink merging from
almost white to a near red. The national crest of the Emperor
is even a flower - it is a crysanthenum called the Kiku. The
crest of the Samurai or the famous war class of Japan is a
half crysanthenum and water representing the product of the
sea called the Kiku Su. Many of the Mon or family crests that
are worn on all of the good garments of Japanese symbolize
flowers.

Nothing perhaps is more beautiful than the dark eyed,
darker haired little Japanese girl who carries in her hair a
single flower to match the sparkle of her spring-loving eyes,
encasing it all in the lovely colored kimono of spring time
which often possesses a flower design.

And this Mother is all that I have to say in my composition. If you can forget the family troubles, personal ties
and even that you are miles away from me and sister then the
ten minutes it has taken to read this will not have been in vain.

All my love and kisses -

                                        elaine

For a while I considered starting a business in Japan. I thought my friend, Mr. Tsuchiya, might be helpful in figuring out how to make the right connections. Brannon thought Tsuchiya hung around us so he could brag to his friends in the Diet (the Japanese Parliament) about his inside "trial knowledge." Tsuchiya appeared to dabble in politics and was a follower of General Ugaki. He was a champion fencer and got his start in business by negotiating a labor-management dispute for a big Japanese company.

Brannon and Logan had to travel to Izu Nagaoka to see General Ugaki. Trying to navigate the Army bureaucracy to make the arrangements for their transportation made me wish other Occupation personnel considered the trial attorneys as "Very Important People." No one appreciated how much we needed Ugaki's testimony. Uncooperative officials seemed to delight in citing endless regulations to me. Complicating matters, Logan and Brannon needed to take their

Japanese interpreters with them, leaving me to justify it all to an Army major who seemed to delight in making my life difficult. But I worked it out through the system for my bosses.

CHAPTER 12 ~ TRAVEL, WORK AND PLAY

An invitation arrived to dine with the prince. Some other invitees were an American major, his wife, one of the defense attorneys, and Marquis Matsudaira. Matsudaira had been secretary to Marquis Kido. General MacArthur's staff had many meetings with Mastsudaira along with other top Japanese officials when the time came for the selection of defendants. He was a courtly gentleman known to have been on fairly close terms with the emperor.

The dinner was not at the Imperial Palace, but at the prince's residence, an amazing dwelling with exquisite paneled woodwork and many elephant tusks. There were beautiful paintings, vases, lacquered boxes, gold and silver figures, and gorgeous upholstery. When we went into the dining room, there was a seating diagram and I noticed the Prince seated me beside him—a place of honor. We talked about sports and were completely at ease. The menu for the meal was printed in French with the Imperial Seal.

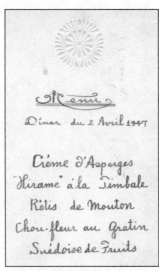

Menu at Takamatsu dinner

Everything on the table was imprinted with the flower pattern of the Imperial Household, the chrysanthemum. The food was western or continental and very good. We started with cream-of-asparagus soup, fish soufflé, and fresh spinach, which the prince referred to as "Popeye." The marquis explained that Japanese children loved the cartoon character Popeye the Sailor.

The spinach was followed by roast lamb, French-fried potatoes, cauliflower au gratin, and Jell-O with fruit. Completing the meal were burgundy and the best coffee I had tasted in Japan.

After dinner the prince and princess showed us a miniature doll collection that filled an entire room. The detail on the dolls was absolutely beautiful. I felt badly that I did not have a camera to record the amazing display. However, I did not need photographs to imprint my memories.

After dinner and coffee we went upstairs to see the doll collection. And, Mother, you've never seen anything like it. If my mind could only photograph these things so I could show you, because this was something rare and unique. They had a special room and there were about 7 tiers that stretched across the length of the room, which was about the size of our living room in Beverly Hills. Everything was in miniature. The emperor and empress on the top tier seated on their throne. Below them the ladies of the court and all these dolls were dressed in beautiful kimonos and wigs -- all in miniature. Court musicians and their instruments, regular dishes, food on gorgeous lacquer dishes, golden chopsticks, soup and rice bowls, and different-shaped dishes. Next was a tier covered with the dressing closets—it was the most perfect black lacquer ware with the Imperial Crest in gold. You open each drawer to find a tiny, tiny kimono. Another drawer had the obi, and then a drawer full of hair dressings, combs, and cosmetics with tiny pots of rouge, one whole chest full of different types of ceremonial wigs. On the bottom tier were the rickshaws and carrying chairs and, oh, it was perfect. A child would go crazy in that fairyland, and I sure could have played with that outfit.

My letter went on about how pleasant the evening was and how much fun I had teaching the prince to play gin rummy.

We went downstairs and the prince wanted to know more about gin rummy, so I opened my purse and took out two decks of cards which I brought along as a present. He suggested we play. I think he was happy to find something to do instead of entertaining those stuffed shirts, so Logan coached him and I was teaching Mrs. Matsudaira. We played a hand and I beat him 100 to 70, and we had a lot of fun. Mrs. Thompson, who I couldn't quite warm up to, wanted to leave—I guess she felt a little left out, but I kind of turned against her after she made the remark at the table that the civilian workers have it better than the dependents over here, and that the poor dependents can't go away to rest hotel. Well, I was ready to explode, but didn't say anything, but Logan did—he said, "We can't go to rest hotel either because the dependents have them all taken over," which is true. Here this couple have an apartment in a lovely apartment house with their own kitchen and the dependents get the best of everything and buy all the food they want in the commissary, and they have their car over here, which is a big Cadillac and she's telling me the dependents have it worse than the civilians—baloney to that.

I was so grateful that Brannon made me continue studying Japanese, because Prince Takamatsu complimented me on my skills with his language.

Another great outing was when Brannon and I were invited by Mr. Shimizu to his villa in the resort town of Atami. He was one of the richest men in Japan and an inventor of precision instruments. Atami was considered the Riviera of Japan. His home was occupied by a rear admiral who was living in the Japanese part of the house, which was lovely. Outside was a beautiful garden where a traditional Japanese tea ceremony was held.

Mother, you ought to see the ceremony that goes into that. You have to take out the various utensils, clean them a certain way. You have to admire the bowl and the brush to mix with the tea, and then fold the napkin. You clean them a certain way and it's quite a slow process. I was served my tea first as the guest of honor. But I had to ask permission of the man next to me if I may drink first, and he says yes. Then you have to drink it in 3-and-a-half gulps, and on the last one you have to make a noise—interesting.

Mr. Shimizu is a self-made man whose father was a farmer. From those humble beginnings he somehow managed to attend Tokyo Imperial University where he majored in electrical engineering and went on to patent two hundred inventions. I told my mother more about him as I learned so much.

We had a lovely lunch. The rice was so good; I had two bowls. One of the guests was in the whaling industry so whale steak was served. No one seemed to like it. This man was the one who invented the Japanese bomb sight after the Japanese captured the Norden bomb sight, and he duplicated it, but that was towards the end of the war. He is anything but a sympathizer with the military. He is a far-sighted humanitarian type and showed us stacks of American magazines he had saved so he can show them to the peasants and the poor people to let them know what a good standard of living should be, how Americans live, and how they must seek to improve. He also spoke in terms of America being the chosen country by God to lead the world into peace. But everyone seems to talk against Russia, almost as if a war with Russia is inevitable, but I still don't agree.

I couldn't compare Atami to the Riviera, not having been there, but it was a beautiful spot. I kept thinking of that American admiral being so fortunate to have Mr. Shimizu's home requisitioned for his use. We could not have had a more gracious host.

One Sunday morning, Brannon and I went to Kamakura to see the cherry blossoms. We walked through entire lanes of fully blooming cherry trees after which we took part in a traditional tea ceremony again at the home of Mr. Shimizu, who had invited us for a second visit. We saw the giant Buddha. It was huge! Walking through entire lanes of cherry blossoms made the day especially memorable.

Despite his accomplishments in the field of armaments, Mr. Shimizu was not militaristic and spoke in glowing terms about peace. It was not unusual to meet men of his caliber who appeared to be genuinely happy at the prospect of changes in the Japanese way of life. I felt pride knowing I was part of something worthwhile and historical.

At work, Brannon was interviewing witnesses. I prepared so many affidavits; I gave up counting. The work seemed to be tearing him apart. He became increasingly moody and impatient. Watching him, I developed an appreciation for what dedication to a client really means. No matter how lawyers feel, the dedicated ones keep going on behalf of their clients, knowing the responsibility and outcome depends on an accurate, articulate, confident, and sincere presentation. Brannon was that kind of lawyer.

Brannon had stayed in touch with Admiral Nagano's widow. She decided to return to Shikoku, her native prefecture. When she came in to say goodbye to him, she brought several cards the admiral had written just after the surrender. They were farewell notes to his friends. At the time, he had contemplated hari-kari, the ritual suicide, but decided he could help his country more by standing trial and claiming full responsibility for the attack on Pearl Harbor.

Sir William Webb antagonized the entire defense staff by accusing the attorneys of spreading enemy propaganda when any attempt was made to introduce evidence against the Russians. As already mentioned, Russia had been in the war against the Japanese for merely six days before the surrender. When it came to atrocities, there was evidence the Soviet troops had also committed many acts.

Ben Blakeney, the attorney for Ambassador Togo, infuriated the Russians when he went to Chief Justice Webb and told him his efforts to interrogate important Japanese witnesses, including nine generals, had failed because they were still held as prisoners in the Soviet Union. He stated that there were many other witnesses the defense would like to summon from "behind the Iron Curtain," but he could not expect favorable testimony "from a man with a gun in his back."

The Soviet prosecutor was so furious; he accused Mr. Blakeney of attacking the Soviet Union. Justice Webb somehow kept control of the courtroom and the problem seemed to go away without further incident.

Around the same time I recorded an interrogation of Ambassador Nomura, well known as the envoy specially sent to Washington by Premier Tojo to personally deliver the message that further negotiations would not stop the war. Although he was supposed to deliver the message to the secretary of state before 1 p.m., he, along with Ambassador Kurusu, arrived *after* Pearl Harbor was bombed. He was never considered as a possible defendant and it was difficult to find anyone who did not have good things to say about him. When he claimed ignorance of the timing of the attack, he was believed. Brannon told me that there was absolute proof that Nomura did not know hostilities had already started before he had a chance to deliver the final note.

Nomura was an interesting man. Physically he was large—at least six feet, and not thin or wasted looking. He knew President Franklin D. Roosevelt and other American diplomats, all of whom spoke highly of him. Reporters recounted witnessing Ambassador Kurusu (who had been sent to Washington shortly after Nomura) actually shedding tears when he found out what had happened.

Nomura was late for an appointment with Brannon, who teased him for his "lateness" (referring of course to the debacle over Japan's failure to inform the U.S. of the attack on Pearl Harbor). Nomura, who had a great sense of humor, said, "There would never have been a so-called 'sneak' attack on Pearl Harbor if Miss Elaine had been the typist at the Japanese Embassy when the note came from Japan saying negotiations were going nowhere." The only Japanese employee available to type the message had done so using the "hunt-and-peck" system, thus the translation and transcription were so delayed that when Kurusu and Nomura reached the White House to deliver the message, it was too late.

John Brannon and Ambassador Nomura

Meanwhile, even with all the activities going on in Japan, I was trying to help my mother—who was miles away and bitterly unhappy in Argentina—obtain passage on a ship and return to America. Although the trial was continuing with no end in sight, I still thought I'd be able to leave by summer. I wondered where my mother and I might settle down. I thought about applying to law school again. I wrote to law schools at the University of Southern California and to the Universities of Miami, Hastings, and Denver. I considered asking one or two of the judges to write letters of recommendation for me but I did not follow through, as it didn't seem urgent. Yet, that idea stayed in the back of my mind waiting for the right time.

One day Judge Norcroft, the judge from New Zealand, invited me out. I refused his invitation, thinking, What would I talk about to a judge who had the power to sentence our clients to death? At the time I was still evading Herbert Norman who continued to call me.

I started acquiring things to bring back home such as a camera, a leather briefcase, a string of pearls. Cameras were available on the black market in exchange for cigarettes. I acquired both a Canon and a Mamiya camera for only a few dollars. Pearls could be purchased for ten dollars at the PX. When the PX had shipments from China, embroidered Mandarin coats were only twelve dollars. Everything was so inexpensive, including merchandise from the States. They were finally getting in some Stateside clothes. My luck in finding Japanese dressmakers left me not wanting for dresses or suits. I was more attracted to the items I knew I would ordinarily not have been able to afford.

As the court drama unfolded, it occasionally occurred to me that the intrigues and personalities of the trial would make a great book. I remember thinking I would probably get sued for libel; in my letters home to my mother I was not always very kind in assessing some of the Japanese I met.

Though I repeatedly wrote to my mother that I would be home in August, the language problem and the need to translate everything into Japanese had extended the trial. As I mentioned, unlike Nuremberg, we were unable to use simultaneous translation. The translation process in the courtroom remained laborious and time consuming.

There was occasional drama in the courtroom, as in the Blakeney-Soviet exchange. That paled in comparison, however, to the war between the chief justice and David Smith. Smith was the attorney for Koki Hirota, who had been premier in 1936 and foreign minister at another time.

Early on, Smith asked for a separate trial for his client saying that having him stand trial with military and naval officers would keep him from having a fair and impartial trial; to have him tried with Japan's military leaders would hopelessly prejudice his defense. His request was denied.

Smith submitted a motion to have the indictment against his client dismissed. He argued that Hirota had never served in the armed forces and when he had become premier in 1936, it was "too late to set the clock back," for this was a period of time when Japan was in such turmoil that the emperor selected Hirota to form a cabinet to control an attempted coup by military men. Mentioning the emperor was something that had never been done in the trial. This generated lots of reaction from other counsel. Once again, Justice Webb denied his motion.

Another encounter between Webb and Smith received a lot of attention and endless discussions. Smith questioned correct legal procedure, stated who was not following it, who should have been following it, and on and on. It started when one of the defense counsel questioned a Japanese journalist who was testifying about a prewar cabinet that had fallen. There was nothing unusual in the questions he was being asked, but Sir William broke in with questions of his own. Smith objected to the Tribunal's "undue interference with the ordinary examination of the witness." The judge was inflamed by Smith's remarks, considering them offensive, and demanded he apologize. Smith refused. The court recessed. When it came back in session, the drama continued as Sir William again demanded an apology. Smith continued to refuse and was thrown out, and excluded from practicing before the Tribunal. It was the first time something that contentious happened.

By this time, I wanted and needed a vacation, but it could only be granted if I applied for sick leave. The doctor wrote that I had nervous tension connected with my work, and I should go away immediately. I traveled to Numazu and stayed at an oceanfront hotel on the Izu Peninsula. I was in a tiny fishing village and the pervasive smell of drying fish reminded me constantly of cod liver oil. The hotel was located in the midst of beautiful pine trees about fifty feet from the ocean. It was lovely and quiet and, since there was nothing else to do, I was able to rest. I got sunburned by spending too many hours on the beach, swimming, and rowing a boat out into the bay.

Ocean shore at Numazu

Fishing Industry in Numazu   **Fisherman mending his nets**

On one of the days, I took a taxi to Nagaoka and visited with General Ugaki and his wife. My Japanese language skills were still limited and they spoke no English, but we enjoyed each other's company. Relaxed and happy in such a beautiful place, I was able to travel without feeling lost, regardless of my poor language skills. Sometimes I got by; other times, I did not.

I could see Mt. Fuji, which looked just as it did in picture postcards I'd seen. I had already developed a deep love for the country of Japan, and I imagined bringing my mother here, showing her the places that were so special to me, and introducing her to people—like Prince Takamatsu.

The River Kana in Numazu with Mt. Fuji in the background

In June of 1947, I received my mother's final letter from Buenos Aires. What an ordeal she had gone through trying to get back home! I promised I would return and go to law school in the fall. But then I began imagining how hard it would be not to see the trial through to its end.

Logan was preparing to present the economic phase of the Pacific War and Brannon would present the military preparations. My desires drew me both ways. Leave? Or stay? My constant dilemma.

Since the Japanese Navy had held out for peace longer than anyone else, I did not mind working so hard for their "cause." Nonetheless, I recognized the problems and what it would take to overcome them if the defense were to succeed. General MacArthur, the supreme commander of the allied forces, had requested American defense attorneys. Now the rulers of the court were getting nasty when we tried to put up a good fight.

In July, I heard from my mother that she would arrive in New York around July 15, so she planned to stay temporarily at her brother's summer place in New Jersey. I decided to make definite plans to join her there as soon as I heard she was settled. Yet, when I considered leaving Japan, I was again torn. I wanted to keep earning more money so I could save for my future education. My desire to stay and travel in Japan was strong, but I was worried about my mother.

Back and forth I went. I finally wrote out all the pros and cons in a letter and asked my mother for advice. I resolved to book a phone call with her as soon as she was back in America. Trying to apply to law schools from such a long distance was difficult, but I was determined.

The weather turned warm and I often swam at the Meiji pool, part of a gorgeous aqua-sports facility built for the Olympics. I also took advantage of the good weather to get in some horseback riding. Mr. Logan was busy putting together Kido's case, interweaving it with testimony and the diary entries. He escaped the scorching temperatures in Tokyo by traveling out to the Kido family's beachside villa.

Brannon and I began to knock off every afternoon around 3:30 to play tennis before getting down to our evening's work. We were deeply involved in preparing the naval defense. I listened to vivid descriptions of the attack on Pearl Harbor. As part of John's presentation, many of the Japanese naval officers had their affidavits prepared for the trial. I jokingly wrote home that, "I had attacked Pearl Harbor so many times in one week I could see the American battleships jumping up and hitting the Japanese planes."

Another fascinating person I met while working with the defense was Paul Wenneker, the German Naval Attaché who spent the entire war in Tokyo. He was a striking, good-looking man, desperately trying to avoid repatriation to Germany. He provided us with a great deal of useful information for the case.

Admiral Wenneker caused me to be aware of how different the Japanese on trial seemed to be from the Germans. Somehow the majority of our clients did not truly seem like criminals. I felt the ones who had been fighting in China for so long probably fit the description of what a war criminal was, but not the others. The only defendants who looked strong, healthy, and commanding were Generals Sato and Muto; these two became special favorites. Thus far, I had not heard of any atrocities connected with them, but because I had not worked on their particular cases, I did not have a lot of knowledge regarding this. I knew Colonel Kenworthy liked them, which lessened feelings of guilt I had for liking them.

After the death of Admiral Nagano, Admiral Shimada became our primary client. His young daughter, Hiroko, often came to visit him. She was about fifteen years old when she first came, and I soon fell in love with her. She was faithful in coming at least once a week to see her dad. She adored John Brannon. It was as if we were a big family.

The admiral had the kindest face of any of the defendants. Something about him set him apart from the others.

Another fascinating, popular person I had the privilege to meet at a tennis tournament in Tokyo was Fritzi Berger—a famous ice skater from Austria. She was married to a Japanese man who was the grandson of Mikimoto, the Pearl King. She offered to teach me how to skate if I would teach her how to play tennis.

Fritzi was Viennese. She was energetic and seemed so happy to be making American friends after spending the war years in Tokyo. At an ice-skating rink in Tokyo I watched her skate. She had actually beaten Sonja Henie, another world-class champion.

Fritzi Berger with son and John Brannon

Fritzi's skating was spectacular. When someone is that gifted I suppose they do not lose too much of their skill despite the absence of skating opportunities in Japan during the war. My trips with her to the skating rink were so much fun.

Fritzi told me about being in Japan during the war and how bad conditions were, but she had never lost her sparkle. She was happy the Americans were the occupiers. She felt certain Japan would clean up the mess the bombing had brought and reuse the opening of this large and beautiful skating rink as an example of the "new" government's progress. She had only one child, a boy. She said she was always looking at children of mixed-race marriages simply out of curiosity to see what they looked like. Her son was very handsome—she was a very proud mother. I liked her so much.

Planning trips was becoming harder and harder. A place I wanted to see was being used for soldiers on leave from Korea. This place was Aso Kanko, the site of a semi-active volcano. The resort hotel in Kyushu was fully occupied. The soldiers there were a lot more important than civil servants trying to escape from work. So, I began to think of going to Karuizawa instead and a trip materialized. It was in the mountains and had horses, tennis, and golf. A trip to Karuizawa materialized. Brannon would go as well for he hoped to see Admiral Wenneker again.

Karuizawa was known as the place where foreign nationals were sent during the war. Before the war, it was a favorite resort for foreigners living in Japan. Logan played golf and he wanted to come along not just to play, but to see this place. Logan thought I would be a natural at golf. Little did he know—I was not. The idea of hitting golf balls was something I had not thought about. I was devoted to tennis. But I reveled in my good fortune to be on a golf course without a required fee.

This benefit was true, too, of my access to horses. By this time, I had become quite confident about horseback riding and was learning jumping with my new teacher, Andy, a cavalry enlisted man. He was a daredevil and regularly put on demonstrations of trick riding. So when I was told there were stables at Karuizawa, I looked forward to having some practice time so I could go back and impress Andy.

Just before we left for Karuizawa, Logan asked me to buy Marquis Kido a birthday present. I chose two books. I figured someone who liked to write as much as he did (thinking of his diary) would also love to read. Whereas Brannon loved to shop and often went to the PX, Logan never did.

On occasions, the PX held a one-time sale of special merchandise. I had to get there at the advertised time and usually wait in a long line, but the sale items, like the Chinese linens, were spectacular. I bought several, including elaborate banquet cloths that were priced at less than fifty dollars each. I bought beautiful nightgowns and lingerie. So there I was—shopping again.

I stayed at the Mampei Hotel in Karuizawa. Brannon still needed to meet with Admiral Wenneker, courtesy of the Japanese government. The admiral was evidently not involved with the Occupation authorities.

Accommodations were very difficult to obtain. The Army personnel who had been put in charge of running the hotels were very slow in following through. I realized how spoiled I had been by being able to say I worked for the Tribunal and then get whatever I needed.

I stayed in Karuizawa for three days, played tennis, went horseback riding and enjoyed the cool weather. I decided to take my first golf lesson with a Japanese pro who was impressed with my natural ability. However, when I tried to play on a real course with Brannon, I couldn't even "find the ball."

Karuizawa was full of Germans; there I met Admiral Wenneker. I wanted to dislike him, but found it hard to do. He was charming, with a delightful wife and adorable children. He showed us pictures taken with our Japanese clients in their prime before the war. I was overwhelmed by the changes in their appearances. When he showed us a picture with a swastika in it, I felt sick inside. Brannon interviewed him and gathered pertinent information for the defense; I recorded it all.

While in Karuizawa, I renewed my friendship with Fritzi Berger (Mrs. Nishikawa). Fritzi and her husband had a summer home there that was a good haven away from the scorching-hot weather in Tokyo. I was thrilled when she told me to stop by the Mikimoto store on the Ginza. Once again it was open for business. My hopes were set on getting a nice string of pearls for a good price.

When we returned to Tokyo I thought I had reached a decision about coming home. I wrote my mother that I would leave Japan at the end of August. I knew the trial would not be over, but I thought the case would be prepared, and I would not let people down too badly if I left then. I hoped my sister and her husband would settle in California and that my mother might join them there. At the same time, my mother seemed to like the New Jersey house belonging to her brother, my uncle, Martin. I was still waiting to hear from law schools and considered going to New York University while living in New Jersey.

Back at the office, we prepared for the reopening of court on August 4th. Logan was to present the "Pacific phase" of the defense; Brannon would come in towards the end. We needed to prepare Admiral Shimada's defense. I did not want to leave any loose ends, but thought that, before the long work hours closed in on me, maybe I could fit in a few more trips.

The 2nd Demobilization Bureau (an outfit composed of all the former Japanese Navy officers) announced their intention to present me with a kimono and obi in recognition of my service in defending Admirals Shimada and Oka. I was hopeful that the Navy officers we were defending would not hang; but I did not think they would get off either. Receiving the tribute from the Navy men meant to me they knew my heart and soul were in the work I was called upon to do.

The Japanese looked for any chance to give a "presento"—a special gift. From the least elaborate that I received from the maids and waitresses, to the silk, the lacquer ware, and the mementos from the lawyers and clients, I always appreciated how thoughtful these people were and how much they showed their appreciation for any kindness shown to them.

Brannon and Logan also adopted the custom. They gave me a "presento" if I did something extraordinary for their comfort. Likewise, I enjoyed giving them small gifts, which I presented to them with a bow, a smile, and "dozo" present.

CHAPTER 13 ~ THE TRIAL PROCEEDINGS

The recess lasted six weeks, not nearly enough time for us to prepare. Court resumed on August 4, 1947. The opening statement was given by Yoshitsuga Takahashi, counsel for Admiral Shimada. He said, "The attack on Pearl Harbor was not long in preparation, nor was it a premeditated act indicating aggressive war." Reporter Arnold wrote in his book *The Other Nuremberg*:

> *Takahashi summed up his view with the observation that 'the powder keg of war with its many fuses was plainly visible for all to see. Who lit the first fuse is all important—not which fuse set off the first blast.' But the metaphor was faulty. The first blast had been along a stretch of South Manchurian Rail way track on September 18, 1931, and the incontrovertible evidence was that the Japanese Army lit the fuse.*

Brackman's observation sounded accurate and confirmed what Logan and Brannon said from the beginning, that Japan's actions in China would be the hardest to justify. We were not called upon to defend the generals who were part of the military's dominance of the country, "hell-bent" as it was on conquering northern China.

As Logan began to launch his defense, he was repeatedly stymied by the Tribunal and managed to have very few documents entered into evidence. Everyone knew what a superb lawyer he was. It was easy to feel that the judges wanted to convict the defendants and were reluctant to listen to the defense.

Logan's frustration sometimes came back into the office with him. He acted as if it was my fault instead of the Tribunal's. The Japanese lawyers were also becoming more difficult. I had to wait weeks for their final corrections before giving up and "cutting the stencil" on an affidavit they were to sign, only to have them arrive with numerous corrections as I was typing the final page. Stencils were machines used for making copies, and they were messy and difficult to use.

Many Japanese officers of high rank testified in order to be helpful. The Japanese lawyers said there was no intention to mistreat prisoners of war—it happened because lines of communication had been cut, food and medical supplies could not be shipped, and it was beyond the control of the High Command. The prosecution, however, pointed out that the infamous Bataan Death March occurred at a time when the lines of communication had not been cut, and Japan was riding high in its efforts to strike the unsuspecting enemy.

One of the high-ranking officers testified that the planning of the invasion and occupation of the Philippines, Malaya, Singapore, Hong Kong, the Netherlands East Indies, Burma, and New Guinea was not part of an overall war effort. That did not ring true, either. It certainly made me wonder how this small nation had struck in so many far-flung places, all at the same time.

What presented the best opportunity for Logan was the testimony from General Okada, who had been chief of War Preparations in the War Ministry from 1940 to 1943. He testified that Japan lacked oil and did not have the capability to supply everyone necessary to secure the many far-flung places initially attacked. He summarized by saying Japan simply did not have the resources for a protracted war.

Sir William Webb then addressed General Okada. Sir Webb stated boldly that the general's testimony actually demonstrated careful preparation for war. This remark led Logan to say, "On the contrary, the evidence shows there could be no war, based on the materials they had on hand."

Sir William disagreed vehemently, saying there was no explanation for the fact that so many advised against war, and yet war took place.

Sir William appeared to have taken over the case for the prosecution; he argued with Logan when he said the United States arms embargo was designed to choke Japan. Webb's retort was, "And your case is because America would not supply you with arms, you were justified in attacking her, although you acquired them to attack some other nation?"

Logan's response was, "That is not my point at all. The West's embargo had strangled Japan at a time when the United States was shipping arms to China, who was engaged in war with Japan -- and the strangulation of Japan led to the war."

The answer came from one of the lead prosecutors that the argument made no sense as the United States was shipping arms to a country that was a victim of Japanese aggression.

There was quite a bit of testimony about the timing of the Pearl Harbor attack, most of it designed to show that certain of the Japanese leaders intentionally set things up so that the delivery of the message would be late and the attack would not be crippled in any way.

Volumes can and have been written on what really happened. The defense evidence was that four days after the fleet set sail for Hawaii, Prince Takamatsu told his brother, Emperor Hirohito, that the Navy thought that in a war against Britain and the United States, Japan could not win. The emperor consulted with Admiral Nagano and Prime Minister Tojo and it was Tojo who expressed confidence that the attack would be a success.

Sir William was known to have been disappointed that the emperor had not been indicted. When he heard the testimony, he said it was the emperor who directed the program to go forward. Logan then said as far as the emperor was concerned, he was following constitutional government. Sir William blurted out that he was saying, "The king can do no wrong under the constitution."

Logan's response was, "If the cabinet advised the emperor that it is necessary for the country to go to war for self-preservation and self-defense; self-defense is a good defense to any crime. They didn't want to go to war, Your Honor. All the evidence points against it. They knew that they couldn't win the war, and the prosecution evidence so shows it, and so does ours. They were driven to it."

When it was time for the individual defendant's cases to proceed, it didn't seem as though the defense had done very well. This was a harrowing time for the attorneys; they had to decide whether or not to put their clients on the stand. As it turned out, fifteen did testify. General Doihara, who seemed the most vulnerable to me, did not testify, nor did three other generals.

I decided to wait until we finished putting in the naval evidence before applying for orders to go home. Despite the hectic pace and demands of Logan and Brannon, I was learning a lot and had begun to write running commentaries and small courtroom speeches. Logan and Brannon treated my ideas and opinions with a lot of respect. I knew how they felt when an affidavit I spent hours preparing was rejected by the Tribunal. The chief judge would not allow Brannon to explain why documents the Tribunal refused to allow into evidence should have been received.

When evidence was offered by either side, the judge determined if it would be received or rejected. Usually the attorney trying to keep a document, photo, or testimony out of evidence stated a reason such as "no proper foundation," "hearsay," or "facts not in evidence." The judge then ruled. The attorney could note for the record that he was taking exception to the ruling, which preserved rights on appeal. But Chief Justice Webb abruptly ruled on the admission of evidence without waiting for the attorney to make whatever point he wished to make. He would not listen to Brannon as he offered argument to support his position. It was utterly dictatorial and almost an abuse of his power.

Brannon had great confidence. He told us, "We won this war on the battlefield; and we're not going to lose it in the courtroom." Logan planned on taking three weeks to present his case, but he was hurried along and finished in seven days. The defendants had a choice of whether or not they wanted to present opening statements before they testified. Admiral Shimada and Admiral Oka did desire to present opening statements. Preparing those special affidavits took hours and hours.

Marquis Kido's turn came after that of the bureaucrat Okinori Kaya (who had been finance minister during some of the most crucial years). Kido was the "star" because of his closeness to Emperor Hirohito. Along with most of the other defendants, he was charged with almost all of the counts in the indictment.

It was permissible to read an affidavit into the record. That was how Kido's defense started—by reading the 297-page statement. Having typed it, I knew the heart of it was showing his separation from the militarists. He said he was against everything that was planned, from the actual plans for war itself to the Tripartite Pact bringing the Nazi government and Japan into an unholy wedding and, of course, the actual commencement of hostilities. The emperor could not know everything, nor could he do anything.

As previously noted, Marquis Kido almost took credit for preventing the loss of American lives in an invasion of Japan when he said, "The dropping of the atomic bombs was a good thing." He wanted it clear that he opposed the war, even though he was the one who recommended to the emperor that General Tojo become premier. His explanation was that, had Tojo not been in charge and strong enough to maintain order, there would have been havoc, assassinations, and chaos.

Joseph Keenan, the American prosecutor, sparred with Kido for days in the courtroom. There were heated exchanges as the same questions were asked in three or four different ways. Logan was exhausted. Marquis Kido went back to prison hated more than ever by the military defendants, who knew his aim had been to target them as the real culprits.

For me, the hardest assignment I had was played out in the massive courtroom. I learned Kido's testimony had been reported in Stateside newspapers because of his proximity to the emperor.

Blakeney represented Togo, Japan's foreign minister. Blakeney was smart, but a disagreeable character who did not cooperate with the rest of the defense counsel. Blakeney, Logan, and Brannon were all known as the "elite" lawyers.

Togo was a tattletale and disloyal to his fellow defendants. Revising the saying "There's honor among thieves," he actually built up the prosecution's case. He started out saying that Japanese foreign policy in 1931 was under the control of the militarists. He then gave examples of how the foreign ministry officials were deceived by the Army and Navy. He said he had never dreamed the Japanese Navy would attack the American fleet at Pearl Harbor. He continued by stating that Nomura and Kurusu proposed that Roosevelt and the emperor exchange messages so it would not be clear that there was an urgent crisis about attacking the American fleet. He claimed that Admiral Nagano and his chief of staff had earlier told him the Navy wanted to carry out a surprise attack. They wanted the negotiations with the United States to be left open so the war could start with the effectiveness a surprise attack would bring. That was all Brannon had to hear.

As Togo continued to testify, he claimed Admirals Shimada and Nagano had threatened him at Sugamo Prison saying he was not to tell the court the Japanese Navy had favored a surprise attack on Pearl Harbor. He further claimed the two admirals had promised serious repercussions against him. Admiral Nagano was already dead and Admiral Shimada had already testified. I wondered, What could these two prisoners have done to him?

Brannon and Logan vigorously cross-examined Togo. Brannon asked him if he was prepared to say that Nagano and Shimada lied.

Togo's answer was he did not have confidence in the memory of those men. He further stated that Admiral Nagano said he would take full responsibility for the timing of the attack.

Brannon was furious that this defendant so willingly turned on his fellow defendants. Togo had portrayed himself as a statesman. He did appear more sophisticated than some of the other defendants. For some unknown reason, the prosecution dropped many of the charges it had filed against him. Those charges would have implicated him in events happening before 1941. Why had the charges been dropped? The other defense attorneys did not know.

As more and more Army personnel poured into Japan, Tokyo became less and less pleasant. Life seemed to be dominated by paperwork. The feeling of being a part of a small community was fast disappearing; we knew the Japanese were busy putting Japan back on its feet. The Japanese had been repatriating the Germans who had languished in their country all during the war.

Initially, Brannon issued a subpoena for Admiral Wenneker to come testify. He thought it might help the defense. However, when the last repatriation boat was leaving, John decided to release Wenneker rather than risk the wrath of GHQ. In addition, during this time, a New Zealand officer announced his plans to marry one of Wenneker's daughters.

On August 21, 1947, I saw Brannon present his opening statement. I was nervous on his behalf, but I need not have been. He made a wonderful appearance in court. He attempted to show how Admiral Shimada had not been part of a military clique; nor had he sanctioned atrocities by any Navy personnel; nor had the Navy ordered a sneak attack on Pearl Harbor. Both he and Admiral Oka expressed remorse that hostilities had started without advance notice. The blame, Shimada said, was the Foreign Ministry of which Ambassador Togo was the chief.

The defense did not go smoothly when evidence was introduced to connect Shimada with misuse of prisoners of war as slave laborers and the use of "hell ships" to transport them. He denied knowing of those things. He did admit knowing of attacks against British holdings without notice having been given. His explanation—he had not attended the staff meeting where the timing had been discussed. Shimada offered his apologies for this having happened, just as he apologized for prisoners of war being mistreated.

It was difficult to know how Shimada's defense appeared to the judges. We had to wait until decision day to see whether the Tribunal believed the Navy had not wanted to go to war and that Admiral Yamamoto had "his arm twisted" by the Council and given in, hoping a successful initial attack would bring negotiations and peace.

From a cosmetic viewpoint, Admiral Shimada looked good. He was handsome with nothing warlike in his looks. His defense had been influenced by the need to protect the emperor, which seemed to be a common goal of all of the defendants.

Admiral Shimada had given Brannon more freedom in planning his defense than any other defendant gave to any other attorney, basically putting his life in Brannon's hands.

The prosecution made a big show about Admiral Shimada being appointed Navy minister; if Tojo knew the admiral would vote for war, it would secure a unanimous vote. Unanimity was a prerequisite to going forward.

We had information that Admiral Toyoda, who was anti-Tojo, had been considered for the position of Navy minister. We went to special lengths to keep this information out of our case. We did not know if it would be necessary to recall Shimada to the stand.

Life went on as Brannon thought about how he would sum up the Navy's position and individually close for Admirals Shimada and Oka. Admiral Oka had been chief of the Bureau of Naval Affairs and vice minister of the Navy and was supposedly responsible for the use of the so-called "hell ships."

Oka's testimony was brief. He denied the Navy ordered a sneak attack on Pearl Harbor. He attributed the failure of the note being delivered in a timely fashion on the Foreign Ministry, which meant Togo. As to the atrocities with which he was charged, he apologized profusely, saying that, considering the history of the Japanese Navy, its teachings, and its training, as well as the education of the Japanese, it was inconceivable that the atrocities charged could have happened. His apology preceded Admiral Shimada's testimony, who said virtually the same thing with profound sorrow at what happened.

About this time, my maid, Yasuko, became ill and I visited her in the hospital in Yokohama. While this stressful defense was going on in our office, I kept wishing I could take Yasuko back to America when I returned. She was the sweetest girl and would do anything in the world for me. I knew she had an unhappy home life and was quite shy. I strongly encouraged her to meet new people. She finally relaxed around me.

Each of the Japanese girls who worked at the Kanda Kai Kan was wonderful. They worked hard, though they looked so tiny, delicate, and pretty in their kimonos. I wanted to help them as much as I could by giving them food and clothing.

I became obsessed with finding the "right" ship home, and discovered the Maritime Commission had ships going to New York through the Panama Canal. These ships had a reputation for nice accommodations; whereas the Army and Navy ships' quarters were crowded, though they did stop in Honolulu. I could not decide whether I wanted to see Hawaii or Panama. I tried to figure out the best deal. It was not urgent so my pursuit was easily sidetracked.

In the meantime, I applied for a trip to Kyushu. A doctor authorized a rest leave to the Island. When the Army called the doctor to see if I was legitimately in need of official leave, I was furious to have had my intentions questioned. The powers in charge wanted me to use my annual leave instead of sick leave. I finally went to the Pearl Farm at Toba Bay. The trip there was tiring, but well worth it. I detoured to visit the Ise Shrine where only emperors worship. It was famous for its simplicity and ability to create a feeling of utter peace.

The scenery on the way to the Pearl Farm was beautiful. There were guides to show how the oysters were implanted with mother of pearl obtained from Chesapeake Bay in Maryland, U.S.A. The oysters were placed in cages in the water where the oyster did its work, making a pearl. The divers were all women, trained in the art of diving, which required holding the breath for a long time as they brought up the cages. I asked to join them in the water and was allowed to do so. I found out I surely was not a pearl diver.

There I met Mikimoto, who was then ninety years old and very active in overseeing the empire he had created. I had my introduction through Fritzi Nishikawa, who told me to bring the gentleman some Black and White Scotch, which he liked. His secretary invited me to lunch and served me, among other things, an oyster. I had to refuse it explaining that I did not eat shellfish. Judaism has a prohibition in its dietary laws against eating shellfish. I knew I could not explain that, so I did not enlarge on my refusal. I found out that the oyster had a pearl inside. Before I left, Mr. Mikimoto gave me a lovely strand of pearls. I was overcome with gratitude.

MIKIMOTO WEARS A LONG BLACK CAPE AND AN ANCIENT DERBY HE BOUGHT IN LONDON

Mikimoto, the Pearl King

Mikimoto's signature

A MIKIMOTO WORKER, CHIEKO KATO, 21, INSERTS A MOTHER-OF-PEARL BEAD INTO AN OYSTER WHICH WILL BUILD PEARL AROUND IT

The Pearl King

Mr. Mikimoto of Japan is making a postwar fortune by irritating oysters

PHOTOGRAPHS FOR LIFE BY ALFRED EISENSTAEDT

If properly irritated in a scientific manner, oysters produce big lustrous pearls. They are called cultured pearls and in Japan the cultured-pearl business has suddenly come back to lusty life, having found a lush and handy market in the U.S. occupation forces. Strings of cultured pearls selling at $20 to $130 are one of the most popular items in the PXs throughout Japan. As a result the man who is Japan's unchallenged pearl king, wizened, 89-year-old Kokichi Mikimoto, made $200,000 during the first year of the American occupation, which gave him the biggest personal income in Japan.

Mr. Mikimoto laid the foundation of his fortune by perfecting a way to force oysters to create pearls. The Chinese had first discovered the technique in the 13th Century but Mikimoto borrowed and improved it. The Mikimoto method is to insert a tiny mother-of-pearl bead into a healthy oyster and then put it back into the ocean, where the irritated oyster slowly covers the bead with layer upon layer of nacre, the lustrous, opalescent substance of which pearls are made. Average-size pearls are formed in from three to five years, big ones in 10. By trial and error Mikimoto discovered the best ways of inserting beads into oysters and the conditions under which they flourish, but

even though his general methods have been copied by other Japanese, nobody yet has equaled his production performance. Mikimoto's cultured pearls are indistinguishable to laymen from natural pearls. By using X-rays and by determining specific gravity, jewel experts can tell them from natural pearls, but to the legions of pearl wearers around the world the difference seems negligible. Part of Mikimoto's secret is that, despite advancing years, he gives every detail of his business minute attention—from directing his girl divers to negotiating sales with American authorities, who now take his entire output. His role in occupied Japan is important because the Japanese government, which has frozen domestic sales of both pearls and silk, hopes that exports of luxuries will help to meet Japan's war indemnities and pay for food imports. In the past year Mr. Mikimoto has sold $300,000 worth of pearls to Americans. Some of his best products, however, are being hoarded for a reopening of world trade. At present he has a stock of tiny mother-of-pearl beads sufficient to raise 15,000,000 cultured pearls. Before that runs out he must send agents to the U.S. because a major source of the mother-of-pearl beads he inserts into his oysters is in, of all places, the Mississippi River where it passes Iowa.

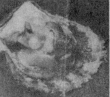

PEARL IN OYSTER IS ABOUT 3 YEARS OLD

CONTINUED ON NEXT PAGE 99

The Pearl King article (1 of 2)

Pearl King CONTINUED

CONJURING TRICKS are done by Mikimoto to amuse girl workers. In his left hand he holds paper to start.

EMPTY-HANDED, he shows that paper has vanished after being torn into small bits and scattered on ground.

PAPER REAPPEARS in Mikimoto's mouth after much hocus-pocus accompanied by usual professional patter.

Lively old Mikimoto loves to do tricks to entertain his factory workers

In his kimono, English bowler and long, dark-serge cape (see opposite page) Mr. Mikimoto is a mirth-provoking figure, but if Mr. Mikimoto is at all crazy it is like the fox. Since 1894, when he developed his own pearl-culture process, Mikimoto has built up an industrial kingdom which had branch offices all over the world until war interrupted. Today he has 1,500 employes, a sizable fortune, 5,000,000 yen worth of pearls in stock and a booming business. He behaves toward his employes with benign paternalism, balancing extremely low wages against free medical care and other benefits that seem to have made them happy workers. On unguarded factory shelves he keeps a fortune in pearl necklaces in paper boxes. "My workers are my children," he says, smiling. "They would never steal from me." He makes them work hard but occasionally entertains them with conjuring and other divertisements. For dinner guests he saves his nicest and most surprising entertainment: while their host smirks, his guests are served oysters in which they invariably find one of Mr. Mikimoto's pearls.

BALANCING ACT is Mikimoto's favorite. He takes off his kimono, lies down on the outdoor table and then balances a paper umbrella on his bare feet as the girls look on. To cap his performance he tries to twirl the umbrella.

Though phenomenally agile for a man of 89, Mikimoto's gymnastics worry his family, who fear he will overdo.

104

The Pearl King article (2 of 2)

He found that gems of purest ray serene come from carefully protected but thoroughly discontented oysters

Mikimoto, the Pearl King

Condensed from
Pageant

Blake and Deena Clark

SPRY 91-year-old Kokichi Mikimoto is one of Japan's most useful citizens. As the pearl king of the world, he brings into Nippon 300,000 coveted U. S. dollars annually.

Many years ago Mikimoto was a humble peddler of abalone, lobsters and dried sea-slugs. He was 33 when at an exhibition of marine products in Yokohama he saw tiny seed pearls selling at exorbitant prices. An accompanying exhibit explained how pearls grow. A piece of foreign matter — sand grain or shell chip — lodges in the oyster and irritates its sensitive membranes. To protect itself the oyster sheds tears of calcium carbonate in thousands of thin layers. These solidify, and eventually the lowly oyster has converted its affliction into the loveliest of gems.

The idea flashed into Mikimoto's mind that it might be possible to encourage the oyster in doing what comes naturally. He headed for Ago Bay, an inlet where the sea is shallow and calm. There, safe from sharks and dangerous water pressure, he collected oysters, pried open the shells a fraction of an inch and inserted a grain of sand between the oyster and its shell. After weeks of work he had spread 10,000 irritated oysters about a foot apart in the water. But when he brought up a batch months later, to his dismay, he found not even the tiniest seed of a pearl.

Mikimoto stubbornly started all over again. He spent weeks and months waist-deep in water, experimenting. He went into debt to pay for divers to help collect mother shells. Into some shells he inserted

Pageant (January, '49), published by Hillman Periodicals, Inc., 535 Fifth Ave., New York 17, N. Y.

123

Reader's Digest **article on Mikimoto (page 1 of 4)**

206

clay beads, into others fragments of mother-of-pearl, glass, copper, paraffin. He varied the placing of the seed, sometimes thrusting it near the hinge, sometimes at the outer edge, or even embedding it in the iridescent inner lining. He submerged the oysters in water of varying depth and temperature.

Two discouraging years passed with no results. During the third year, multitudes of microscopic plankton, which feed on oysters, swept into the bay and killed all the mother shells except one batch in an isolated cove. With little hope, Mikimoto and Ume, his wife, spent six dispirited days opening these, as usual finding nothing. Then on July 11, 1893, a day Mikimoto will never forget, Ume opened a shell and there lay an iridescent semispherical pearl!

Laughing and crying at the same time, they feverishly opened the remaining oysters, and found four more pearls. Though far from perfect, because they were not completely round, they were nevertheless rare and valuable, and they were Mikimoto-made. Hurrying home, they placed the shining gems on the family altar and thanked the gods for their success.

Mikimoto patented his process and set out to cultivate pearls on a larger scale. At a little uninhabited island called Tatoku ("Many Virtues") he and his wife and their five children started an underwater farm of 690 sea acres. Each April for the next four years he deposited 50,000 mother shells on the floor of the bay.

His first harvest was poor, but the second was impressive. And in April 1901, when Prince Komatsu attended the Coronation of King Edward VII in London, he caused a sensation by presenting a selection of Mikimoto pearls to the King.

Mikimoto was honored by an audience with Emperor Meiji, who wished to hear from the miracle-maker himself exactly how he grew the water jewels. After the audience he went to the tomb of his recently departed wife and reported the esteem he had been accorded.

Mikimoto had not yet succeeded in making circular pearls. But in January 1905, to his astonishment, his crop yielded five perfectly round ones! Cutting them open, he found that they had formed around nuclei which had accidentally lodged in the mantle of the oyster itself. Here protective, concentric layers of smooth nacre had been thrown entirely around the irritating seed — forming the perfect gem Mikimoto had sought so desperately.

At last he had the secret. His mistake had been in placing the seed between the shell and the mantle, instead of in the flesh itself, making it physically impossible for the oyster to coat the nucleus evenly around all sides.

Now Mikimoto began inserting the bead directly into the mantle of three-year-old oysters. It had to be introduced with extreme care — not too deep lest it kill the oyster, yet deep enough to prevent its being disgorged. When the oysters were

Reader's Digest **article on Mikimoto (page 2 of 4)**

grown Mikimoto found six round pearls of breath-taking beauty in the first 100 he opened.

To protect his oysters from natural hazards Mikimoto suspended wire-mesh cages from floating rafts. There, safe from hungry eels and devilfish, the oysters could feed themselves and could be hauled to safety when threatened by plankton or unfavorable currents. Moss, seaweed and barnacles were scoured off the cages every four months, and the oysters themselves were carefully inspected and scrubbed.

"Pearls, like wine, have a vintage that is dependent upon temperature, cloudiness and rainfall," says Mikimoto. "A mild temperature, combined with just the right current flowing through the bay, can produce a perfect crop. An earthquake one year changed the current, a cold spell was ruinous to another. Heavy rains can cause lackluster. My 1948 crop should be excellent. We've had the best pearl weather in ten years!"

As his industry expanded Mikimoto could not find enough oyster larvae, or spats, for his needs. Too often they were eaten before they became large enough to undergo the culture operation. He determined to snare the spats before their enemies did. This led to another important invention — a wire screen coated with adhesive lime-cement. Lowered into the water in July, the screens are raised in November, teeming with millions of tiny spats which are transferred to protective cages where they will grow up.

Three-year-olds that grow "wild" on the ocean floor are collected by robust women divers known as *Ama*, or "Girls of the Sea." They can dive three or four fathoms, and some can stay under more than a minute. Mikimoto claims that women are better divers than men, and that their golden years are from 40 to 59. His champion is 58-year-old Kitamura Oroku.

When Mikimoto first offered his pearls in Europe at one fourth the price then current, they created a sensation. Buyers found it impossible to distinguish his more beautiful specimens from natural pearls except by using special X-ray machines. Jewelers in Paris were furious: they had a vested interest in high-priced natural pearls. The dealer who had brought in the new gems was boycotted.

A lawsuit followed. Organized jewelers attempted to prove Mikimoto pearls false. Eminent biological scientists, however, after exhaustive tests, pronounced them genuine in every respect. The only difference between nature's pearls and Mikimoto's pearls was that the part that was *not* pearl — the tiny center pellet — was introduced naturally in one and scientifically in the other. There was no real reason why they should not have the same value.

Although Mikimoto emerged victorious, he insisted upon labeling his pearls "cultured"; he wanted the world to know he had produced them.

Mikimoto opened his own salons in Los Angeles, San Francisco, Chi-

Reader's Digest **article on Mikimoto (page 3 of 4)**

cago, New York, Paris, Bombay, Shanghai and Kobe. At the height of his career he had 12 million oysters producing approximately 75 percent of the world's supply of pearls. He carried on a far-reaching American-type promotion campaign. At Philadelphia's Sesquicentennial Exposition in 1926 he displayed a five-storied pagoda, over three feet high, made entirely of pearls and worth $250,000. To Chicago's Century of Progress Exhibition in 1933 he sent an exquisite pearl model of Mount Vernon, two feet long and 18 inches high, which is now a cherished exhibit at the Smithsonian Institution.

When Mikimoto's major patent on the pearl-culture process expired in 1921, the waters in his neighborhood soon swarmed with the rafts of competitors, most of them Mikimoto-trained. Some of the newcomers dumped inferior pearls on the market. On July 10, 1933, to shame them and to demonstrate that he dealt only in the best, Mikimoto set up a furnace in the middle of one of Kobe's busiest streets where, before an incredulous public, he poured in some 750,000 second-rate gems.

Mikimoto's prize strand took him 20 years to collect. Worth $350,000, its superb center jewel is the most magnificent he ever produced. Its 47 pearls equal the length of the standard strand of 100.

During the war Mikimoto was in effect a conscientious objector. Government officials advised him to invest his money in booming war industries. "I'm a peacetime business-man," he replied. An army officer sent him a sharp Samurai sword, suggesting hara-kiri. Mikimoto ignored the gesture and moved his family to his pearl island where they lived in seclusion. His luxury industry languished until there were fewer oysters in the water than 45 years before, when Mikimoto discovered his first perfect pearls. He sells his current output, about 2000 strands a month, to the men and women of the American occupation forces, at bargain prices of $3 to $100.

Mikimoto denies the familiar belief that pearls must be worn to preserve their luster. "Like the beauty of lovely women, the soft luster of pearls fades with time. They will last for several generations if you merely caress each gem, first with a cloth dampened with alcohol and warm water, then with another dipped in water only. Never leave even a drop of moisture on your pearls. Never submerge your strand in water or any other solution; the pearls might absorb some liquid from the string and become stained or discolored. Beware of polishing powders," he concludes, "rubbing is useless. The moonglow of pearls comes from within the heart of the gem."

The old gentleman laughs at people who believe that the gems have curative properties. "But I find," he says with a twinkle, "that a woman suffers few ills which are not greatly relieved the moment she receives a string of pearls!"

Reader's Digest **article on Mikimoto (page 4 of 4)**

Pearl diver postcards

Pearl divers

Pearls were sorted and strung by hand.

I wanted to see Mt. Aso, a dormant volcano in Kyushu. Hearing that parts of Kyush resembled the Swiss Alps, I certainly wanted to go there. I left from Tokyo Central on the morning of October 1, 1947, and traveled for the first time in daylight beyond Nagoya and Kyoto.

Mount Aso

Along the way I saw a rugged and beautiful coastline with bays, islands, and little fishing villages. The ground was a plush carpet of lush, green vegetation with rolling mountains and quaint Japanese-style homes. The train made a major stop at Shimonoseki, the last city on the island of Honshu. Then it went through a tunnel under the straits to Kyushu to the last stop—Hakata.

After thirty-six hours of traveling, I arrived at the resort where I had a private room and bath. I was truly in the mountains. This hotel looked somewhat like pictures of lodges in the Swiss Alps. Many rooms were off the spacious lobby, which seemed to be set up for relaxing in front of a fireplace. There was a large dining room with large windows all around. There was a cold rain. I relaxed and forgot about the trials as I enjoyed the hot sulfur baths—a glorious treat!

Hotel Akakura

213

Warm-water swimming pool

I had a new camera to play with—it was a Canon and one of the first to be produced since the war—supposedly an exact copy of a German Leica. More than just a camera, it was a sign that Japan was emerging from the devastation the war had wrought and was getting back into production.

I resolved to go horseback riding again. Most of all, I wanted to take my time and be lazy. It was great to be miles away from the IMTFE, such a relief after the weeks and weeks of preparation for the trial. I wanted to stay away as long as I possibly could.

Riding or swimming, I could not stop admiring the extraordinary views of the mountains that were literally covered with a soft blanket of trees and foliage. Rice paddies and waterfalls were everywhere. Smoke from the volcano mushroomed up into the clouds. It was as if all this had been prepared for my enjoyment. I shopped in Kumamoto where I bought an opal for my mother. I went to a steak fry at Tochinoki. I spent hours sitting in the sun and taking some beautiful photographs.

Before returning to Tokyo, I stopped in Beppu. I risked getting into trouble without official permission, but I was so happy I took the chance. I found a hotel right on the beach.

This trip heightened my desire to see more of Japan. I began planning my next escape from Tokyo. Sendai sounded nice; I wanted

214

to spend a few days there riding horses with Andy. I wanted to see Matsushima, one of the three most scenic spots in Japan, which was only twenty miles from Sendai. Seeing the beauty of Kyushu and all the other places gave my spirits a lift.

Matsushima

The Occupation of Japan was so peaceful that reporters did not have enough to write about, so they constantly sensationalized the most trivial things. This terrified my mother in New Jersey who wanted me to come home. Even earthquakes and typhoons were blown out of proportion.

People were predicting the end of the trial in December. I felt I should see it through, and my mother agreed.

We began to hear rumors that there might be a congressional investigation about the length of the trial. I knew Logan had not contributed to the delay, remembering he had prepared twenty witnesses but did not call any of them. After the prosecution had objected to two of the affidavits, Logan withdrew the rest. Still, Kido had testified for almost a week—perhaps he contributed to the length of the trial. With the translation problems alone, a longer trial was understandable. More witnesses would add to the length, as well.

I promised my mother I would leave Japan on January 15th and not a day later, going so far as to say I would sign a sworn affidavit to that effect. I repeatedly wrote to my mother that I was eager to start law school and begin making a home with her again; but I was torn because I had fallen in love with the Japanese countryside. I begged my mother to take a trip for a few months until I could get home. I was now hearing that the trial might not completely wind up until April.

Brannon and I had the privilege to be entertained in the home of Chiba Satsuko, one of Japan's most famous movie actresses. She was an expert koto player and I enjoyed her renditions of Japanese classical music. We sang songs and I found the Japanese melodies lovely, including "China Nights," which had been banned by the occupation authorities because it told the story of a Japanese soldier who fell in love with a Chinese girl while the Japanese were invading China. Although no one was able to record it anymore, SCAP could not prevent orchestras from playing it.

One of the other guests that evening was Captain Inuzuka, a distinguished Japanese naval captain who had served as attaché for two years in Paris. He had been stationed in Shanghai and become involved in helping the Jewish refugees there. He believed the Jews were the oldest type of Japanese aristocracy. I could have spent an entire night listening to him.

I went with Logan and Brannon to the sumo-wrestling matches. It was therapeutic to witness these two lawyers relaxing and having fun. Sumo consisted of a formal ceremony before the two gigantic opponents engaged each other. It was so different from American wrestling and difficult to understand the studied movements.

Sumo wrestling

During this period, there was rampant inflation in Japan. In a year and a half the price of a carton of cigarettes increased from 300 yen to 1200 yen. The legal rate of exchange was fifty yen to the dollar, but ninety percent of the people exchanged their money on the black market. My main objective in shopping at this time was to see if I could buy things to send to my mother who could use them to impress a car salesman. It was next to impossible to buy a car in the States; manufacturing large quantities of any merchandise was proceeding slowly. Perhaps some Japanese merchandise would soften a car salesman's heart and my mother would be able to buy a car.

CHAPTER 14 ~ WILL I EVER GET HOME?

By November, 1947, I had been in Japan about a year and a half and was far removed from what was going on in the United States. I was dying to know what styles people were wearing Stateside. I was buying up the lovely lingerie and linens from China featured in the PX. Cheap and beautiful, these were things that I could bring back home knowing they would be out of my usual price range. Handmade clothes were affordable in Tokyo so I would have lovely, individually styled clothes for school once I returned home. I had never considered myself a shopper, but I went after bargains with the zeal of the newly converted.

I asked my sister to send fashion magazines; my mother's friend sent material for suits and coats. Having clothes made just for me was great fun. I constantly marveled at the skill of Japanese tailors. A shop opened briefly right near the Kanda Kai Kan, but the tailor was not that good. When I found one with whom I could easily communicate, I was delighted with my new clothes. I wanted to be well dressed yet cool in the summer; the summer heat took away all thought except the desire to be cool.

Tokyo PX (Post Exchange)

218

I worried about my mother being alone in her brother's house at Cupsaw Lake, New Jersey. If I had gone home, we would have been looking for a new place together. I loved my mother so much and often thought of how she had become a widow at such a young age and raised my sister and me without any help or guidance. She gave us so much in the way of education, athletics, and travel, never thinking of herself.

In Japan, I worked hard, but it was a good life, free of the pressure of finding a place to live or planning a budget. Yet there she was, all alone in a strange place so different from California.

The defense was supposed to finish presenting its case by the end of December. I remained torn between waiting for the trial to end and reaching a point where I could leave without feeling I had abandoned my two bosses. The stronger force holding me in Japan was the love I had for the beauty of its people and landscape. I was determined to traverse the country from one end to the other and see everything. I did not want to go home feeling I missed this singular opportunity to explore as much of the country as possible.

I knew enough Japanese to introduce myself and get around. I loved walking the streets and visiting areas outside Tokyo. Most of the people were no longer so loyal to their former leaders, nor could they understand why American lawyers were working so hard to defend those who had led the country to war. I saw a change from the eager lines of spectators waiting for admittance to the trial.

Most of the Japanese I associated with, and certainly those with whom I worked, knew me as the diligent secretary. But when Brannon was around, I was more than a secretary. His presence gave me status in their eyes and I was treated like an "assistant lawyer."

As time passed, I socialized more with the Japanese than the Americans, though thousands of American soldiers, dependents, and children poured into the country. Tokyo was now a miniature version of the United States. Transporting all these people to Japan, and building schools and communities in which to house them, was costing the military a fortune. I could not help wondering who was really paying the bill. Supposedly it was Japan, but I knew the Japanese economy was poor and would take a great deal of time to rebuild. No matter how peaceful the Occupation, expecting Japan to pay for it seemed unrealistic.

The Japanese were always so friendly and courteous; it was impossible to know what they really thought about us. I wavered between feeling sympathy for them and fury for the havoc wrought by the war, justifying to myself that liking the Japanese was okay because "they're not like the Germans."

At the end of November we prepared for Admiral Shimada's return to the courtroom; Brannon planned to recall him if needed to counter any damaging testimony. Logan was thinking ahead to the summation he would deliver for Marquis Kido. Logan and Brannon were immersed in preparations for not only a brilliant defense, but one able to convince the judges that their clients should not be judged guilty.

The work consumed them. I tried to placate them and apportion my time so neither felt neglected. But that was not easy. Logan became furious if I was not available the minute he needed me. Brannon was equally demanding. I knew in my heart that I was a good secretary with skills, endurance, and patience. When I felt discouraged, I remembered my mother's favorite expression: "If you think you're indispensable, take a walk through the cemetery." How true it was then and now!

What compelled me to work those long hours, and negotiate between two lawyers who were working their hardest, was the understanding that Admiral Shimada's life was at stake. I was touched whenever his little girl, Hiroko, came to the office and hesitantly asked questions about her father. He was a real person—a husband and father, not just a war criminal charged with horrendous crimes. I felt we were there to save his life. When the presentation of Shimada's case was complete, I could look forward to an easier workload, and maybe even get away to play some tennis again.

The defendants all testified that they wanted peace. Everyone eschewed planning the war and claimed a desire to promote friendly relations with the U.S. and Great Britain. I thought it would be refreshing if just once, someone would stand up and say, "I did it, and I'm glad I did it."

Each defendant had a good story to tell. We heard endlessly about how they were decent men who found themselves in bad company. Were any of these little old men the "bad company?" The defendants had distinctive personalities and many were quite likeable. I felt sad if I thought about them being hanged. Some days, there was endless testimony in which nothing was clarified, and I still was left to wonder: Who started the war if all these guys were innocent?

During a break in preparing the case, I enjoyed a break from Occupations food during a sukiyaki dinner at the home of our interpreter. His English was excellent. He had been schooled in Shanghai; his wife was from South Africa. He told us an anecdote about a Japanese scholar whose "book-learned" English was ridiculous in the extreme. When his professor's wife served this scholar tea, the scholar replied, "Thank you dear sir or madam as the case may be."

One of the American defense lawyers, Owen Cunningham, struck me as pompous and not nearly as smart as my two bosses. His client, Oshima, was the former ambassador to Germany, a man who was in quite thick with the Hitler leaders. I asked Cunningham if Oshima was going to testify and he replied, "Ambassador Oshima—please."

Oshima was the one defendant towards whom I had no feelings at all. When called as a witness, he dressed in a tailored suit and wore a bow tie. It occurred to me he must have gotten his clothes in Germany. He certainly did not admit any personal relationship with Hitler, Goering, Himmler, or any of the Nazi leaders, and denied he had been close to the military clique in Japan. Oshima's American attorney was a civil lawyer from Iowa who snobbishly insisted to the other defense attorneys that his client was a "diplomat," and not a military man.

General Sato's case would be on soon. His lawyer, Buck Freeman, was from North Carolina and had been an attorney with the U.S. Navy. He was not considered one of the heavyweights of the defense staff. When he decided not to put General Sato on the stand, Logan and Brannon both thought that was the right strategy.

The case against the general was based primarily on the importance of his position as chief of the Military Affairs Bureau in the War Ministry from 1942 to 1944. His department was responsible for the way POWs were handled and the disbursement of slave laborers. Mr. Freeman found witnesses who testified that Sato's role in the War Ministry was minor. Yet when the general had been interviewed at Sugamo Prison he had not said that at all. I worried about him because he was one of my favorites -- full of personality and a great sense of humor.

I did not know it at the time, but he wrote his own memoir of the trial, which was referenced at some length in Arnold Brackman's book. General Sato recognized that the chief American prosecutor, Joseph Keenan, and Sir William Webb did not like each other. He described Webb as brilliant and strong, and Keenan as vulgar and arrogant. However, he understood that it was Keenan who made certain that Emperor Hirohito did not share any blame for the events that happened when the accused were in power.

General Sato said, "Had the emperor been tried as a war criminal or been summoned as a witness, we would not have felt we were alive." The biggest surprise Sato revealed in his memoir was that Justice Pal, the Indian judge, visited him at Sugamo Prison after the trial ended and told him, "You were the leaders of Japan. Through that leadership, Asia was liberated. With that in mind, I express my respect to the accused." Knowing Justice Pal had thus spoken, it is no wonder he wrote such a lengthy dissenting opinion.

On December 2nd, I wrote home about our preparation for Admiral Shimada's defense.

> *Everything is just about ready, and tomorrow will be the clean-up of our preparation for Shimada's case. The old admiral thanked me today for the work I did. Honestly, John had a real good explanation of Shimada's connection with the prisoners of war, and Shimada didn't like it. He wants to take full responsibility; so the affidavit is his and was changed to what he wanted. The Japanese believe in saving face, but Shimada ought to start thinking about saving his neck.*

This affidavit was in the form of rebuttal evidence. It could not contradict his earlier testimony lest he lose credibility. I worried about how he might come across. Brannon's "hands were tied," as you cannot force a client to testify in a certain way—a lawyer can suggest and suggest, but in the end there is a saying that "the defendant is entitled to his day in court."

The defense case continued to be dictated by the need to protect the emperor, who had not been indicted and was still the nominal ruler of Japan. Apparently the prosecution had actually received orders to keep the emperor out of it. None of the individual defendants would admit he had the slightest culpability, but somehow there was a feeling that the judges might infer otherwise.

In the meantime, my thoughts returned to going home. I gave up on any idea of going to China, even though there were opportunities and trips offered through the Occupation authorities. I took someone to the airport and, hearing announcements of planes coming and going from different cities in the Orient, such as Shanghai, Singapore, and Hong Kong, I thought that, if I did not take advantage of my chance to go there, I'd be sorry. I'd probably never have the chance again.

Between working with the Japanese lawyers, Logan, and Brannon, I was exhausted and had grown sick and tired of the whole thing. The pressure made me think back to the time when I had worked for Major Frost, who was mainly responsible for the training of flight engineers on B-29 aircraft at Sheppard Field in Texas, and at Lockheed Aircraft in Los Angeles. In hindsight, being Major Frost's secretary had been a far more pleasant experience than trying to keep my current bosses happy. Sometimes I wondered what drove me to keep trying to be "the best." I didn't think I was overly egotistic or ambitious. Something, though, in the way my mother raised me, whispered, "When you say you're going to do your best, you had better just do it."

The trial was moving along and only five cases remained before the Tribunal; they were Shiratori, Suzuki, Tojo, Togo, and Umezu. Of the five, Togo was the only civilian. I thought he had already testified and he was not our client, anyway. I had no personal feelings about the others, only Tojo. After these cases were concluded, there would be final arguments, summations, and rebuttal evidence.

Once again I picked a date, January 10, 1948, as the date on which the trial would end, but I had been wrong so many times. By December 9th, the presentation of Shimada's case was completed. Overall he had done quite well. He looked so much like an admiral; there was something distinguished and kind about his appearance. I was haunted by the thought that he might receive a death sentence. I could not imagine him being hanged. I felt sad to even consider it.

With some of the trial pressure off, I was again concentrating on travel plans in and about Japan. As luck would have it, I met someone who had connections on the island of Shikoku where Mrs. Nagano lived. Few Americans visited there, so I had something to look forward to when the break came and I could go.

Meanwhile, I spent my leisure hours shopping and writing my mother about coming home. I felt a bit crazy, always talking about going home and never doing it. I knew this could not go on forever. I was happy when my mother wrote to tell me she was saving my letters. I thought my letters might be a good record of my experiences for the book I might write someday. I felt I was seeing into the hearts of the defendants and could understand their thought processes.

Most of the defendants appeared not to care whether they lived or died. There was no desperation about their demeanor; yet they still wanted to convey their innocence. Some were dour, others were placid, and still others were lively and interested. It was quite a mix.

I wanted to see Admiral Shimada when he testified. Seeing how happy he was when his daughter visited him made him seem more like a devoted father than an accused war criminal. One of the days that I saw him in court, he was asked if Marquis Kido tried to influence him in any way. His answer was, "I'd bark at him and throw him out like a dog if he tried to do that." Shimada's wife later came into the office and said that "God sent Mr. Brannon here" to defend her husband; and the admiral sent a note of thanks to me for helping with his case.

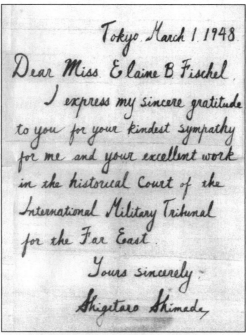

Letter of thanks from Admiral Shimada.
Original hand lettered on silk, 2I" x 31"

In the middle of December, Fords and Chevrolets were sent to Japan. Six months earlier, they had announced a lottery and I had put down $1,000 in the hopes of getting an automobile. The new priority system favored people like me who had already put their money down and waited patiently for good news. I was elated by the thought of taking a brand new car home with me. All I had to do was wait for the call.

On January 20, 1948 I wrote home:

Now, about the car deal, there was an announcement today in the paper that from now on it will go by priority. They are having a drawing the 23rd to determine your permanent place on the list. This drawing will be divided into groups which go according to the way you put your money in. I was in the group that put their money in near the very beginning, so I will have a good chance, but I may get disqualified as the rumor is that you have to agree to stay for six months after you get the car. Because I work at the trial, which could end anytime, I have to make a deal with Brannon as it's his money in the pool under my name.

Getting a car was so much on my mind that I wondered why I wanted a Chevrolet more than a Ford.

No kidding, Mother, if I actually had the car and was sure about this, I'll be a different person. It will mean everything to me to have a car here for the next few weeks. I'll be able to go ice skating and horseback riding and shopping and just everything. I'll be the happiest person. It will be wonderful and I'll end up in a blaze of glory. I heard the government ships them home. Of course I'm not excited yet because they might refuse me, as I'm not going to stay six months.

It was impossible to get a new car in the States. I still told my mother that she should promise the salesperson that her daughter in Japan could send souvenirs.

I did not just dream of getting away; I actually did something about it. I got orders to go to Sendai, where my friend Andy, who had been my riding instructor at Camp Drake, was now stationed. Andy's love of horses was so apparent that horses loved him back. He was the best teacher, so patient; I wanted to show him that I was improving so he would know what an excellent instructor he had been.

I could not have gone to Sendai without asking for help in getting there. At this point, good contacts were essential to navigate the red tape of the Occupation. In order to make trips outside of Tokyo, I needed to navigate one bureaucratic office after another. Those in charge "loved" to make things difficult for the civilians; it was the dependants to whom they catered.

CHAPTER 15 ~ TOJO TESTIFIES

Finally Tojo was called as a witness. There was an electric buzz of excitement due to his infamy. He was the most well known of all the defendants. During the war, Hitler, Tojo, and Mussolini were evil personified for Americans.

Overnight, the trial took on some color. During the day, the lawyers had to be in court, listening to the testimony. When they came back to the office, Brannon and Logan both wanted to dictate. We desperately needed more office help, but no one else was available. I went a bit crazy with hours and hours of dictation and even more hours of transcribing. I felt at once privileged, overused and taken for granted.

We knew General Tojo liked Admiral Shimada. We hoped his testimony would help the defense rather than hurt it. Were our defendants guilty or innocent? My thoughts were inconsistent on this subject, veering wildly between the two extremes. It was difficult to connect the dots.

The indictment went back to 1928. Shimada had not achieved prominence in his career or worked closely with most of the other defendants until 1940 or 1941. That being the case, how could he possibly be guilty of the charge of conspiracy, unless it did not matter when you entered a particular cabinet or worked with a particular defendant or minister? It would depend on what the law of conspiracy was. Kido was different. He had been in close touch with the emperor and the people surrounding the emperor for many years. I wanted the trial to end without any of the defendants I personally liked being hanged, including Generals Sato and Muto, although I was not closely involved in their cases.

Tojo testifying

On December 26th, General Tojo took the stand. He was represented by George Blewett, the Philadelphia lawyer, though his Japanese lawyer, Dr. Kiyose, had prepared his defense and read his opening statement, which made one wonder if we were all at the same trial.

Dr. Kiyose asserted that Japan had not prepared for war against the United States, Great Britain, or the Netherlands; Japan had no ambitions to take China; Japan joined the Axis in Europe to avoid war; the attack at Pearl Harbor had been provoked; the Greater East Asia Co-Prosperity Sphere had been designed to free all the people in Asia; and there were no military cliques.

Continuing on, he submitted a 250-page statement that said the U.S. had broken the Japanese code and knew all of its plans, so the attack on Pearl Harbor was not a surprise. Further, he asserted that the Doolittle Flyers violated international law. He went on and on as a filibusterer and finally concluded by saying that he believed this was a war of self-defense that did not violate international law. He also absolved Emperor Hirohito of responsibility saying, "...full responsibility for the Pacific War rested on the cabinet and high command and was not the responsibility of the emperor; the responsibility for defeat rested on him as premier."

General Tojo's true feeling that Japan was not at fault came through loud and clear in his testimony. In the book, *Tojo, the Last Banzai* by Courtney Browne, Tojo was quoted as saying:

Never at any time did I conceive that the waging of this war would or could be challenged by the victors as an international crime, or that regularly constituted officials of the vanquished nations would be charged individually as criminals under any recognized international law or under alleged violations of treaties between nations...I feel that I did no wrong. I feel I did what was right and true.

One of the defense attorneys spoke out, condemning the whole idea of the trial, saying that democratic governments did not, and do not, exist in all countries of the world and that branding other governments as evil meant that the victorious government was casting judgment based on a criterion of its own choosing. This led that government to castigate the leaders of Japan who truly believed they were carrying out their patriotic duties.

After the direct examination was finished, the cross examination by Chief Prosecutor Keenan went absolutely nowhere; in fact, he was bad to the point of embarrassment and left the courtroom at one point. When he finally finished, he had to live with the bad reviews of his performance, while Tojo's performance was applauded. What became obvious was how the emperor's role in the war would be that of one who had no control; therefore, he was blameless. Whether or not this was true would be debated at another time—not in this Tribunal.

The trial was heading towards its conclusion. Admiral Shimada took the stand again and sought to clarify the testimony about threats supposedly made by him and Admiral Nagano against Ambassador Togo. Shimada's explanation was that he and Admiral Nagano had told Togo he should be more careful regarding the truth. Togo's testimony had dishonored the Japanese Navy. Shimada went on to say that Togo was trying to avoid charges that he had bungled the delivery of the December 7th note. When Shimada returned from the witness stand back to the dock, George Yamaoka announced to the court that the defense had no further evidence.

The new year arrived and I sought some new diversion. My idea was to visit some place that was not being talked about as a place to see. I chose to visit Ueno Zoo. It amazed me to think any animals survived the war, but there they were. This was a truly fun experience—short but memorable, then back to work.

My mother asked me to explain Admiral Shimada's crimes. I did not know how to answer her. All of the defendants were being charged with being members of a conspiracy to wage aggressive war and of committing crimes against peace, crimes against humanity, and murder. Admiral Shimada was the Navy minister, specifically brought into the Tojo cabinet to support going to war. However, prior to taking that action, Shimada had no history of intrigue, and no relationships with others in the government or military who favored war. Would the judges recognize this? I hoped so.

My mind was on traveling. On a weekend, I journeyed again to Sendai. I walked for hours, exulting in the wonderful clean air and peaceful surroundings. This totally refreshed and renewed my mind, body, and soul.

Upon my return from Sendai, I took part in an interesting event—the first anniversary of Admiral Nagano's death. A Shinto priest conducted a special service. The ceremony took place at Mr. Sogi's home—a wealthy man who was Admiral Nagano's brother-in-law. There was an elaborate altar with arrangements of fruits and vegetables and a picture of Admiral Nagano. The presiding priest was dressed in white silk robes and a "funny" black hat. We sat on the floor.

The priest bowed, approached the altar and started chanting. It was unlike anything I had ever heard before, vaguely reminiscent of animal sounds. The priest took a bowl filled with green twigs and offered it to the mourners, who crawled towards the altar where they bowed, clapped twice and placed one of the twigs on a platter. Logan, Brannon, and I followed their example. As I sat on my knees, I forced myself to think about Admiral Nagano giving the order to attack Pearl Harbor. He never seemed to have any particular hatred for America.

As we went upstairs after the ceremony, Mr. Sogi told us Admiral Nagano would have been happy that his American friends took part in observing the anniversary of his death. We ate a lovely dinner, after which I played with Mr. Sogi's adorable little grandson. Later, we excused ourselves to go home. I was happy returning home to the Kanda Kai Kan knowing I had been a participant in an honorable, sacred event.

Each day the trial continued, the more I thought of General Tojo's appearance and how we had joked that if Tojo continued to testify so brilliantly, the court would be forced to hang Mr. Keenan and free Tojo. I could only conclude that all of the defendants testified well; after all, they had once brilliantly led a nation. No, they were not just the little old men they appeared to be, in ill-fitting clothes surrounded by military police; they were so much more.

When I first came to Japan and became involved with the trial, I asked some of the Japanese what they thought of their former leaders. Their response was usually that they hated them. However, General Tojo was their hero. They loved him when he led them to wartime victories and their love was reignited by his fantastic courtroom performance and dignified demeanor.

Before a full house replete with reporters, Tojo testified how the Japanese had been forced to go to war because of America. America had given Japan an ultimatum about China. The Americans told Japan to get out of China or they would not have access to any of the world's oil. However, the Japanese had been fighting in China for more than ten years and invested significant military and economic resources in this battle. Japan was not amenable to being threatened or forced to leave.

When the last defendant, General Umezu, testified, I realized how different the trial and my job would be when there was no longer pressure to prepare for the next day's happenings in court. Mr. Logan and Mr. Brannon worked far harder than I did. My work was labor; their work required them to be and do so much more. They had to absorb literally thousands of facts and pieces of information and to have their brilliant, creative minds continually engaged in order to save their clients. When the trial was over, even if their clients were exonerated, no one would thank them. (Conversely, the loss would be a terrible blow to their professional pride.)

Again I had a little bit of free time; I took a short respite to Matsushima. I was seeing almost the same things and places I saw on my first visit. I concluded that for true scenic beauty, I liked Kyushu better.

Back in Tokyo, my friendship with Fritzi Nishikawa flourished. I felt fortunate that such an accomplished athlete was willing to teach me how to ice skate. She dazzled me with her superb skating; it was no wonder she had earned an Olympic berth. My involvement in sports had always brought so much to my life. From learning to swim and dive when I was a child, to tennis and Ping-Pong, and now in Japan, I was learning to ice-skate and ride horses. These many sports gave me such pleasure as well as wonderful associations and fond memories.

Work loomed ahead as we prepared for the summations and final arguments. With an end in sight, I applied for orders to go to the Japanese Alps. Though it was my dream to see this beautiful country and then go home, I tried some self-analysis to find out if I really wanted to leave. I knew I had become a big fish in a little pond at the trials. The life I had been leading was totally unreal for a secretary, an assistant, or whatever one might call me. The hard work was balanced with lots of play and fun. In addition, I never forgot—I was *participating* in an historic event.

I thought the war trials and their outcome would be extremely interesting to people. Other times, I thought, *who really cares; this war is over*. I was watching a new Japan rise from the ashes. Rebuilding was very slow, but people were working hard to move into a new future. As I traveled within the country to places run by the Occupation forces with help from the Japanese, I no longer saw wheat and grass growing in the cracks of the sidewalk and streets. When I took the train to Yokohama, I was shocked to see a modern first-class rail station in place of the rubble that greeted my arrival two years earlier. By now, I had become quite experienced in riding the trains, though I was hoping soon to have my own automobile. I could drive places and not use the trains until it was time to return to the States, when the car and I would have a fully paid one-way ticket.

One of the "nice-things-that-happened-to-me stories" was running into Sir William Webb, the chief justice of the Tribunal. He was a curt, abrupt type of judge, ruling from his "throne" during the trial. When I went to his chambers to have him autograph a picture for Mr. Logan, he asked how Mr. Brannon was. I said he was fine, but working hard. The judge then told me to let Brannon know how much he had enjoyed his opening argument; that he found Brannon's language beautiful. This was a huge compliment. It reinforced the pride I felt working for such a fine lawyer. No wonder the Japanese were nice to me. My two bosses were famous, respected, and genuinely liked.

My mother was interested in the trial's outcome. I wrote her a long letter in which I tried to explain the difference between Togo and Tojo. I repeated all my observations at some length, explaining that Togo was the foreign minister and Tojo was the prime minister. Togo was the one responsible for sending the final "too late" message to Washington declaring Japan's intention to go to war, and then took advantage of the fact that Nagano was already dead and thus could be blamed for all of the notice problems. He went a step further in placing the blame on Admiral Shimada. According to Shimada, the story that the Navy wanted to attack without warning was a fabrication on Togo's part. It appeared to me that Togo was interested in saving his own life and to "hell with the others." It was humiliating to see Admiral Shimada forced to sink to the level of Togo in order to set the record straight. Togo seemed to enjoy implicating as many of the other defendants as possible.

I thought the defense was making progress until Kido and Togo testified. The prosecution claimed there was a military clique planning a war of aggression. Kido and Togo tried to show that, as civilians, they had nothing to do with the military and thus escape blame for the war.

Tojo was an outstanding witness. Hearing him speak and seeing his carriage and demeanor, it was not difficult to picture people following him. The defense believed he spoke up and took the blame because he thought there really was no blame. He was fiery and sharp and showed up all the other defendants with his performance. I did not consider General Premier Tojo that different from the English leaders who hundreds of years ago believed in manifest destiny and wanted to expand their empires. He was simply a few centuries later.

To break up the hectic schedule of work, Captain Watanabe's wife made a lovely sukiyaki party for all of us. I greeted our Japanese friends by bowing to the floor. I reciprocated the Watanabe's hospitality by having a Japanese girl who ran a beauty parlor I frequented cook a sukiyaki dinner at my place. Sukiyaki, with lots of meat and plenty of vegetables in a tasty sauce, was my favorite dish. I was anxious to bring the recipe home and dazzle my mother. I continued having more beautiful clothes made by an excellent Japanese tailor. I kept thinking the trial was winding down and my departure for the States would be imminent; but…

On January 20, 1948, I wrote a long letter to my mother in which I again summarized all the preparations that had gone into crafting our defense for the trial. The prosecution presented their case using a phased approach. They started with the Manchurian incident and from there moved on to the China incident and the conquest of the countries in the Far East.

The prosecution was especially relentless about the Japanese aggression in China. They also explored Japanese relations with the United States, the British, and the Soviets. Before resting, the prosecution presented evidence against each of the twenty-five defendants.

> *Now when an accused finished his case—say when Shimada's testimony was over and all his witnesses had testified and we got documents in evidence—that doesn't mean Shimada is through and then they try someone else. He's just finished for the moment. At this stage of the proceedings, all of the defenses for the twenty-five accused have been represented, and the defense is through presenting evidence. The prosecution is now on rebuttal—their answer to the defense. When they finish that, and it should take another few days, they will present their final arguments. After that is done, the defense will answer and present what we call summations. Then the case is over and the judges write their judgments. They sentence them or free them, whatever the case may be, and so I hope you see that these twenty-five men are, and have always been, the only ones on trial in this particular case. When the trial ends it will end for all twenty-five, and it has not yet ended for any of them.*

CHAPTER 16 ~ BEGINNINGS AND ENDINGS

At the end of January, 1948, the prosecution finally presented rebuttal evidence followed by final arguments. After that, the defense planned to present its own summations and then wait for the judges to rule. Would the defendants be sentenced or set free? The idea of actually winning acquittals was wishful thinking on our part.

Meanwhile, I went to Akakura in the Japanese Alps and had my first exposure to the sport of skiing. There were no sleeping cars on the nine-hour train ride from Tokyo. The train was filled with many skiers already dressed in their ski clothes. At the train station, a transport called "the weasel" picked us up. Twenty-five minutes later, I was at the hotel, surrounded by snow and sunshine. I met the Swiss instructor who had been with the Swiss ski troops and was known as a fantastic teacher.

Skiing in the Japanese Alps

I skied and fell, skied and fell, skied—and fell some more. Thank God, the snow was soft! I could not believe I found a sport at which I seemed to have absolutely no talent. Still, I enjoyed the whole experience.

On my return to Tokyo, I learned that my name was on the short list to get an automobile. Of course, there were rules and regulations with which I had to comply, but there was a car in my future!

On a visit to Fritzi Berger's, she confided that she had once lived in London where her husband had managed the Mikimoto Pearl Store. She originally came to Japan to give a skating exhibition and met her future husband on the ice. He was the Japanese skating champion. Fritzi said that, although she was not initially attracted to most Japanese men, she found her future husband quite handsome. Now they had a son who dreamed of someday going to America. Being with Fritzi was always exhilarating. Viennese women were known to have lots and lots of charm, and she had more than most.

Despite the fact that the final defense was underway, Brannon, Logan, and I went to Izu Nagaoka. We drove there and stayed in a beautiful Japanese hotel. (I could not help thinking again how wonderful it would be if my mother could experience Japan with me.) Although we traveled together, upon arrival, my bosses and I entertained ourselves separately.

Mr. Logan's family had arrived in Japan for a visit. He was so nervous about preparing for his final arguments and summation that he sent them to a resort hotel in another part of the country while he escaped from Tokyo with Brannon and me. I think it soothed him to be in the company of Brannon.

Once word got out that the two famous American lawyers, Logan and Brannon, were in Izu Nagaoka, their privacy and peace were short-lived. They were considered popular celebrities. Their names were often in the newspapers and, when radio transmission became part of Japanese life again, news of the trial kept them in the spotlight. The Japanese lined up for autographs.

Logan had earned the genuine love and respect of the Japanese people by defending their countrymen so passionately. The defeated nation embraced him for his hard work, brilliance, and sincerity. When we returned to the trial from Izu Nagaoka, Logan asked for an adjournment to prepare concluding arguments. The judges were not enamored of him for making this request without much notice.

As mentioned so often before, Brannon was frequently temperamental and difficult to work with, but he could also be generous and often expressed his appreciation with thoughtful gifts. His favorite

Japanese jewelry was pins, so he gave me gifts of pins. He had also began writing directly to my mother, asking her not to pay attention if I wrote that he was working me to death. When he was good, he was very, very good; and when he was bad he was...

My feelings toward John were difficult to put into words. I had never had a "steady" boyfriend in Tokyo despite the fact that I had so many chances to enter into romantic relationships. It started with David Hornstein who said he was in love with me. I thought he was crazy; he was so young—what did he know about love? Then there was Cog, whose friendship I treasured, but we had never carried it farther than him saying I was an important person in his life. I had "fallen" for Herbert Norman, but I had quashed those feelings very quickly when I found out he was married. When Brannon came along, I had not been swept away by his good looks and athletic ability. Eventually, however, he grew on me.

Brannon genuinely concerned himself with my life and how I was living it. He went with me to Jewish services although he was Catholic. Those services never seemed to be in the same place each week, but I somehow found out where they were being conducted. He delighted in any victories I had on the tennis court. He loved that I was friendly with Prince Takamatsu.

Elaine and John Brannon in kimonos

237

As a boss, John was demanding, critical, and cold to the point that I wondered if he was the same man who complimented my work and "went to bat" for me so I could get a raise. When he called me his "Baby-girl," I melted. When he talked about me becoming a lawyer, I wanted to take him home with me and show my mother he was every bit as wonderful as I said he was in some of my letters (and not nearly as mean as I said in others).

Brannon spent so much time with me that he made me feel he did indeed love me. I always wanted to be with him, particularly when we explored the streets and spoke to the Japanese people. The strangest aspect of our relationship, though, was that he did not want me to miss out on chances to meet other men. I knew he thought that I wanted to meet a wonderful Jewish man. Perhaps he was telling me we would not be together when the trial was over.

One day in an interview, Mr. Keenan, the chief American prosecutor, said, "John Brannon was the most promising lawyer at the trial." Even though I had a front-row seat at the trial, it was rarely exciting, anymore. Just when I thought we were nearing the end, more work had to be done.

When Mr. Logan needed me to continue his defense of Marquis Kido, I almost resented it, as I still did not like the marquis. I did not like his Japanese lawyers much either. However, I was fond of Kido's mother and grandmother. I also enjoyed the younger Kidos, whom I came to know when I accompanied Mr. Logan to their beach house. I realized that the defense offered on his behalf did make a lot of sense, as he certainly was not a military figure.

Logan was totally engrossed in his defense of the marquis, just as Brannon was involved in the cases of the Japanese Navy.

Bill Logan with Marquis Kido's mother and wife

Marquis Kido family

Bill Logan with Marquis Kido's mother

I now had a different personal feeling about the naval defendants. It desperately mattered to me that they not be hanged. On occasion, I reminded myself that my brother-in-law spent three-and-a-half years fighting the Japanese in the Pacific. Despite their courtesy towards me, the Japanese were responsible for the deaths of many of our American soldiers and close friends. I was increasingly ambivalent and nursed a guilty conscience. Yet I stayed on, postponing my departure once again.

Whenever everything revolved around work, an unexpected break and surprise came. I was invited to go duck hunting at the Imperial Palace Preserve. Following the hunt, Logan and Brannon were invited to a buffet dinner dance and included me in this invitation. The Russian judge (who was also a major general), two Russian officers, and two Russian women joined us for this occasion. The Russian judge could not speak English, but he tried to make up for it by giving me lots of hugs and kisses. All this made me ponder the lack of peace in the world and the many misunderstandings among various nations. We were already in the "Cold War," yet the Russians seemed warm to me.

The Imperial Palace

Villa on the Imperial Palac Reserve, site of the duck-hunting party

February 5, 1948, was a momentous day for me—I GOT MY CAR—a Ford "super deluxe" eight cylinder, with a radio and a heater. I felt extremely lucky to have a brand-new car, just when I was beginning to believe it would never happen. The total cost was $1,950, which was the same cost had I bought it in the States. The men at the old Japanese Navy offices said they would take care of the car for me. So I wrote home asking for Simoniz and chromium cleaner to keep it new and shiny.

Elaine and her new Ford

About this same time, I was amazed to get fresh milk to drink. I had missed milk; it had not been available in Japan to this point. I found it so rich and dense I could only take a few sips.

Along with a new car and fresh milk came the chance to see *The Mikado* by Gilbert and Sullivan performed for the first time in Japan. It had been banned previously because it made fun of the emperor. The presentation was absolutely wonderful.

Despite these wonderful experiences, I started making plans to go home. This time I estimated that the trial would definitely be over by March. I presumed my work would end in about three weeks because we were working on final arguments and summations. My plan was to obtain orders to visit the northern island of Hokkaido and then take an extended tour of southern Japan. I felt as if all the extra hours I worked entitled me to time off. Once I could tour more of the country, I would certainly be more than ready to go home.

The prosecution was ready to give their summations. Then the defense would give final arguments and the trial would end. Mr. Logan had already applied for orders to have his family go home. I started selling my older clothes in order to accumulate enough Japanese yen to buy pearls, souvenirs, and gifts to take home. I was thrilled at the thought of taking my new car back to America, picking up my mother and traveling across the country with her. We would have one glorious vacation before settling down.

In the meantime, there was still a lot of work at the office. We finally hired extra help.

One day Brannon asked me to take a box of candy to Admiral Shimada. Shimada did not smoke, but he loved candy. As I walked through the Tribunal corridor, I ran into Colonel Kenworthy, who was responsible for the safety of all the defendants. He told me how sad he would be when the sentences came down. Brannon and I had taken candy to Admiral Shimada before, but this time Colonel Kenworthy said he had orders that we could not give the prisoners anything. I am sure they were taking special precautions, because in Germany some of the prisoners had committed suicide.

The weeks we were spending in preparing the closing arguments were hectic. Both my bosses seemed totally exhausted and in a stupor, yet they worked around the clock to get the summations finished. The review of testimony was exceedingly time-consuming. The Japanese lawyers had to be consulted and conferences had to be arranged by and between the lawyers representing their clients. Arguments were drafted and redrafted. It did not seem as if the end was in sight at all, but it was.

I developed a real affection for my Ford and ordered seat covers from Montgomery Ward by mail. The car was my only diversion during this period of intense work. Yes, the defendants were all guilty of something, but the thought of them being hanged still did not sound or feel right.

When the verdicts came down in Yokohama where Class-B and C war criminals (enlisted men who committed atrocities) were being tried, a lot of hangings were ordered.

I wrote home that I wanted to get my picture taken with Admiral Shimada and with the two generals whom I thought had the most personality. Looking back, I suppose it was childish, but at the time I wanted to have some remembrance of these special defendants.

I survived the incessant demands of work by dreaming of more escapes. I wanted to see Noboru Betsu, a beautiful hot springs resort on the island of Hokkaido. Hokkaido was supposedly laid out by an American and allegedly contained some wide-open spaces similar to the American West. Not many Americans visited that island...all I knew was I wanted to go.

Noboru Betsu Spa is located in wooden mountains on the island of Hokkaidol.

**On the road from Noboru Betsu is Jigoku-dani, the "Valley of Hell,"
composed of boiling muddy water and sulfur steam.**

*I hope to get out of here in March and wish you would go
to California as it will be warmer and I can meet you there.
The work will be over in 3 weeks and I want time enough to
play and travel. Then [I'll] get the first boat and that will be
it. Right now we're writing our summations and final arguments. The trial is really almost over—honestly.*

The trial was moving along and Mr. Logan was developing his
"economic" argument, attempting to show that Japan was cut off from
her foreign markets by the U.S. tariff restrictions; she had really fought
the war in self-defense to protect her economic interests. My thought
was that if you work at this long enough, you believe it; certainly the
attorneys believed it.

Ironically, the United States had won the war, but after almost destroying Japan, the U.S. was now obliged to spend a fortune putting her back together. We were rebuilding the country.

The War Ministry Building was fairly far from the city, but now I could get in the car at lunchtime to do errands and go shopping. That did not sit well with Messrs. Logan and Brannon, but they were stuck with me. I pounded away at the typewriter, writing and rewriting the speeches on which they were working. I wondered if the other attorneys were working as hard for their clients. I knew other lawyers were working hard and they were good lawyers, but not as extraordinarily good as Brannon and Logan.

I knew *LIFE* magazine had a story about Tojo in their January 26, 1948, issue. They had a good picture showing Colonel Kenworthy standing next to Admiral Shimada. Shimada was extremely well liked by all of the MPs and he was the colonel's pet.

At the pace we were going, I felt secure in thinking it would all be over by March. I knew it was best to not wait until the end for the sentences to come down; I knew it could take months for the appeals to MacArthur.

Towards the end of February, I finished working on the economic summation for Logan and the conspiracy argument for Brannon. Everything was typed on a stencil and printed out. It was not an efficient way of turning out copies, but it was the only method we had. Whoever used the machinery ended up with purple hands; and special soap was needed to clean up.

On March 1, 1948, the defense started its summation. Logan went away from Tokyo to work in peace and took a secretary with him, providing me with a brief respite. This was the only time the Defense Section was allowed extra stenographic help. I was thrilled when Logan inherited the secretary of a defense attorney who had been rebuked by the Tribunal and sent home. Brannon presented his huge paper attacking the conspiracy counts in the indictment. His arguments attracted attention.

John Brannon in courtroom

I planned on making some final purchases of pearls and china bowls. Pearls were controlled by the PX and hard to get. They were always available on the black market, but I was terrified to venture there. The Occupation authorities were constantly trying to control this illegal commerce. I frequented the Japanese stores, which were opening everywhere. Japanese lawyers working with us were happy to help me with my special shopping needs. The opportunities to shop were otherwise limited as Brannon and Logan revised and rewrote their arguments until I thought I would lose my mind.

I worried about Admiral Shimada and whether the judges would be persuaded by the prosecution's accusation that he had voted for the war and thus was as guilty as the others. I wanted to make sure I was not in Tokyo when the judgments came down. I knew I would fall apart if a death sentence were imposed. My objective was to leave as soon as the testimony and arguments ended.

By the middle of March, pressure was intense; I was working on Admiral Shimada's summation. When it was halfway finished, I delivered it to the admiral in the prisoner's holding room. Each of the screens separating the prisoners from their visitors had a slot in the center to insert papers.

I wanted to talk to the admiral about additions and corrections, but when he saw me carrying the huge sheaf of papers, he ran up to the screen and grabbed the papers so he could start reading immediately. The papers contained his best hope of avoiding execution. Brannon and I both had strong feelings about this gentle, intelligent man.

While I was in the room, Colonel Kenworthy spotted me and asked if I had seen the latest pictures of him in the paper. (Whenever scenes of the trial were pictured, the colonel was always there.) I was in a room with two special people—an American colonel and a Japanese admiral. Here I was, Elaine Fischel, secretary, standing between two worlds—the old and new countries of Japan. I was truly looking at history being made.

CHAPTER 17 ~ FEELINGS AND FRIENDSHIPS

Colonel Kenworthy and I remained friends. He always came over to joke with Admiral Shimada a bit when I visited. When I was leaving one day, this hardened combat veteran who had fought four battles in the Pacific War zones followed me and said, "I don't know what I will do if they hang that man. I just love him."

The colonel shared my hope that Shimada's life would be spared. Having joined the Japanese Navy at eighteen, Shimada was a naval career man—intensely patriotic and devoted to his country, yet possessing gentleness. He had attended the Naval Academy, was a veteran of Japan's war in China and had a brilliant record of military successes at sea. However, facts were facts. I knew the Tribunal judges would say he was brought into the Tojo cabinet because he was not strong enough to resist their urging to make their vote to go to war unanimous.

The real issue was to determine whether it had been a war of aggression initiated by these defendants. To find in favor of the defendants would mean the U.S. and Britain were the aggressors. I wondered if the judges would even listen to Admiral Shimada's explanation.

There were others among the defendants who had also held out to the last minute, not wanting to give in and vote for the hostilities to begin. I believed some of the defendants were guilty, but I anxiously awaited the Tribunal's ruling. There was no possible way to anticipate or predict the thinking of eleven judges from eleven different nations and cultures.

Adding to the last-minute workload, Brannon took over the defense of General Sato. Sato was one of the defendants I thought would escape unscathed; there was so little evidence against him. Sato had a sparkle in his eye. He was the kind of man whose buddies would be sure to plan an elaborate party to celebrate his release from prison. He was always giving a nod of approval to his attorneys and to any American with whom he had contact, including me. Along with General Muto, Sato was one of my favorites.

The men still treated General Tojo as if he were their boss, while no one liked Foreign Minister Togo because he had blamed all the other defendants. I could not help but feel sorry for him as he really had not wanted the war. Yet he had some complicity with regard to communicating that last message to the White House; therefore, some of the guilt and blame was his.

I had written home that I thought the crux of the whole trial was the guilt of the emperor. It was a tremendously farsighted and wise policy on the part of General MacArthur to keep him in power. I, along with many others, attributed the peaceful Occupation to the emperor's continued reign. The judges could not touch him, but occasionally I got the feeling they considered the emperor to be the number one criminal.

Logan applied for orders to return to the States. It seemed that the trial would soon be over. I wanted to apply to law school if I went back to California, and my choice was the University of Southern California (USC). However, I was not anxious about law school just yet. Once I got home, I would have time to apply. There were still some trips I wanted to take within Japan. Prior to leaving, I sought letters of recommendation from judges such as Sir William Webb and others who knew about my work at the trial from start to finish.

I rarely mentioned the Yokohama trials, but I did write home that those trials were for atrocities committed by the military. In one day, they brought in verdicts of death by hanging for forty out of forty-six defendants. These trials went before military commissions. I thought those defendants deserved to be hanged for their violent and atrocious conduct.

In the Kyushu University trial, a Japanese nurse was tried for cannibalism and vivisection experiments on Americans. I had attended those trials once or twice and felt strongly that the prisoners deserved their harsh sentences. This was in contrast to our defendants, whom I regarded as policymakers and far removed from the worst atrocities.

Towards the end of March, 1946, I realized I was still not going home as soon as I planned. I wanted some time off. I had my car now, which meant freedom and time to shop and explore.

A mandated change in currency also applied to transportation tickets. Money and tickets were to be turned in. Through this exchange, I got a ticket to Sapporo, the capitol city of Hokkaido, the northern island of Japan. I was able to do this without going through the Army, thereby avoiding all the red tape.

When I arrived in Hokkaido, my accommodations were at a ski lodge built into the mountains. The ski season was over, but the 11th Airborne Battalion was there for R&R—rest and relaxation. On the train going up, I met some sergeants who reintroduced me to skiing. I was an awkward, clumsy beginner, and lucky to find excellent teachers. Each morning I was on the slopes by 8 a.m., reveling in the clean, fresh air. This was my second chance; I hoped to forget my earlier skiing attempts in the Japanese Alps.

While at the resort, I met "Wild Bill," a seasoned combat veteran and paratrooper. He was a tough master sergeant, a hard-drinking, hard-swearing type who could not believe I didn't smoke or drink. He introduced me to everyone and was proud when I beat the club champion at Ping-Pong. He could not do enough for me. He took me in a jeep to the base PX where he bought me pajamas, blouses, nightgowns, and other souvenirs.

Unfortunately, he had to go back to Tokyo, putting an end to my first good time in months. I took great pleasure in watching "Wild Bill" melt from a tough soldier into a caring and gentle man. After he left, I stayed on and skied for four more days. Climbing to the top of the slopes was a workout, but the sun was out and it was so temperate I didn't even need a sweater.

Skiing in Hokkaido

In Sapporo, I watched the troops at Camp Crawford make jumps. Seeing the parachutes open was thrilling. The paratroopers said one didn't have to be crazy to jump out of a plane—but it helped. They were all so calm after the jump. I went to brunch with two of them, and after that to the PX where I bought beautiful pearls for $11.50. I found out that "Wild Bill" left orders for his boys to take good care of me because I was his fiancée. This was news to me, but who cared? It was all so happy and carefree. Eventually, I called Tokyo, spoke with one of my bosses and was assured that all was well.

Watching the paratroopers

After leaving Sapporo, my plan was to travel to the hot springs resort at Noboru Betsu for a weekend. I was introduced there to the Ainu people, who were treated almost as a caste -- referred to as "The Hairy Ainus." They were excellent woodcarvers and fishermen. This two-week absence was an oxymoron; I was both revitalized and exhausted from the trip. I needed more vacation time!

The Ainu, aborigines living in Hokkaidō, look fierce, but really are friendly. They still maintain primitive manners and customs of long ago, including the 188 famed Bear Festival. Standing on the right is the tribe chief in his formal attire.

The Ainu are aborigines, living in Hokkaido, who maintained their traditional manners and primitive customs. The tribal chief, standing on the right, is in traditional formal attire.

While I was at Noboru Betsu, "Wild Bill" called, telling me he had returned from Tokyo and wanted to see me. He asked me to postpone my departure for another day or two. He was so nice; I agreed, although I did not really believe he came all the way back from Tokyo just to see me. Later, when Bill took me to the train station, he actually asked me to marry him. I thought he was crazy! I told him so, but I did agree to see him in Tokyo.

When I got back to Tokyo, I started planning a trip to Shikoku, the southernmost island of Japan. Yet, amidst the happiness, I still felt tired and guilty that I was not helping out at the trial. I abandoned my idea of traveling to Korea, but I was determined to see as much of Japan as I could. I knew the trial was almost over. I wrote home, "It's wonderful not to work, and I don't know how I did it. I'll give myself a medal." I signed the letter, "your lazy daughter."

Back at the office, there was a farewell party for Bill Logan. If he was going, it meant I, too, would soon go. (John Brannon planned to stay for the verdict.) I now took things at a more leisurely pace. I checked in at the office, did a little work and then left. I played tennis, went horseback riding, had more clothes made, shopped, sent packages home and simply relaxed. I rationalized that this was my reward for working so hard.

Logan told me he'd look up my mother when he got to New York. So, of course, I wrote her a letter begging her not to divulge all the things I had written home about him, especially that he was such a nervous person. After MacArthur, Logan was the most famous American in Japan. All the Japanese knew him and thought he was wonderful. I was proud and privileged to have worked for him.

> I'm glad you'll meet Logan...don't forget not to tell Logan anything except I said he was real nice. Don't worry, or rather, I don't have to worry as I know you're a lot smarter than any of them including Logan and your brother.

I was hoping that my mother's brother would be there when they met because he had been in business in several countries and had shown interest in economic developments in Japan.

On April 18th, the trial was supposed to formally end. They had even begun to clear out some of the offices. The trial actually ended on April 16, 1948.

One of my final goals was to get autographs from all of the defendants, so I looked for Colonel Kenworthy. I had my picture taken with Admiral Shimada and John Brannon. I went to Yokohoma to see Mr. Logan and his family off for their return to the States.

With no indication of when the verdicts would be reached, I sensed Brannon's restlessness. By now Logan had, true to his word, met my mother in New York. He continued to write to ask me to do little things for him. He missed being with Brannon and the Kido family. Logan had worked hard on Marquis Kido's defense and was experiencing a letdown. It was inevitable there would be no more Defense Section as the attorneys began returning to the States.

Those days of leisure were wonderful. I had a golf lesson and attended the Bugaku, the ancient Japanese court dances at the Imperial Gardens. While there, I was able to view the double cherry blossoms — the yaezakura. I missed the ordinary blossoms, which had bloomed while I was in Hokkaido, but the double blossoms were sometimes considered even more exquisite and supposed to bring good fortune to the viewer.

With my schedule now more flexible, I played tennis with a British three-star general, General Gardner. I had not played for months. With the trial over, I further indulged my dream of seeing Japan, a dream that never disappointed me. No one frowned on my taking time off, so I was happy and carefree.

"Wild Bill" called from Sapporo to let me know he broke his arm. Somehow his kindness and innocence coexisted with his belligerent swagger. I met so many nice soldiers on my Hokkaido trip -- all men with big hearts. Many had been in the war's most crucial battles, but I never heard them talk about combat. They were happy to enjoy a different kind of military duty.

Opportunity continued to abound with the cessation of work. One week, I had a full day at the golf course; another day, I worked half time and at night went ice-skating with Fritz Berger Nishikawa.

Some of the lawyers planned to stay on in Japan and cash in on business opportunities. Mr. Logan had been a partner in a New York law firm before the war that represented wealthy Japanese clients. His partner, George Yamaoka, was being courted for his contacts in the business community.

Some of the defense attorneys just wanted to get back to their Stateside law practices, while others were more adventuresome. I thought Brannon, who had become acquainted with many wealthy Japanese business people, might be interested in staying on, but he was not. I knew I'd be leaving soon; I had no intention of taking another job, and the War Ministry Building appeared to be closing down.

One day, three of the defense attorneys were discussing Japanese psychology. The subject was "on," which, roughly translated, means "obligation." (It is difficult to find specific English words to describe this Japanese cultural concept. Sometimes it is translated into English as a whole series of words including obligation, duty, loyalty, kindness, and love; but these words are not indicative of its true meaning.) Virtuous men in Japan, contrary to what we say in America, never brag that they do not owe anything to any man. On the contrary, the Japanese man is indebted not only to the past, but for the day-to-day contacts he makes with people.

Japanese are taught about "on" at an early age. An "on" is actually a life of continuous indebtedness. For the Japanese to say, "I carry an 'on' for you" means, "I carry a load of obligation to you." The recipient of the "on" is called the person's "on-jin." The payment of the "on" is called "gimu" or "giri." When the Japanese pay homage to their parents, whom they respect and for whom they exercise filial piety, they are exercising "gimu."

Such obligations are always present in the Japanese and can be observed in the homage they pay to the emperor, the law, and the country itself. Duty to one's parents and ancestors, together with duty to one's work, carries different names such as Chu gimu, Ko gimu, and Ni mu. These obligations are never discharged and are carried by Japanese throughout their lives.

There are also obligations that are considered temporary in nature, such as the receiving of a gift and the giving of one in return. If a Japanese receives a small present from his mother, within a week or so he will reciprocate with a present.

Trying to understand this concept brought with it the realization that there are vast differences between the Oriental and Occidental ways of thinking; understanding the difference does not necessary resolve the basic incongruities that exist between our cultures. Learning about this facet of Japanese life helped me appreciate their cultural heritage and history even more.

CHAPTER 18 ~ THE BEAUTY OF THE COUNTRY BECKONS

After months of hard work, my slower schedule held the promise of fun and adventure. I drove along the coast on one of the few paved roads in Japan to Yokosuka Naval Base, about an hour and fifteen minutes away. Despite the early hour, the streets were full of people parading and singing. It was May Day—a holiday. Red banners were flying and soldiers were out in case Communists or Koreans decided to make their presence known. However, nothing happened. It seemed nothing ever happened; still, rumors of trouble persisted. When I bought tennis balls and souvenirs at the PX on the Naval Base, there were no lines —an unexpected bonus.

I spoke to Major General Kramer's aide. Kramer was the American general on the Tribunal. I asked the aide to have Kramer write me a letter of recommendation to USC's law school, even though I still wasn't sure where I'd end up once home. I was a bit frightened to think about going back to the States after so long. I would be returning to a new, unfamiliar world.

In the meantime, I was engaged in a social whirl. Fritzi Nishikawa invited me to tea at her house, after which we went to the skating rink to watch an exhibition and a hockey game. Fritzi performed flawlessly!

That night, the emperor's son, Prince Akihito, was in the audience. He looked like a Japanese schoolboy. There were so many people guarding him I knew he must be "the real thing." One of the GIs said, "All this fuss for a little guy like that," but Fritzi said not to forget he would grow up and become emperor some day.

As the evening wound down, I had a chance to talk with Fritzi's husband. His comment was, "All the Americans think they can make a million dollars without investing anything, just because they're Americans." He went on to say if an American had a half-a-million dollars and invested it in setting up pearl culture stations in the appropriate water sites throughout Japan, in five years they would have a fine return on their investment. It takes five years to culture a pearl, but he thought the "get rich quick" mentality of the Americans meant that very few would be willing to invest their money and time in such a venture. He also told me that the hotel I was planning to stay at on my upcoming trip to the Japan Sea was absolutely gorgeous.

> *Boy this trial is a farce in some ways as it sure isn't going to prove anything. I think most of these guys on trial are plenty guilty and deserve all they're going to get, but it will only make them heroes to the Japanese. I wonder how much the Japanese have learned and whether they think they didn't love the war. It's hard to figure this out, as this is the most peaceful occupation anyone has ever known and the Japanese cooperate all over the place. But—what are they really thinking?*

I wrote this knowing I felt differently about some of the individual defendants, and also knowing I would be devastated if they were found one hundred percent guilty and hanged.

My trip to the Hakunro Hotel in Kaga was memorable and the hotel was as gorgeous as I had been told. There were lakes, stables, tennis courts, swimming pools, and dependents—lots of dependents. Every recreational spot was filled with dependents. They could best be described as family members of military or civilian personnel working for the Occupation. I think I was the only single person at the hotel.

I took an overnight trip from Tokyo with stops in Kyoto and Nara, home of breathtaking gardens and the tamest deer. I was thrilled to take this trip. I stopped in Kyoto and found Amy Yoshikawa, a Japanese-American young lady I knew when I lived in Santa Monica. Her family owned lots of produce markets there. We talked and talked and got caught up on each other's lives. She had returned to Japan when the war broke out and had been there through all the hostilities. Being a fluent speaker of English, she was working at the hotel.

I planned trips to the Japan Sea and other spots. My cameras were my friends; taking pictures was absorbing and joyful.

Boys swinging on gate

This woman was cooking on a small wood fire in the street.

An open-air market: bikes were common mode of transport.

Yet there were some cars to be seen.

When I got to Osaka, I found out that I could travel to the beautiful Hot Springs Resort of Beppu again by taking a boat that traversed the Inland Sea. The Inland Sea was a Japanese treasure filled with more beautiful islands. I traveled on an overnight train occupied only by Japanese, and I discovered they were actually more relaxed in ways Americans were not (i.e., Breastfeeding their infants in plain view. No one thought anything of it in Japan, while in America it would have been frowned upon.). It surprised me, however, to find the crowded trains so dirty.

Beppu Hot Springs

Coming back from vacation, the atmosphere at Ichigaya had changed to what can be best described as winding-down. Many of the lawyers and secretaries were gone. The quiet gave me time to reflect. I had worked for Brannon for two years at this stage. He was always there; I saw him day-in and day-out. We worked and played, enjoyed memorable outings and encounters, and traveled together. Yet, I never thought of him as a "sweetheart." I could always hear my mother—"Elaine, don't sleep with anyone unless you are married to him."

I wanted one more trip—to the southern island of Shikoku. I could go home knowing I'd seen all four Japanese islands: Honshu, Hokkaido, Kyushu, and Shikoku.

With so few demands at work and a swimming pool opening at my billet, I decided to swim early each morning to get back into condition. During the months and months of sitting at a desk, typing had been my only exercise. I was determined to get back in shape. I began getting regular massages and was fascinated to learn that blind people were taught massaging as a trade in order to be self-supporting. A young girl was led to my room to give me my massage. When she finished, she said to me in Japanese, "You are sick." Somehow I thought she was right as I seemed always to be tired. I thought maybe I was simply out of condition. I went to the Army doctors for a physical and was told I was fine. This made me work even harder at getting fit, even though it meant really pushing myself when all I wanted to do was lie down.

The news came that a list was circulating, naming people who had to vacate their offices and leave Japan. However, this was reversed when one of the generals at headquarters said: "In order that there may not be the slightest charge of injustice to the accused, the date of relief of the American counsel employed by the United States to assist the Japanese counsel for the defense is modified to take effect when final judgment is pronounced by the Supreme Commander for the Allied Forces."

All this free time was wonderful. I shopped in the PX and had more clothes made. My biggest purchase was a set of Gorham sterling silver at a bargain price—something like thirty-six pieces for $93. Shopping was a diversion amidst the rumors of lawyers ordered to stay and lawyers ordered to leave. Brannon was one lawyer ordered to stay. By June 1st, I heard that my orders to leave would be coming soon.

The lawyers who were ordered to leave were upset. If their clients were given death sentences, they would not be there to plead for clemency. The fate of the defense was in the hands of high-ranking judges, so there was nothing to do but wait and see what orders came before making any plans. I was fairly certain I was not going to stay until the verdicts came in. Knowing I was being ordered to leave gave me the momentum to actually tend to all the little things I'd been putting off.

Towards the end of May, I became involved in a sad drama that did not have a happy ending. During the many months Brannon had worked on the defense of the Japanese Navy, he had become quite close to Juji Enomoto. Enomoto had been the legal advisor to the Japanese Navy for several years. In that role, he had attended disarmament conferences all over the world. He was the nicest, kindest man you could ever meet. He had two sons in their twenties who were six feet tall. When we asked how these boys came to be so tall, his answer was they had spent much of their childhood in Switzerland where they drank lots of milk.

Mr. Enomoto was the first Japanese person besides Capt. Watanabe with whom Brannon and I established a true working relationship. John loved him. I had written home to my mother about Enomoto, saying that she would have loved him, too.

Juji Enomoto

Enomoto had a quiet dignity and a twinkle in his eye. His twenty-seven-year-old son, who had just graduated from Tokyo University, often came to our office with his father, so I felt I knew him as well. Imagine our shock when Mr. Enomoto told us his son had been stricken with a rapid-acting strain of tuberculosis. Streptomycin had just been made available. I went to the dispensaries of the Army, the Navy, and the Marines in both Tokyo and Yokohama begging for the drug. It was there, but under lock and key. My efforts were in vain. I pleaded with four different colonels, but to no avail.

Brannon took food to the Enomoto's home, but we knew it was hopeless. Enomoto's son died. We learned the body of the departed does not lie in state for viewing; instead a picture is displayed while incense is burned. The family sits while the mourners pass by and bow. They must not cry. I could not imagine suppressing sobs when your heart was breaking, but that was the proper custom. Brannon told me it was customary to give a monetary offering at a Japanese funeral. He gave the family two thousand yen in my name. I am sure he gave a lot more; it was typical of him to help people.

Brannon was a stern lawyer—with a soft heart. One day he brought me a beautiful bedspread with all kinds of embroidery that the Enomoto family wanted me to have. He said if I wanted to do something nice, I should take Enomoto's wife and daughter out driving and perhaps buy them a gift at the PX.

> *Boy, this has me crying all over the place. I don't understand these people at all and that's all there is to it. The old man has something for Brannon and gave him a gorgeous brocade table scarf and then a letter saying he was giving him this lacquer box that his son liked. It's the most gorgeous carved red lacquer and the old man stands there and smiles and laughs. Mother, these are strange people [and strange customs] you'll never know. Their heart can be breaking and they'll smile and not show their feelings.*

Mr. Enomoto affected me greatly. His writings on pacifism and stopping the war were both meaningful and clear. I felt extremely privileged to know him. I wanted to give him a gift and so I asked Brannon for suggestions. He said cigarettes would be good. I gave Enomoto a carton as soon as I could, but then I worried that he would feel he had to give me something in return. This is how the Japanese are with gifts; it's part of the "on." The bedspread was so beautiful and had been in his family for many years. I so desired to comfort the family in this tragedy, but instead they comforted me.

CHAPTER 19 ~ THE TRIAL JUDGMENTS

Confusion reigned as orders came through for the Defense Section to disband. The orders were then recalled. I was the only secretarial help that remained for the entire Defense Section, and I was on the list of people ordered to leave. It seemed stupid for the government to have spent so many millions on the trial and then try to save a few thousand dollars by ordering the defense lawyers to abandon their clients. I wondered whether General MacArthur considered the implications of sending the defense home before the verdicts had been reached.

One day, Brannon took me and another secretary to an exclusive tea party at Shinjuku Imperial Gardens, a place frequented by the emperor. The gardens were in a gorgeous setting in a huge park. Brannon had become friendly with Marquis Matsudaira who was part of the imperial household staff. The food was extravagant, accompanied by hot sake and Japanese beer. Americans were "falling all over" the rich Japanese; demonstrating the old adage "money speaks a universal language."

George Yamaoka, the Nisei attorney who was a partner of Logan's at the New York law firm of Hunt, Hill, and Betts, was present. He knew everyone. There was a wealthy Japanese woman whose home the Army had taken over. They were now spending lots of money to make improvements before returning it to her. Yet there were still many Japanese living in parks and shacks. If anyone had asked for my opinion, which of course they did not, I would have suggested sending all the civilians out of Japan and doubling the people in military government and intelligence. Tokyo and other centers of the Occupation had become "Little Americas" and the taxpayers were stuck with the bill.

My Japanese friends might not be rich, but they were distinguished, kind, and caring. The American civilians might be working, but their presence meant building housing that conformed to that found in the U.S., plus schools for their children, imported food from home to stock the grocery stores, which were part of the housing complexes and making sure that there were garages and gasoline stations to service their cars. They demanded their comforts and would not do without every convenience they had at home.

Each day I came to the office even though there wasn't much to do—an odd contrast to the nonstop pace of work a few months earlier. The lawyers could no longer visit their clients out at Sugamo Prison and no one knew how long it would take for verdicts to be reached.

I had saved up about $3,500. I was waiting to hear from several law schools. I teased myself that, if I became a lawyer, I would be ready in time for the next war crimes trial. I'd had a lot of exposure to the practice of law and to the differing styles of Logan and Brannon. Logan was in court all the time and spoke up constantly—no one could shut him up; but he did not possess Brannon's brilliance. Logan was a plugger with rough edges, while Brannon was as smooth as Japanese silk.

Toward the end of May, Brannon wanted to entertain his Japanese friends and he asked me to serve as the hostess. A special friend, Ambassador Nomura, was there smiling and gracious as he always was whenever I saw him. Throughout May and June of 1948 there were many social events with the Japanese people.

One day I was able to accompany Brannon, George Mizota, Enomoto San, and his lovely daughter to the golf course, where I enjoyed seeing the lady caddies. I felt close to the Enomoto family after witnessing the tragic death of their son. Another outing was a party to entertain two prominent Japanese not connected in any way with the trial. Brannon was the host and the honorees were Mr. Nagasaki and Mr. Imai. Mr. Imai had never been out of Japan and yet spoke beautiful English with a slight British accent. He had been taught English at a Catholic school and he was a Catholic. He was the chief of the Liaison Section of the Japanese Board of Trade and worked with Mr. Nagasaki, whom I learned was considered the most important businessman in all of Japan.

Elaine with lady caddies

267

Japan was making a comeback and prominent Japanese had to staff the bureaus of the new government that was emerging.

All Japanese production was under government supervision. If a manufacturer wanted to manufacture a product for export or even home consumption, he had to go to the Trade Board to obtain the allotment for the necessary materials. When raw materials came into Japan, it was Mr. Nagasaki who distributed them to various manufacturers for production. In other words, nothing could be manufactured or produced without his approval and help. Of course, everyone sought his favor. He was held in high esteem by General MacArthur, and the Japanese government likewise recognized his status.

Personally, I thought Mr. Nagasaki was a sweet, ugly old man; and that Mr. Imai was a handsome, smooth-talking operator. Mr. Nagasaki told Brannon he would introduce him to anyone in Japan he wanted to meet. I tried to analyze my own feelings and realized the people I felt most at home with were the Japanese Navy men who had been to the office and had some idea of what we were doing. Since these two gentlemen had never been part of our defense work, I was more reserved around them. However, Brannon, who always went out of his way to shine some of the spotlight on me, told these men that I was playing in a tennis exhibition. I told Mr. Nagasaki that I planned to go to law school when I went home. He kindly said, "Do well and come back; I'll get you lots of clients."

These were happy, relaxed days. I met some interesting Americans at the tennis courts. One of them, who spoke Japanese and was in foreign trade, expected to make millions in Japan. He said these were formative years and it was the right time for men of ambition to jump in and take advantage of an opportunity to make money. It started me thinking about becoming a representative for a sporting goods company, until I learned that sports equipment was a luxury item and would not be high on the list of imports. The emphasis was more on manufacturing things to export, not on what to import into the country.

In order to get rich, it was helpful to know the right people—someone like George Yamaoka. He had been in contact with important Japanese before the war. He then put in time as a defense attorney. Being wonderfully fluent in Japanese, he was in a perfect position to benefit from the postwar boom. *Good for him*, I thought.

On June 9, 1948, I submitted the paperwork to terminate my employment and requested transportation on a ship leaving Yokohama July 17th. I heard the ships were all going to Seattle, but there were other possibilities, such as a ship stopping in Honolulu where I could get off and take a mini-vacation. After getting somewhat excited about the prospect of vacationing in Honolulu, I learned the following day that if someone went to Hawaii on an Army transport, they would have to pay their own way to the States from there.

Cars were being shipped home on a space-available basis; they would be unloaded and safely held in Seattle. Another alternative involved getting on a ship that stopped in Guam. It might have been exciting, were it not for the Army red tape.

An opportunity for a return trip to Nikko presented itself and I put off all my plans to go home. I planned my third visit to this beautiful and famous spot.

The last week of June, I traveled to the southern Island of Shikoku with my stenotypist friend, Frances Way. We made contact with Army people before we left and found ourselves well received on arrival. One of the officers declared himself the Ping-Pong champion of Shikoku. I promptly beat him. There were no hard feelings. Frances and I were given a jeep to go sightseeing and were taken on a boat ride. The scenery was beyond description; we both absolutely loved it. The next stop was supposed to be Beppu, but I overslept and missed the boat. I did not care as it meant another day enjoying the beach and the wonderful weather.

Waiting to board our boat to the Island of Shikoku

On boat to the Island of Shikoku

On the way to the Island of Shikoku

Island of Shikoku

Island of Shikoku

The weekend before going to Shikoku, I took my Japanese secretary with me on the train to Nikko. A group of New Zealand soldiers were going to the shrine on a weekend pass. One of the soldiers had a guitar. He was joined by three others in singing American songs throughout the journey. I learned a little about New Zealand. I knew Judge Northcroft as the New Zealand judge on the Tribunal. It surprised me to learn how few people lived there—only a million.

The soldiers proclaimed New Zealand the finest country on earth. It sounded like a land of plenty with food for all and stunning scenery. The guitar player was Maori, a native New Zealander, and he teased his fellow soldiers, calling them immigrants who lived off the natives. He told us that Mormon missionaries had visited the country and that he was a Mormon. He said his grandfather had traveled to the Mormon Tabernacle in Utah, which made him a "big shot" among the Mormon Maoris. The Maori soldier was tall, handsome, and darker-skinned than the other soldiers. It was funny to hear their accents—their speech sounded Australian but more pronounced. They told us there were millions of sheep there (more than people) and to be a successful sheep farmer all you had to do was be a little smarter than the sheep. What a lovely trip Frances and I had!

Back in Tokyo, Frances and I went to a swim meet featuring competition between three universities. We took one of the Japanese elevator girls from our billet with us. The Japanese packed the stands at Meiji Park. We were shown into the Allied section but, because we had a Japanese girl with us, one of the duty-happy GIs ordered us out, so we sat with the Japanese. I was angry and embarrassed by the behavior of the Americans. There were still some German nationals in Japan who could go anywhere and do as they liked because their skin was the right color. The Italians also had a diplomatic mission and they were able to move about freely. Yet the Japanese were restricted in their own country. This did not make sense to me. What was the right color? Years later I read a book called *I Saw Tokyo Burning* written by a French correspondent, Robert Guillian, who spent the war years in Tokyo. He discussed the policies that propelled Japan to war:

> *Japan was bursting with a desire to prove itself as much a world power as the Western countries of which it had so long been the docile, patient pupil. This Asian people was*

determined to force its way to the stage of history by chasing the white race out of Asia.

Perhaps to the Japanese, "white" was the wrong color. Surely we were discriminating against them.

The hero at the swim meet was Furohashi, a twenty-year-old student at Nihon University. He broke the world record in the 800-meter freestyle. The Japanese girls swooned over him just as the American girls swooned over their favorite idol. I was told that swooning over a sports hero was not the accepted thing to do, but the girls did not seem to care. I wondered how he could be such a marvelous swimmer eating mostly a rice diet. Then I learned that the Japanese diet was the healthier one.

The three teams came out with their flags and bowed to each other. The exuberant cheering sections seemed completely Americanized. I could tell the Japanese people loved sports. Baseball was so popular that even the young waitresses at our billet were fans. This was fun to see. I wondered when the Japanese had learned about America's national past time.

What seemed even better to me was that I could understand more of the language. Brannon had forced me to listen to the Army records we had on conversational Japanese and insisted I do some serious studying. Finally, with more leisure time, I was able to wander around, always looking for opportunities to practice my Japanese. The Japanese were always delighted when I attempted to speak to them in their own language. I presented my business cards and told them I was a secretary working for William Logan and John Brannon. Then I told them how beautiful their country was and thanked them for making me feel so at home and comfortable.

I was amazed on my southern trip to see how quickly the country was recovering. I knew Kyoto and Osaka had not been bombed as relentlessly as Tokyo, which accounted for the fully operational hotels and stores. After my return to Tokyo, a large earthquake struck the area I had just visited.

The trip to Shikoku exceeded my expectations. Frances and I were invited on a recreational launch to one of the islands in the inland sea. The water was so clear you could see all the vegetation. Shikoku looked untouched by the war. The city parks were exquisite; no wonder they were so famous. We visited Matsuyama, which derived its name from the pine forests (Matsu) and hilltop (Yama). The prettiest homes were still lived in by Occupation dependents and soldiers.

We went back to Beppu Hot Springs on Kyushu. No one talked about or even seemed interested in the trial or its pending outcome. Perhaps the people had lost interest; I surely did not know. This left me with nothing to do but enjoy the scenery. The sulfur springs colored the various lakes, turning the area into a virtual rainbow. There was a green lake, a blue lake, a red lake, and a white lake. Wandering around Beppu, we inadvertently entered the "Red Light District," which was technically off-limits. It was colorful and full of ornately clad Japanese ladies who bowed and smiled at us.

We headed back to Tokyo, stopping at Hiroshima. Despite the devastation of the bombing, Hiroshima also showed signs of recovery. There was an enclosure, which was supposedly where the atomic bomb landed. Souvenir shots capitalized on the horrific event. It was mostly still barren although certainly not devoid of people, making me think that it, too, would be revitalized in a few years. I could not imagine what happened when that bomb exploded. It was almost always mentioned in the context of the fact that when it dropped, the war ended. Did that make it a good thing?

Souvenir shop at atomic bomb site

Entry site of the atomic bomb dropped on Hiroshima

Once back in Tokyo, I began to seriously consider my trip home. I wondered if the priority given to returning veterans would keep me out of law school, and if my mother and I would be able to find housing in California, which I had always considered our home. Things had changed so much during my absence.

I knew these problems could be solved and the most important things would be for me to reunite with my mother and family and register for law school.

Hiroshima Peace Memorial, commonly known as the Atomic Bomb Dome or A-Bomb Dome (The dome is the skeletal ruins of the former Japanese Industrial Promotion Hall.)

CHAPTER 20 ~ CHINA CALLS

The trial was in the final phase. Everyone was still waiting for the judgments, which continued to give me a great deal of leisure time with many choices. Tokyo was very warm in the summer, but the heat did not bother me; I went to the beach and sunbathed to get tan. I arranged some riding time at the stables with Andy Lock, who had come back to Tokyo for ten days. Then a chance to fly to China and see Shanghai and Peking for only two hundred dollars opened up to me. I met some Chinese who offered to help me make contact with their friends in Shanghai if I decided to go.

When I contemplated the trip to China I began thinking about race and color again. The Japanese, who had taken over Shanghai, could see the International Settlements carved out by the white man who had driven out the "yellow" Chinese. Had they thought it was their turn to drive out the "white" Europeans and Americans just as author Guillian said? World problems would not be easily solved; what would the trial contribute to the solution? Probably nothing. Regardless, I began looking forward to my impending trip.

When I was out at the Setagaya Racetrack with Andy, he scolded me for having neglected my riding and arranged for me to go riding three mornings a week. I was in heaven—riding, shopping, relaxing, and still getting paid. How good could it get?

Andy introduced me to a Japanese rider at the stables who excelled at an entirely different style of riding called *dressage*. It was beautiful to see how he synchronized every movement with the horse. This man had phenomenal horsemanship and was an excellent teacher.

When Judge Roling found out I was riding, he asked me to arrange for him to go out to the stables as well. He wanted to know about local beaches and whether he might be able to enjoy sunbathing while avoiding local recognition. I had supposed all the judges were working on the final verdicts day and night; apparently this one also wanted recreation and relaxation.

Judge Roling was such a handsome man. His background in judicial circles was impressive. I felt certain being a part of the judicial panel at this historical trial was totally different than anything he had previously experienced. (Just think of the articles and treatises he could write when it was all over.)

My paratrooper friend "Wild Bill" came down from Sapporo, and we all went to the beach together. Being a "he-man," he refused my offer of suntan oil. I learned later he was hospitalized after our day at the beach with second- and third-degree burns. After my repeated lectures about the benefits of physical activity and the dangers of drinking whiskey and beer, "Wild Bill" paid dearly for not taking my advice.

Time off in July gave me an opportunity to assess what I had accomplished. During the months when I was working day and night, I was productive in other ways as well. I was happy to have absorbed so much of the history of Japan as the trial unfolded. Now I was focusing solely on pleasure and rest; I no longer read or had as much interest in world events. Between ice skating, tennis, swimming, riding, and shopping, there were always fun things to do. It was like being on a perpetual vacation in a glorious playground and, instead of costing me, I was getting paid to do all this. I wrote home that perhaps God was repaying me for two years of hard work.

Brannon enjoyed teasing me; he said the reason I wanted to learn new things was so I could show off for my mother. He may have been right.

At the end of July I flew to Shanghai on Northwest Airlines. We left Tokyo at 8:30 in the morning, had a one-hour layover in Okinawa and arrived in Shanghai at 4 o'clock. The plane was full of interesting people, including a British colonel on his way to liquidate funds that had been sent to China by the United Nations Relief and Rehabilitation Association. There was also a veterinarian who was going on to Nanking.

Brannon arrived in Shanghai two days before I did and made arrangements for me at the hotel. I wrote home to my mom telling her I did not want to be one of those foreigners who spent a few days in a country and then acted as if they were experts; I wanted to truly see the real China and people. I would have only about ten days to do this and wanted to use my time wisely.

My initial impression of Shanghai was the noise. I believe even Times Square was quieter. There was also the awareness that I was no longer affiliated with an Army of Occupation. In China, *I was a foreigner!*

Before the war, the Americans, British, French, and Germans carved their own International Settlements or Concessions, and each was policed by their own forces. They built Shanghai, maintained law and order and thought of it as a fine, clean, cosmopolitan city. Since the surrender of Japan, China lost many of the institutional structures and services these foreign countries had provided. The city was filthy and crowded beyond description. Car horns blew continuously. The chief mode of transportation was still the rickshaw or the pedi-bike driven by the poorest of the poor Chinese.

Chinese rickshaw driver

Amidst the general din and commotion, there was none of the politeness or gentility I was used to in Japan. I saw naked Chinese children running around with severely distended bellies, and people living in houseboats on the Whangpoo River. The river was so crowded I wondered if it was even navigable.

However, the city had not been bombed and the contrast to Tokyo was startling. There were shops bulging with goods and big department stores loaded with everything from food and clothing to household appliances—even late-model cars. The late-model cars were driven by the Chinese.

I did not know how to come to terms with poverty and wealth in such close proximity. On the streets, beggars were everywhere. Rich

Chinese people stepped over dead coolies in the street as if they were not even there. Coolies were the poorest of the poor who did the kind of work no one wanted to do. The reality of all this evaporated my preconceived notion of finding glamour in China.

The money situation was bizarre—the typical tip was one million dollars of Chinese currency. On the day I arrived, the exchange rate was 6,800,000 Chinese dollars to one American dollar.

I was warned not to go out alone, but my curiosity got the better of me and I did a lot of exploring by myself.

One of the lawyers with the Chinese group in Tokyo had given me an introduction to his law clerk and he invited me to his home for dinner. He had a brand new car, a chauffeur, and an apartment on the finest street. When we went shopping, he carried the money. When I went out by myself, I carried money in a cosmetic case.

Inflation in Shanghai was rampant. We needed piles of money to buy anything. I bought luggage and some exquisite Chinese linens that were available at half the price they were sold for in Tokyo. I spent less than one hundred dollars for two fine suitcases and two fine tablecloths. The wealth was dazzling.

Brannon returned to Japan shortly after my arrival. Because American females appeared to be scarce, meeting people was not a problem. I met an American pilot at the hotel. One evening we went dancing at the hotel roof garden with other Americans who also were mostly pilots. Every month these pilots flew in goods to the Chinese. I was shocked when the pilot said the Chinese do not fly planes—they just let them sit; if anything goes wrong, they lack the knowledge of how to fix them.

There was talk that fighting was going on between the Communists up north and the Nationalists in the south. These were some of the last days of "old" Shanghai before the Communists took over.

China is greed, graft, and corruption with Chiang Kai Shek and the Soong family getting most of the money, and the people getting nothing. The customs won't let them import Sunkist oranges because that's a luxury, but it's O.K. to import these big cars now because that's a necessity. It's all the way you look at it, isn't it?

I traveled on to Peking. It was a four-hour flight during which I kept looking for the Yellow River. The drive from the airport into the city reminded me of Mexico with its adobe houses and people with stands along the road. I checked in at the Wagons Lit Hotel, which was considered the best in the city. I learned "Wagons Lit" meant the same as a Pullman (i.e., a wagon with a bed).

I set off in a pedi-cab pedaled by a Chinese man to do some exploring. The inflation was a little less than in Shanghai, but I still got between seven and nine million yen for one dollar. Peking was quieter and cleaner than Shanghai. I was told some of the streets were replicas of streets in Paris. There were foreigners everywhere—Americans, Russians, and British were highly visible.

I planned on going to bed early, but instead I received a surprise phone call in my room from a stranger who said he was from Pasadena, California; he had noticed my name in the hotel's registry and asked if we might talk. He turned out to be very interesting. He, too, was a pilot with CAT, or China Air Transport, which was General Chennault's airline. Its purpose was to bring freight and supplies to the Nationalist government. He had a British pilot with him. Both told stories of how impossible it was to work with the Chinese. Yet they were making a fortune. Pilots were normally not supposed to fly more than eighty hours a month and here they were working twice that and being paid by the hour. They also were paid extra money for landing at what were considered "dangerous" airports. They looked exhausted to me and I could not believe they were scheduled to fly out at 3:30 the next morning. They said their flights were termed "shuttle-runs." After chatting for about an hour, they left and I was happy and ready for some sleep.

The next day I ventured out like a typical tourist armed with camera and leaflets. I saw the Forbidden City and the treasure-laden Emperor's Museum. I went to the Temple of Heaven, stopping at pagodas and museums along the way. For the first time, I saw women with bound feet who could not walk, but hobbled pitifully along. I had heard three versions of why the feet were bound. One was as a sign of beauty to help a girl catch a rich husband. Another was as a sign of luxury. (Women of the working class needed their feet; if you were rich, you did not need to walk.) The third reason was to keep women from running away. It was very ugly to see the bones crowded together and bulging above where the ankle was supposed to be. I found myself totally repulsed and bewildered by the sights. I would walk down a dark, dingy alley and come out upon a beautiful store or home. They must not have heard of city planning.

Chinese Temple of Heaven showing Altar of Heaven

Chinese Temple of Heaven

Chinese Winter Palace, the White Pagoda

That evening the British pilot (Harry), who I met with the American from Pasadena, came to see me. I enjoyed his visit. He told me a story to illustrate how the Chinese put a prize upon "saving face." Once when his Chinese copilot was landing a flight, he overshot the field. Instead of simply going around again, he landed by slamming on the aircraft's brakes, burning them out and rendering the plane totally unable to fly. He had "saved face" because he did not have to fly around and try again.

That morning Harry had been flying a plane loaded with mortar shells to Nationalists in Mukden when the rudder locked. Harry was resigned to not getting airborne when the Chinese radio operator said, "Should we call the tower and ask for a departure signal?"

Harry had replied, "No! Wire St. Peter for an arrival signal." They flew around for a while trying to lighten their load in anticipation of a crash landing, but the rudder suddenly began working again. He was still drained by this experience and asked if we could go for a walk. We went along the city streets to a special market place — a black-market street where there were huge cans labeled UNRRA, United Nations Relief and Rehabilitation Association. Harry said all the stuff sent by Americans to Shanghai wound up in the black market. American clothes, shoes, powdered milk, and canned milk were all being sold instead of being distributed to those in need. However, if the UNRRA stopped aid to China, the Communists would take over. Once again it seemed as if the rich kept getting richer, and the poor kept getting poorer.

> *I really don't mind being by myself, but China is funny. In Japan if you're away from Tokyo in a strange place, where there aren't many Americans, and you see an American, you smile and are friendly. But in China nobody gives a damn about you; if you smile they look at you like you're nuts.*

Some people I met said we should have allowed the Japanese to take over China, as they were the only ones who could deal with the Chinese mentality. I felt people should be given a chance to develop their own countries, but I had no idea how to fight the graft and corruption that inevitably ensued throughout this massive country. Communism was how it was fought!

From Peking, I traveled on to Hangchow. I'd heard it was a particularly scenic spot to visit. At the airport, I watched a huge, modern aircraft unload a group of refugees in pajamas and peasant clothes, even a very old lady with bound feet. Everyone up north was being evacuated as the Communists advanced. It would not be long before China would be closed to the western world and completely out-of-bounds for travelers.

Hangchow was very pretty with lots of pagodas, shrines, temples, and monasteries. It was hard to appreciate the ornate richness of these structures when the people seemed so extremely poor. Maybe this is why Communism seemed to be succeeding.

Back in Shanghai, I took a cab to the Park Hotel. The taxi ride cost four million yen and I gave a million yen as a tip, but it did not seem like enough. I was exhausted and, rather than stand on the street trying to decide what to do, I ran into the lobby. After resting, I changed clothes and went back down to the lobby where by chance I met up with another American pilot and his flight crew. We all ate dinner together and afterwards went up on the roof garden to dance to a Chinese orchestra playing American music. These Americans did not seem to be bothered by the inflation, which had my brain spinning with the huge amount of Chinese money that was received for an American dollar.

I always met lots of people coming and going to airports. The strangest person I met was a British man on his way back to Tokyo. He had been a Japanese POW and had lived in Shanghai for several years. Surprisingly, he was not bitter towards the Japanese. It was almost as if he felt no one could get along with the Chinese and perhaps the Japanese were not so bad.

The Chinese were nominally on our side. I knew very little except that Chiang Kai Shek had a wife who had been very demanding when she visited the White House. While the U.S. supported Shek's government, there were always questions as to whether or not it could succeed.

When I arrived back in Tokyo, I realized I had only two weeks left in Japan, so I concentrated on fitting in a final bit of fun. Judge Roling wanted me to play tennis and go horseback riding with him again, so I did. He was such a fine person. Everyone seemed to respect him and talked of his role as an educator in his home country. I liked him because he was not a bit stuffy and instead was thoroughly down to earth, wanting to enjoy his time away from the bench.

Justice Roling, Elaine, and her Ford

I was scheduled to leave August 20, 1948, and flying home by way of Guam and Honolulu, but I had to land near the port where my car would land. Brannon planned a big party for me with my Japanese friends: Ambassador Nomura; Mr. Okuyama, our Japanese lawyer; Mr. Enomoto; and Captain Watanabe, who had become a close friend. I felt a genuine affection for these people.

While in Shanghai, I bought presents for all the Japanese girls at the Kanda Kai Kan. I still wasn't sure of my own feelings towards the Japanese except that they were not at all what I had thought of them when I first found I would be coming to their country. I wanted to return with my mother because she had a gift for knowing people and judging their true characters.

I hoped Mt. Fuji would be clearly visible on the day I left. It was said seeing Mt. Fuji brought good luck and meant you would come back some day. At my goodbye party, I intended to give a speech in Japanese, so my days were spent in preparation.

Mt. Fuji

To my surprise, the Kido family invited me to their home for a party. Even though I had never had any warm feelings towards Marquis Kido, his son was one of the Japanese lawyers with whom I had worked and I felt somewhat close to him. The family was wonderful, giving me a "presento"—a lovely pearl ring. Mrs. Shimada gave me a tiny jewel box with the Imperial Crest on it.

There was time for one last picnic in Meiji Park with my Japanese secretary and Brannon's maid from the Dai Ichi Hotel. We had fried chicken and potato salad. By now, my car was already on a ship heading home. At my goodbye party, Ambassador Nomura sat on my right and I wrote my mother that she would have been proud and amazed to see me discussing foreign affairs and world problems with him. The people at the party were my Japanese family. I truly loved them!

The car's journey took it to Seattle, while I would end up at an airfield in California. On my last night in Tokyo, there was another party at Mrs. Tohara's house attended by Prince Takamatsu, Captain Watanabe, and John Brannon. I sat with the prince and, as always, he was alert and interested in everything. People said he was the informal eyes and ears of the emperor; an article had appeared in *TIME* magazine reporting on his recent tea with General Eichelberger, second in command to General MacArthur.

Brannon, who knew how much my mother's approval meant to me, said he would have given a million dollars for my mother to see me in this setting. I had learned a Japanese street song and dance; the prince and I got up and danced, then everyone joined us. The prince took me home in his chauffeur-driven car and gave me a wonderful goodbye with lots of bowing and smiles. Leaving Japan made me melancholy and unbalanced—happy to go home, and sad to leave a place I loved.

My car was not due in Seattle until September 8th, so the sergeant who took care of my transportation fixed it for me to get "bumped" at Guam and Hawaii to kill some time.

On one of my last days, I went horseback riding with Judge Roling. We talked about the trial again in terms of having participated in an historic event. He did not discuss any specifics, nor did I expect him to. He told me again how much he admired John Brannon, saying he was one of the few lawyers with whom he wanted to be friends. My memories were made even richer when Judge Roling took me home, planted kisses on each cheek and told me to work hard and become a lawyer.

Elaine and Justice Roling on horseback

To cap everything off, I had written General MacArthur requesting a formal meeting before I left Japan. My letter said I had worked in Tokyo for two-and-a-half years and it would be sad to tell my mother that in all that time I had never met my boss. (At that age I guess I had more nerve than sense.) What a surprise when his aide, Colonel Bunker, called in response to set up the meeting.

At noon on August 21, 1948, I met "God"—the Supreme Commander for the Allied Powers. He talked to me for two "long" minutes. He looked just like his pictures. Even though he was gracious and polite, I knew he wanted me out of his office as soon as possible. He deigned to see me out, walking me to the door and shaking my hand. I wrote home and said, "You see, he's not 'God,' just a little bit higher."

MacArthur was surprisingly young looking and had a wonderful carriage. He exuded authority, leadership, and all the qualities needed for the position of supreme commander. There were always Japanese who waited at the Dai Ichi Building to see him in person when he left for his home at the American Embassy. They knew the emperor had met him on one or two occasions and the worship they had for the emperor was seemingly transferred to this powerful man.

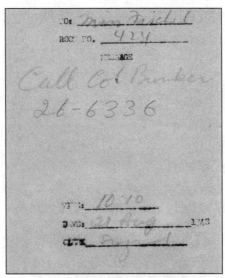

**Message arranging appointment
with General MacArthur**

I was having problems getting out of Tokyo due to an explosion on Guam, but that did not stop Judge Roling and me from going to the GI beach and having lots of fun splashing around. He told me about his life as a judge in Holland and about being on the Tribunal.

During those last days, I still went to the office. Brannon was thinking of filing a writ with the Supreme Court if there was an unfavorable verdict. Judge Roling told me he was glad I was going home before the verdict. That worried me because the judge knew how much I liked Admiral Shimada. He did say the admiral had impressed the judges more than any of the other accused, but no one could forget Shimada's role in joining the cabinet in order to give his vote for war.

It was now the end of August and I still had not gotten onto a flight. Finally, on September 1, 1948, I left Tokyo at ten o'clock, arriving in Guam on September 2nd. Because my car was not due to arrive in Seattle until the 8th, I hoped to visit Guam and stay in Hawaii for a few days.

Of all the coincidences that happened throughout my stay in Japan, here was another on Guam. A nurse I met mentioned a Colonel Frost. I gasped in recognition and started asking questions. He was the same Major Frost with whom I had worked at the B-29 Flight Engineering School in Texas and Kansas!

CHAPTER 21 ~ FINAL JUDGMENTS

Running into Colonel Frost was wonderful. He brought his jeep and off we went. I found Guam to be not only picturesque, but a beautiful tropical island. (I had the same thought when we stopped there on the way to Japan so long ago.) I still remember the unique experience of watching rain fall through bright sunlight.

Colonel Frost had achieved a high rank at a young age. He was looking forward to returning from the service. I told him about my work and adventures in Japan. After a few hours of catching up, I had to say goodbye to him. Seeing him once again made me nostalgic for the months I spent at the B-29 Flight Engineering School. Working with the colonel had been my first really important, demanding job, and I had risen to the challenge.

There were so many young pilots killed in the Pacific War who would never be coming back. Again, I was sobered by the thought that I had assisted in defending the enemy who orchestrated their destruction. There was no way to get around the fact that for the past two-and-a-half years, I helped to defend "the enemy."

Life presented me with a true puzzle. Does peace make you forget the past? Or do you relive it again and again and try to gain some wisdom in the process? I had no answers, only questions.

After an overnight stop on Guam, I was back on the plane for the flight to Hawaii. We landed at Hickham Field. For two glorious days I enjoyed the wonderful weather and explored Honolulu. Then on to California and Tacoma, where my car awaited me. Somehow, I managed to unravel the miles of red tape and endless paperwork necessary to reclaim my automobile.

At last I was headed for my sister's home in Mar Vista (a Los Angeles suburb) where I would reunite with my mother, my sister Ruth, and her husband Bill. After all their wartime traveling, Bill was out of the service and preparing to take the California Dental Board examinations to obtain a California license.

The drive home was an uneventful, yet lovely journey down the coasts of Washington, Oregon, and California. I finally arrived only to be completely and emotionally "crushed." My mother thought I looked just awful. She kept wondering what had happened to me. She kept asking me if I felt all right. I started thinking back and remembered on my trip in China, I had struggled to climb a small hill. At the time I had attributed my lack of energy and exhaustion to the heat. My mother worried about me constantly and was concerned that all I wanted to do was sleep.

This homecoming was not joyous as I expected. We could not find housing in the Los Angeles area so we decided to drive to New Jersey. My mother's brother Martin had a lakeside home at Cupsaw Lake, which he used when he visited the New York area on trips from his home in Argentina. My mother had visited there when her brother came to the United States. Martin said he would be happy if we lived there. I had applied and was accepted at law school at New York University and it was possible to commute to school from the lake.

The home was more than adequate for our needs and quite pretty according to my mother. So we drove across country in my trusty new Ford and moved into our new home on the lake. This was going to be "home" for the duration of school. I knew, though, someday we would return to Los Angeles.

Elaine and her mother at lake

Living out in the country and being on the lake was pleasant, but the yard needed much attention with massive amounts of leaves to be raked. I hated to gather them up and I found it frustratingly difficult. Even the slightest physical effort left me exhausted.

293

I continued to worry about the outcome of the trials and wondered if our clients would be sentenced to death when the final verdicts were announced. On November 12, 1948, the long-awaited verdicts came in. The Tribunal passed sentence on all twenty-five of the defendants; seven were given death sentences. As expected, Hideki Tojo was the lead story. The New York Times reported:

Editorialists for the main Tokyo newspapers will state tomorrow that these sentences were not merely punishment of the guilty, but a lesson for the whole Japanese people to abstain hereafter from aggression and concentrate on the preservation of peace.

New York Times **article on verdicts**

General Tojo leaving the International Military Tribunal;
on November 11, 1948, after hearing himself sentenced
to hang for conspiracy to wage aggressive war and for
atrocities against prisoners (U.S. National Archives).

General Muto was one of the seven receiving the harsh sentence.
He was the defendant whose fate had troubled me the most. During the
meetings we had in the holding room, he was very serious, until some-
thing was said that would turn him into a smiling, very alive person.
He commented often on how well I had progressed with my Japanese;
I often checked with him to see if I was bowing in the correct style.

Given the atrocities that occurred in the Philippines and in
Sumatra, it was inevitable that a death sentence would be handed
down. In the Philippines, Yamashita and Homma had already been
tried and hanged. General Muto had been on Yamashita's staff when
the Americans retook the Philippines.

Justice Pal, the Indian judge, in his mammoth dissenting opinion, had detailed comments on the prosecution's evidence. He referred specifically to Exhibits 1355 to 1489, the exhibits received in evidence to establish the acts of atrocities. He said they showed General Muto was not in command of the Army in the Philippines and Yamashita had already paid the price. General Muto was not in Sumatra, either, when the atrocities toward the civilian population took place. He said firmly that General Muto, along with the others, should have been acquitted.

I wondered about the sentences. If the trial was to try those who had planned a "war of aggression," then the generals on trial in some instances could have been tried as Class-B or C war criminals. General Doihara had spent most of his military life in China. The Chinese would want someone to pay for the constant fighting in their country. Japan had been battling in China many years before Pearl Harbor. Many of our defense counsel argued that the United States' demands that the Japanese get out of China were extremely brazen—after all, those were Pacific nations and we in the U.S. were supposedly not concerned with that theater of war. Were we truly unconcerned? It did not seem that way.

I remembered fondly how General Muto gave me his "Go" set, just as he had promised. The Japanese were singularly elegant players of this game, which required great skill and ingenuity. It was said that "Go" started where chess left off.)

General Sato and Ambassador Shiratori playing GO

296

Admiral Shimada received a life sentence, as did seventeen of the other defendants. The two lightest sentences were given to Mamoru Shigemitsu, who had signed the surrender document on the U.S.S. Missouri, and Shigenori Togo. Togo was the only prisoner who had flatly blamed his fellow defendants for the war, claiming he had been left holding the bag for the botched delivery of the note to the White House. His sentence was twenty years.

I was relieved that General Sato did not receive a death sentence. He was the youngest—only fifty-four—and he expressed relief that he was going to live. He was torn apart and reduced to tears when he knew General Tojo was to be hanged.

Mamoru Shigemitsu received seven years. Joseph Grew, former ambassador to Japan, had signed a deposition on his behalf requesting leniency. Shigemitsu had not been found guilty of "Count 1" as a "leader, organizer, instigator, or accomplice in the formulation or execution of a common plan or conspiracy to wage wars of aggression, war, or wars in violation of international law." The only other defendant acquitted of that count was General Matsui—yet he was sentenced to death.

It was a tremendous eye-opener to read the full dissenting opinion of Justice Pal some years later. He meticulously analyzed all of the evidence. This attention to analysis and detail was not forthcoming from the other judges, so how could I know what was in their minds? Justice Roling had written a separate opinion, as did the French judge.

Admiral Shimada was convicted on five counts. As Naval minister, he was held responsible for planning and executing the successful attack on Pearl Harbor. (I never did believe in his guilt, nor did Brannon, who considered Shimada a weak link brought into the cabinet to insure a unanimous vote for war.) I remembered his testimony regarding his thoughts when he joined the cabinet of Premier Tojo:

> *...I did not have the impression that I was joining a war cabinet under which the nation would be plunged into the bitter and tragic struggle that followed; but rather I believed it was an appointment in a government which, by its very military strength, control, and attitude would seek to exhaust the last possibilities in a peaceful effort to settle the grave international dispute.*

Justice Roling approved of the life sentences handed out to sixteen of the accused. He wrote in his separate opinion that Admirals Shimada and Oka, Generals Hata and Sato, and Marquis Kido all should have received death sentences. They should have been found guilty of "conventional war crimes." He was the only judge to ask for the death penalty for the naval defendants. An interview with him in 1982 was recounted in Arnold Brackman's book in which Justice Roling said:

> *It is difficult to explain judgments; the question why one gets a death sentence, and the other only imprisonment. The behavior in court may have played a role [as well as] the tactics of defense counsel. Even the question at what moment the court had to make up its mind may have been significant. If accused "A", (a not-so-notorious person), is dealt with just after the deliberations and sentence concerning a notoriously cruel accused, [then "A"] will benefit from the fact that the Court will be inclined to give expression to the difference between the two.*

Chief Justice Webb wrote a separate opinion denouncing Emperor Hirohito as the real "leader of the crime." He indirectly criticized the Allied leaders for the fact that Hirohito, "although available for trial, had been granted immunity." Webb wrote separately that none of the defendants should have been sentenced to death, because "it might prove revolting to shoot or hang such old men." (Perhaps he was not as mean as most everyone thought he was.)

In Justice Pal's 240,000-word dissenting opinion he declared all of the defendants should have been acquitted as a token of "magnanimity and understanding charity." The judge from the Philippines took the opposite view and said some of the sentences were not harsh enough. The French judge partially dissented. It was his opinion that some of the counts for which the defendants were convicted were not prohibited by international law. He recited all the appropriate language in the international treaties that supported his position. However, his opinion was merely a dissenting opinion and had no control over the sentences.

Several newspaper articles claimed that the current leaders of Japan (now at the end of 1948) were only interested in the verdict's implications on those who were involved as shown by the evidence. There had been speculation that the emperor might abdicate, particularly if he appeared to lose face through the conviction of his entire cabinet. In actuality, this was the case. No one was more conscious of it than Prime Minister Tojo. His attorney, Dr. Kiyose, said, "Tojo's mind is eased very much by the verdict and by knowing he has given no additional trouble to the emperor."

In Tokyo it had been common knowledge that General MacArthur wanted to keep the emperor out of the War Crimes Trial because the emperor's continuing reign insured the Occupation would be peaceful. Certain Japanese observed that, according to the evidence, the emperor was undeniably involved in the war conspiracy, but the judgment handled him very lightly, leaving the impression that he was a man who was forced to go along with the flow of events, rather than a leader or member of a conspiracy.

General MacArthur and Emperor Hirohito in *Today* **magazine**

According to reports, the Japanese leaders now in power were concerned about the implications of the decision on the Zaibatsu. The Zaibatsu were big family trusts that held a monopoly on Japanese industry. These trusts had been broken up by the Occupation. They no longer were reputed to have the power and strength of their prewar dominance. Who knew if that was true? I had discussed this with Brannon. He had compared the Zaibatsu to the Fords, the Rockefellers, and the DuPonts in the United States. Brannon believed that even though the economic advisors to the Occupation had "broken up" the Zaibatsu, they would be back. He said when commerce started up again, there was no way General Motors would want to be doing business with the corner storekeeper; the very nature of big business did not work that way.

The Tribunal held that, although the Zaibatsu were not accused, two of their largest companies (i.e., Mitsui and Mitsubishi) had exercised virtual control of the narcotic concession in Asia under the Japanese Army. The Zaibatsu leaders had been purged by the Occupation, but they were still family and remained extremely influential.

General MacArthur had the power to alter the sentences. He set the deadline of November 19th for receiving petitions on behalf of the defendants. He could not increase the sentences, but he could decrease them; some Japanese thought that he would. The leading newspaper at the time, the Mainichi, said:

> *The Japanese people have received a great shock by the sentences. Unless the whole of the Japanese people make the outcome of the trial food for reflection, all damage done by the Japanese in the various countries during the war and the serious effects suffered by the Japanese people will be a meaningless sacrifice.*

The *New York Daily News* had a cartoon showing a general watching Tojo and some other defendants on their way to the gallows with the caption, "There (but for the grace of heavier armaments) go I." Their editorial said, "WATCH YOUR NECK, OMAR." It then said:

> *Without excusing any atrocities committed by some of Tojo's underlings against Allied prisoners of war, let us not kid*

ourselves about the real reason why Tojo and six other wartime Japanese big shots are to dance upon the air unless General MacArthur commutes their sentences on appeal. These gents real crime was that they lost the war. Certainly, they waged "aggressive" wars; the term applies as well to them as it did to the German war criminals—Goering, Hess, and the rest in the Nuremberg trials. But do you think for a moment that this was the primary consideration—or that the Russians would be even as fussy as we were in interpreting the word "aggressive" Even now Stalin and Co. are accusing us of planning an "aggressive" war. All we can say is WATCH YOUR NECK, OMAR.

The message of the editorial ended with a warning to General Bradley and the cabinet members to build the best war machine possible.

DAILY NEWS

NEW YORK'S PICTURE NEWSPAPER

Saturday, November 13, 1948   Tel. MUrray Hill 2-1234

Published daily except Sunday by News Syndicate Co., Inc., 220 E. 42d St., Borough of Manhattan, New York 17, N. Y. Daily mail subscription rates: U. S., $15.00; Canada, $15.00 a year. For the Daily and Sunday News, U. S., $20.00 per year; Canada, $22.50. President and general manager, F. M. Flynn; executive editor and secretary, Richard W. Clarke.

MEMBER OF THE ASSOCIATED PRESS
The Associated Press is entitled exclusively to the use for republication of all the local news printed in this newspaper, as well as all AP news dispatches.

WATCH YOUR NECK, OMAR

Hideki Tojo came full circle yesterday, or almost. Once he was Premier of Japan; now, after a long-drawn-out trial by his country's conquerors, he is under sentence of death by hanging. His crimes: planning for aggressive wars—mark the word "aggressive" —on Russia, China, and the United States.

Without excusing any atrocities committed by some of Tojo's underlings against Allied prisoners of war, let us not kid ourselves about the real reason why Tojo and six other wartime Japanese big shots are to dance upon the air unless Gen. MacArthur commutes their sentences on appeal.

Hideki Tojo

These gents' real crime was that they lost the war. Certainly they waged "aggressive" wars; the term applies as well to them as it did to the German war criminals—Goering, Hess and the rest—in the Nurnberg trials. But do you think for a moment that this was the primary consideration—or that the Russians would be even as fussy as we were in interpreting that word "aggressive"? Even now Stalin & Co. are accusing us of planning an "aggressive" war.

All we can say is: Watch out for your own neck, Omar.

The Omar referred to is Gen. Omar N. Bradley, our present Chief of Staff, who thinks he is discharging his patriotic duty by pushing his country's drive for military preparedness. He is doing just that—IF we get into a war with Russia, and IF we win that war.

If we lose, Bradley will be declared a war criminal by the Reds, who will undoubtedly insist they are well within their latter-day legal rights if they hang him by the neck until dead, dead, dead, and may God have mercy on his soul.

The same goes for Defense Secretary Forrestal, his three secretaries for the Army, Navy and Air Force, and all our other high-ranking armed service dignitaries. It goes, for the matter of that, for President Truman. The Allies would have hanged Hitler if he hadn't cheated them of that pleasure by committing suicide, as Tojo tried to do.

So Omar & Co. had better build us the best war machine they possibly can, because in the next great, glorious conflict it will be table stakes, and among the stakes will be our military and political leaders' own lives.

Perhaps this has already occurred to these gentlemen. Anyway, they are pressing us without letup to spend billions for defense in amounts previously unheard-of in time of peace. Maybe, in addition to doing their patriotic duty as they see it, they are trying to take out the best possible life insurance for themselves. If so, they're smart.

Watch Your Neck, Omar, *New York Daily News*, November 13, 1948

Cartoon *New York Daily News*, **November 13, 1948**

The verdicts left me bewildered and sad. Realizing only one non-military person, Koki Hirota, had been given the ultimate punishment, while others who had held diplomatic or civilian posts escaped the death sentence, I had to ask myself if I believed the prosecution was truly successful in targeting those who had planned and waged a war of aggression. If so, why were only military men given the death sentence? I did not have the answer. I was pleased Brannon's defense of the Japanese Navy was successful. None of them were going to be hanged for the Pearl Harbor attack. This had to be a huge disappointment for the prosecution.

Once resettled in New Jersey, I contacted Bill Logan and began working as a secretary in his law firm. It was a prestigious place that had represented many Japanese businesses before the war. With the peace, it was inevitable that the Japanese would be back and need lawyers to assist them in renewing their commercial interests.

This was my first experience working in a private law office and I found it fascinating. The office was in one of New York City's most glorious high-rises. A lovely woman attorney was on staff practicing there. Her presence inspired me to believe that I, too, could become a successful lawyer.

While at work, I read in *The New York Times* on November 14, 1948, that the guilty Japanese had barred a clemency bid. I did not understand that, as Brannon had written to me that Ben Blakeney, on behalf of all of the defense counsel, was submitting an appeal to General MacArthur, repeating much of what had been said at the trial.

1. The trial was unfair.
2. The verdict was not based on the evidence.
3. Guilt had not been proven beyond a reasonable doubt.
4. The verdict would not achieve the Allied Powers' purposes.

The document was short, but did say that international law was not clear on "crimes against peace." If losers were to be tried for losing, the law should be clearer so the victor would know how to inflict the proper punishment. Under this last category the appeal said, "The verdict looks too much like an act of vengeance to impress the world with our love of justice and fair play." It went on to say a lot more, but did not do any good in moving General MacArthur.

The Japanese press printed less and less about the trial, but it did publish poems by thirteen of the defendants. They had given the poems to their Japanese counsel after hearing the verdicts.

Tojo wrote:

Oh, look and see how the cherry blossoms fall mutely.

Hirota wrote:

In the spring, men, like cherry blossoms fall; in the autumn men, like sparkling dews, purge themselves.

The former Finance Minister, Okinori Kaya, wrote not a poem, but a statement:

My conscience is clear as the sun and the moon.

Sir William Webb, the chief justice of the Tribunal, conceded that immunity for the emperor was probably in the best interests of the Allied Powers. His comments on what he really thought spoke volumes:

> *No ruler can commit the crime of launching aggressive war and then validly claim to be excused from so doing because his life otherwise would be in danger. The emperor's real power was displayed when he intervened in 1945 to terminate the war and 'save Japan.' In this instance he was acting as an absolute monarch. Previously he had refrained from exercising his real power.*

It was difficult to disagree with this statement. Evidence of the emperor's hold on the Japanese people was made abundantly clear in the final days of the war when he had announced on the radio there would be a surrender. Then surrender had followed.

Kichisaburo Nomura, Japanese Ambassador to the U.S. (left), with Secretary of State Cordell Hull (center) and Saburo Kurusu, Japan's special envoy for a "final attempt at peace," arriving at the White House on November 17, 1941 (United Press International Photo).

CHAPTER 22 ~ GOING TO THE U.S. SUPREME COURT

On the anniversary of Pearl Harbor, I thought obsessively about these men being hanged. Before the final step, there was hope, however, as the American lawyers were going to take this case to the United States Supreme Court. Logan put me to work preparing papers that would be filed with the Supreme Court. Of the lawyers still in Tokyo, Brannon planned to return and argue the case as did George Yamaoka, counsel for Hirota, and George Furness, counsel for Shigemitsu.

December 7th came and went. The Supreme Court hearing was scheduled for December 20th. Since I was working in the law office where Logan worked, it was natural for him to ask me to continue work on the project.

With Logan and the others, I traveled to Washington, D.C., by train from New York and arrived at the court around 10:30 a.m. The building was dignified and grand. Court was scheduled to start at noon. Several of the lawyers who had been in Tokyo had returned home and were in Washington, D.C., for the hearing. Cameramen and reporters were everywhere.

It was just like old times; John Brannon and William Logan were dictating to me and I searched madly for a typewriter so everything would be transcribed and ready for use when the case was called.

On December 20, 1948, at 3:30 p.m., the court announced it would hear the case. I had finished my work and could only hope it would be helpful in the oral presentation. Joseph Keenan, the lead prosecutor in Tokyo, appeared for the United States, together with his assistant Frank Tavenner. The lectern where the lawyers stood to present argument looked a lot like the War Ministry Building (but without the headphones to provide translation).

Fred Vinson, the Supreme Court's chief justice and the eight other judges listened to the case with attention and interest. The basic presentation was fairly informal; a lawyer would speak, a judge would interrupt and ask a question; the lawyer would answer the question and continue with his arguments.

Logan was the first up and explained the background of the Tribunal as well as the framing of the charges against the defendants. One of the justices was Robert Jackson, who had been the chief prosecutor at the Nuremberg trials. The only question he asked was whether or not copies of the Tokyo judgment were available. The arguments went on for three hours. At the conclusion, it was impossible to gauge the reactions or predict the outcome, but it felt like the defense had been given a fair shot at presenting our case.

The New York Times had published a letter on December 19 written by Valentine Deal, one of the attorneys who had departed Japan with Captain Coleman. He claimed that he and the others who left with Coleman believed the defense would not be up to the task of truly representing the accused. He also implied that the lawyers who took on the task were unskilled. All in all, his letter was a bitter blow and seemed remarkably uninformed. He also brought up the fact that, at the time of their arraignment, only a few of the defendants had been represented by counsel, which he believed was an early and decisive indicator of the trial's innate unfairness.

Some of Deal's points had validity. It was true that members of the defense were treated like stepchildren; we never had enough help and we worked long hours. Yet, despite these handicaps, I considered the defense counsel to be courageous and dedicated. Not all of them were superb lawyers, but they had put their hearts and souls into the fight for justice, and the Japanese people knew it.

On December 20, 1948, the Supreme Court made its decision:

> 1. The military tribunal setup in Japan by General MacArthur as the agent of the Allied Powers is not a tribunal of the United States, and the Courts of the United States have no power or authority to review, affirm, set aside or annul the judgments and sentences imposed by it on these petitioners, all of whom are residents and citizens of Japan.
> 2. For this reason, their motions for leave to file petitions for writs of habeas corpus are denied.

Justice Jackson did not participate in the decision. One judge dissented, but died before writing his opinion. That was Justice Rutledge, who I thought was the most attentive to the arguments.

Justice Douglas concurred with the decision, but wrote some chilling words:

> *That resorting to the criterion of 'jurisdiction' was too narrow and it was indeed dangerous as it left no room for judicial scrutiny of this new type of military tribunal, leaving the powers of those tribunals absolute. Prisoners held under its mandates may have appeal to the conscience or mercy of an executive, but they apparently have no appeal to law. I cannot believe that we would adhere to that formula if these petitioners were American citizens.*

He came right out and said that the Tokyo Tribunal was "a political forum, not a judicial action." His opinion closely concurred with that of the Indian judge, Justice Pal. Justice Douglas even cited Pal's observation:

> *It did not therefore sit as a judicial tribunal. It was solely an instrument of political power. Insofar as American participation is concerned, there is no constitutional objection to that action. For the capture and control of those who were responsible for the Pearl Harbor incident was a political question on which the president as commander in chief, and as spokesman for the nation in foreign affairs, had the final say.*

None of these words meant anything to the defendants. In fact, his opinion was submitted six months after the defendants had been hanged in Tokyo. Had they wanted to rule favorably, the hangings would not have taken place; the court would have intervened. But it did not....

It was thrilling to see these judges in action. I was proud of Bill Logan and John Brannon. Both were unfazed and stalwart in their appearance before the highest court in the land.

It pained me to know that those condemned to death were not led to the gallows in uniform or even in halfway-decent clothing. The official report of the Japanese executions by the Supreme Commander Public Relations Branch said:

They were not permitted to wear their own uniforms or even clothing of their own choosing. Instead they went to their deaths wearing United States Army salvage work clothing completely devoid of insignia of any kind.

Of the sixteen defendants who received life sentences, six died in prison. Mamoru Shigemutsu, who had received the lightest sentence of seven years, was the first to go free, followed by Shigenori Togo, whose sentence was twenty years; the others were all pardoned in 1955. Shigemitsu's seven-year sentence started from the time he was arraigned. He was released in November, 1950. In December of 1954, he became foreign minister and negotiated the release of the other prisoners. Their release, however, did not come until April, 1958, when the Japanese government granted their appeals for parole.

CHAPTER 23 ~ LIFE ON HOLD

After the hearing at the Supreme Court, I went back to New Jersey. I realized I had to put the trial behind me and concentrate on what might lie ahead. I had been accepted by New York University School of Law. Knowing I wanted to eventually return to California, it would have made more sense to attempt to enter USC's Law School. But my mother and I had tried unsuccessfully to find housing in California when I first arrived. The house in New Jersey was so pretty that living there for the three years of law school was a welcome solution to our problem.

I had several weeks of leisure before I started my first semester. I was still exhausted and could not figure out why. My mother insisted I get a physical exam before starting school. I saw a doctor who said he wished all his patients were as healthy as I was. He gratuitously threw in the remark that "it was too bad I had gotten lazy"—this when my mother said she was worried as I had just come back from two-and-a-half years in Tokyo, which was full of malnutrition and tuberculosis (TB). With the reassurance that I was indeed healthy, I next had to figure out the train schedule from Erskine Lakes, New Jersey, to law school in downtown New York City.

School started. I used the hour-long commute by train to study. I was cheered by the fact that my trusty Ford would be waiting at the train station when I arrived home. Soon, however, the cold began to overly irritate me and I coughed incessantly. I had just been told by a doctor I was healthy, so I figured I coughed just because it was cold. My mother insisted on another physical. I was all set to go when I received a call from John Brannon that he was coming to New York. Brannon and I arranged to meet after school, and I skipped my doctor's appointment. We had a wonderful reunion. I had just completed six weeks of law school. He was eager to hear about my experiences.

I left Brannon that evening and was on the bus heading to the train station when I started coughing. I soaked a dozen tissues with blood. I was terrified, but did not know what else to do except board the train at the station and try to get home. As soon as I told my mother what had happened on the bus, she arranged for me to see the doctor whose appointment I had skipped. I do not remember how I got there or whether I called Brannon to tell him what happened.

The doctor's diagnosis was shattering. He told my mother in front of me that "your daughter has advanced active tuberculosis and you can send her to Denver and start praying." He went on to say my hemorrhage on the bus indicated I had a large cavity in my right lung and needed immediate treatment. He showed us the lesion on the chest x-rays. Denver had many tuberculosis sanitariums and was known as a place where that disease was treated.

Tuberculosis was about the scariest word we could have heard, because my father had died of this disease in 1929 when he was only thirty-seven. My father was a fine athlete and I still remembered him standing with his stopwatch as he timed my sister and me swimming in pools and lakes.

My mother was still haunted by my father's death at a sanitarium in Saranac Lake, New York. She was determined not to send me away for treatment in Denver. She telephoned her favorite cousin, a well-known physician who was an authority on premature babies and an author of medical texts. After hearing about my illness, Mother's cousin told her he would get the finest lung doctor in New York to see me.

I saw Dr. Harry Wexler, who told us that streptomycin was a new antibiotic that worked wonders. Dr. Wexler planned to inject me with the drug for ninety days and to try to collapse my lung, a treatment technically known as artificial pneumothorax. The cavity was low in the lung, but if he could collapse my lung and the antibiotic killed the bacteria, I would eventually recover. Aside from streptomycin, there were no other antibiotics for tuberculosis. My only question was whether I could play tennis again, someday. He assured me I would be fine; however, I needed to be peaceful and calm with a minimum of two years of bed rest.

We moved into the Croyden Hotel in New York City. Dr. Wexler came every day for ten days. With help of a special machine and a nurse, he put air into my lung day after day. I was then taken to his office. The x-rays revealed that my lung had indeed been collapsed. Putting air in every ten days would keep the lung compressed, allowing the cavity to heal. This meant coming to New York for the refill on a regular basis.

Dr. Wexler repeatedly stressed the importance of bed rest. This was enforced in the strictest sense, which meant not getting out of bed at all unless for an emergency. Neither my mother nor I knew anything about giving injections, so when we arrived back at the Lake, we called the Visiting Nurse's Association to report the case and ask for help. A nurse came out and asked us to practice using an orange and a hypodermic needle. I learned fast and was able to give myself streptomycin injections daily for ninety days. Everything I touched had to be sterilized until tests of my sputum were negative.

I thought of Mr. Enomoto's son who died of tuberculosis. I was struck by the irony that, although I had been unable to obtain the streptomycin for him in postwar Tokyo, treatment that might have saved his life, the drug was freely available to me. My life was saved; his had not been. This has always haunted me.

After I had left Japan, Enomoto San was one of the people with whom I started corresponding and I loved receiving letters from him. What a truly fine gentleman he was!

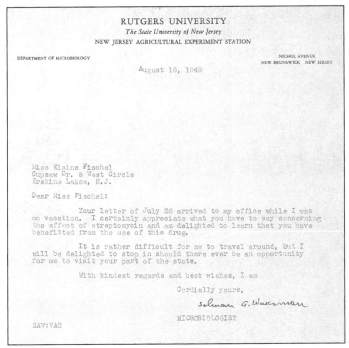

**August 16 letter from from inventor
of streptomycin at Rutgers University**

313

Having been forced to drop out of law school, it was a treat when two fellow students came to visit me in New Jersey. Brannon had been there when the diagnosis was made. Now he assured my mother he would file the proper paperwork insuring government help with our medical bills and living expenses. He was true to his word, putting in a claim through the office of Congressman Coudert. What a relief to not have to worry about the medical bills!

During my convalescence, I had plenty of time to think. I knew I wanted to return to law school and to California, but for the moment, my main focus was on getting well. I could not have asked for a better caregiver than my mother. One of the symptoms of TB is loss of appetite and weight. To counteract this, my mom found a great butcher one town away who provided us with certified raw milk and superb meat. I was able to spend hours reading silly books and not feel guilty.

Television was in its infancy then; we watched Dione Lucas, the former cook for the House of Windsor and the proprietor of the Cordon Bleu Cooking School in New York. I often sent for her recipes. This began a lifelong fascination with baking, which I put to good use when I was finally able to resume normal activities.

Making Dione Lucas' Chocolate Roll and Praline Cake was so much fun! I realized the truth of the saying that "no one gives more pleasure than a good chef." I was constantly asked for the recipes and told I should open a bakery and have those two specialties. I want to share them with you.

CHOCOLATE ROLL RECIPE DIONE LUCAS

Ingredients:

6 large eggs; 7 oz. sweet dark chocolate; 3/4 cup granulated sugar;

6 tablespoons made coffee; 2 cups whipped cream (1/2 pint); 1 teaspoon

vanilla; cocoa

Procedure:

1. 350 degree oven.
2. Line jelly roll pan with waxed paper after first oiling bottom of pan. Then lightly oil the waxed paper.
3. Melt the chocolate with the coffee in a double boiler – low flame so chocolate doesn't burn
4. Separate the eggs and in the yolks add the sugar and beat till thick.
5. Mix the melted chocolate into the egg yolk mixture..
6. Stiffly beat the egg whites and add to the mixture above and mix gently – try to fold in the egg whites.
7. Put the batter into the jelly roll pan and bake for 15 to 17 minutes. Turn off the heat and let the roll stay in the pan for five minutes. Then cover the top with a wet cloth – you can use paper towel if you wring it out - and let it stand till it is cool.
8. Carefully lift each end of the pan but don't remove the chocolate roll. Cover the top with cocoa which you sift on to it. Then turn the roll onto foil cut longer than the roll. Carefully remove the wax paper which is now on top of the roll.
9. Mix the vanilla into the cream which you have beaten till it is whipped.
10. Spread the whipped cream over the jelly roll. Then carefully roll it up – don't get upset if it cracks as you can push it together but it should be easy to roll. Roll up like a jelly roll and you can serve it or put in refrigerator and serve later. Cut it carefully.

Dione Lucas recipe for Chocolate Roll

PRALINE CAKE RECIPE BY DIONE LUCAS

Ingredients:

For the cake: 5 egg whites; 3/4 cup sugar; 1/4 teaspoon salt; 1 and 1/2 cups finely ground browned almonds.

Prepare pans as follows: Use 3 8 inch cake pans and invert them and cover them with foil and butter the foil and sprinkle with a bit of flour.

Beat egg whites until very stiff. Mix almonds and sugar together and fold gently into the egg whites. Add the salt. Spread the mixture onto the top of the 3 pans and put in 300 oven for 20-25 minutes. Leave in the oven overnight so they dry out. You will spread coffee butter cream frosting over the layers and on top.

Coffee butter cream: Ingredients are:
5 egg yolks; 2 tablespoons strong coffee; 3/4 cup soft butter; 3/4 cup sugar; 1/2 cup water.

Put sugar and water in a pan and stir until dissolved. Turn up the heat and allow it to cook until when you let some liquid fall from the spoon it spins a light threat. This takes a while and you will know when the mixture bubbles and is reduced.

Beat the egg yolks well – in a mixer and slowly pour on the sugar syrup beating all the time. Continue beating until it is cold and starts to stiffen. The butter is then added a little bit at a time, not more than one tablespoon and also add the coffee. It should thicken and look like a mouse and be of spreading consistency. Put in refrigerator a while before serving. Cut carefully as it should be crisp. The coffee cream is a little tricky to make and if it starts to separate add a little melted butter and it should come together.

Dione Lucas recipe for Praline Cake

I wrote to my Japanese friends about my illness. Brannon also wrote to Admiral Shimada, Captain Watanabe, and Prince Takamatsu and told them of my predicament. It was not long before I received letters from Japan and beautiful packages of seaweed to help me in my recovery.

Having been told by the doctor that I was to spend as little energy as possible in doing anything, for the first time in my life I was spending time doing nothing. My mother was wonderful company and time passed quickly. Every ten days we had an eventful trip to New York. I very slowly got into the Ford and my mother drove me to Dr. Wexler where he put air in my lung so it would collapse. We then drove to her cousin's apartment to have lunch and rest before the trip back to New Jersey. I wasn't contagious after the first ninety days of streptomycin.

316

Visitors were welcome, which helped us not feel isolated. I could read dime novels; turning pages didn't take a lot of strength and being lazy was actually taking me down the road to recovery.

From time to time, I read articles about the trial and was shocked by one entitled "The Major Evils of the Tokyo Trial" written by one of the Tokyo defense lawyers who had spoken at a convention of the American Bar Association. Among other things, he said the objectives of the trial were vengeance, vindication, and propaganda. This conclusion was the same as that reached by others who reported on the trial and called it "Victors' Justice." The lawyer was Owen Cunningham, who'd had a run-in with Chief Justice Webb and was banned from participating during the trial's last stages. He thus followed David Smith.

I found Cunningham's remarks particularly insightful. I recalled how furious many of the defense lawyers had been that the Soviet Union was allowed to fully participate in the judging of the defendants when it had declared war on Japan a mere six days before the war ended. Owen Cunningham had guts, and he was not afraid to implicate the emperor.

The role of the emperor and the application of the novel principal of individual responsibility for acts of state are irreconcilable. If the prosecution wanted the truth as to individual responsibility, why did they not call the emperor of Japan to the witness stand? Did they have the courage to do so? They have asked the Tribunal and the world to believe that the emperor didn't know what was going on and, if he did, that he did not have the power to prevent it. I do not think the Tribunal will be carried away with such legal acrobatics.

I thought of the lines of ordinary Japanese citizens outside of Ichigaya, standing each day waiting to get into the court and of how faithfully the Japanese newspapers reported the happenings at Ichigaya. I felt in my heart and soul that the trial brought the truth to the Japanese people as to why this devastating war had taken place, and why Japan had to start all over again to join the so-called "Family of Nations." Maybe that was the "good" of it all.

It was 1948 and the world was in turmoil. Making up for the deprivations caused by the war, Americans were becoming consumers, fascinated with all the newly available goods they could purchase. I did not want to keep a wartime mentality going forever, but in the midst of the new prosperity, I worried that people might forget the lessons of war. I was haunted by the fact that our defendants were sentenced to death not for waging war, but for their participation in mass-scale atrocities. Why had they not listened to Justice Pal and sentenced only the truly bad ones where there was proof of their involvement in the atrocities? Instead, it was Justice Webb's words that ruled:

> These far reaching plans for waging wars of aggression, and the prolonged and intricate preparation for and waging of these wars of aggression were not the work of one man. They were the work of many leaders acting in pursuance of a common plan for the achievement of a common object. That common object, that they should secure Japan's domination by preparing and waging wars of aggression, was a criminal object. Indeed, no more grave crime can be conceived of than a conspiracy to wage a war of aggression, for the conspiracy threatened the security of the people of the world, and the waging disrupts it. The Tribunal finds that the existence of the criminal conspiracy to wage wars of aggression has been proved.

As I lay in bed hour after hour thinking about the trial, I thought of my friendship with Justice Roling. He had specifically written that Oka, Sato, and Shimada should have been punished with the supreme penalty. Was I conceited enough to believe because Justice Roling and I had ridden horses, played tennis and gone to the beach together it would mitigate in any way the sentence he handed down?

Brannon had told me about visiting Admiral Shimada in Sugamo and saying to him, "Admiral, you should have been hanged according to Judge Roling."

Admiral Shimada had replied, "I'm glad you were my lawyer and not my judge."

Despite my occasional dark thoughts about the trial, life was not unpleasant. Justice Roling, who was at the United Nations, came to see me. It was wonderful for my mother to meet him. I think she was impressed that a chauffeured limousine brought him from New York to this hideaway in New Jersey—just to see me. Wow! Logan, who lived not too far away, also came with his wife Frances and one of his sons.

I had sent an application to UCLA, but the law school, which began in 1950, was only admitting students who were newly matriculated and I had been out of college for ten years. So I applied to the University of Southern California School of Law and was accepted on the condition I take the LSAT (Law School Admission Test).

The LSAT was being given at Princeton, New Jersey. I drove there with my mother to take that exam. It was the first time I had been out of bed since 1949. Some months later, I was notified I had been admitted to the USC School of Law, so I must have passed.

Before my mother and I returned to California, I needed to know I was no longer contagious. I could not risk infecting anyone. My sister had recently given birth to a son and we would be staying at her home.

We left New Jersey at the beginning of the summer of 1950 and, driving my trusty Ford, made it to California in six days. We stayed with my sister and her husband until we found an apartment near USC. I met my new doctor, Samuel Sills. He said I could go to school in the morning, come home, stay in bed and go back for afternoon classes, avoiding anything strenuous. I could live with that!

Before I knew it, school had started and I was a freshman. At last my dream was shaping up. There is a quote "dreams never retire" and my dream had not. I was now living my dream and planning my future.

Law school is a different experience for everyone. For me it was more the idea of getting through rather than having a love affair with the law. I was surprised at the diversity of the student body. Some seemed absolutely brilliant while others were mediocre. Some students were taking advantage of the GI Bill; many were married. Sometimes I felt completely out of place. Perhaps I was not used to being in an academic environment as I had graduated from UCLA ten years earlier.

Eventually, I made some friends and the time passed quickly. There were about five or six females that first year. I never knew why, but in year two, I was the only female in the class.

I attended both summer sessions so I could finish in two-and-a-half years instead of three. The three-day bar exam was both an endurance contest and a test of knowledge. I passed on the first attempt. Admission to the bar meant going to work. In 1953, no one was hiring women lawyers. I had anticipated this setback, which was one of the reasons I tried so hard to get good grades and qualify for the Law Review.

Despite the timing, I had two job offers. One was to work for a commission investigating the differences between the court of lowest jurisdiction (the Municipal Court) and the one of unlimited jurisdiction (the Superior Court). The other was a job with California Supreme Court Justice B. Ray Schauer. The Supreme Court job would mean moving to Northern California.

I was intrigued and tempted with the Supreme Court job until someone warned me that Justice Schauer liked to hire women attorneys who had previous experience as secretaries. A red flag went up, and I turned down Justice Schauer's offer. I wanted to be out in the world practicing law, not confined to the hallowed offices of the California Supreme Court.

The trials and tribulations of starting a law practice vary. With my mother's encouragement and the money I saved, I finally opened my own office. In time I had clients and the opportunity to go to court. My mother was a good coach. She said, "Keep it short, keep it simple, and don't talk that lawyer talk."

For the first few years I struggled, but I finally established myself and settled down to practicing law. Pneumothorax had ended around the same time I passed the bar, so I concentrated on the law and on forgetting I'd ever been sick.

In 1960, I thought about going back to Japan. I had my wonderful albums and letters from my friends there. I decided to take my mother to the place that had such special significance and so many happy memories for me.

I wrote to Hiroko, Admiral Shimada's daughter. Although she was now a grown woman, I still thought of her as a little girl. I notified Captain Watanabe and Prince Takamatsu that I would be returning to Japan and staying at the Imperial Hotel. After Japan, I hoped we could travel on to Thailand, Angkor Wat in Cambodia, Singapore, Indonesia, and Australia. Winning a large jury trial made it possible for me to pay for the trip.

CHAPTER 24 ~ RETURNING TO TOKYO

When I started my law practice, I had only my mother and my books to help me. However, I learned you could not run away from reality. I liken scary experiences to going to the dentist: you make your appointment; you do not want to go, but you do; and usually, when it is over, you feel better. Practicing law was scary.

During my first civil jury trial and my first criminal jury trial, I was honored that my clients put their trust in me. Their confidence fueled my determination to win each case. If at all possible, I was not going to let them down. I won four trials in a row and then lost the next two. I tried to think like a juror. This approach helped me know how to communicate what I wanted jurors to believe.

The fact that I could now go back to Japan because of my professional success made the trip even sweeter and more exciting.

It was 1960. The flight to Japan seemed endless, but so much shorter than the first trip in 1946 and the flight home in 1948. On our arrival at the Imperial Hotel, I was thrilled to find a message from Prince Takamatsu requesting I telephone him immediately at his palace. Now my mother would know everything I had written to her was true. The prince sent his car and chauffeur to pick us up, and we were taken to his palace for dinner. Princess Takamatsu was a patroness of the silk industry and gave us lovely gifts.

We had a wonderful reunion. Throughout dinner, we could not stop talking and reminiscing. Prince Takamatsu wanted to know about my law practice and my health. He said he knew I had weakened myself by working so hard for Admiral Shimada and Marquis Kido. He was anxious to have me reassure him that I was indeed healthy. I could not have asked for a more perfect evening. The prince and princess were so kind and gracious to us.

Messages from the prince to meet with mother

Captain Watanabe, Hiroko Shimada, and Ambassador Nomura also called. Ambassador Nomura told my mother he had never seen anyone type as fast as I did. He also told her how sorry he was that I had not been working at the Japanese embassy when messages had to be typed. We knew he was referring to the last message to President Roosevelt, which was not typed fast enough at the Japanese embassy to permit it to be delivered before the Pearl Harbor attack. He promised to visit us in Los Angeles (some years later he did).

Captain Watanabe planned our itinerary to Osaka and Nagasaki. In Osaka we planned to visit a china factory. Japanese china had become extremely popular throughout the world. Nagasaki was known as the city where Madame Butterfly supposedly took place. We also wanted to see the Atom Bomb Museum that had been built there.

Captain Watanabe accompanied us to Beppu Hot Springs. This was my third trip there and a "must see" for my mother. The captain was now chief of the Japanese Maritime Services, akin to our Coast Guard. He had our train schedule and told us that, when we reached his home city, he and his family would all be on the train platform to

322

greet us. I was thrilled that my mother could enjoy this warm welcome from my friends.

When we visited Nagasaki, one of Captain Watanabe's aides told us he had arranged a boat tour of the harbor for us. We were escorted by three other boats and enjoyed a show of cascading water plumes as we traveled across the bay. I knew this was done as a tribute to my mother.

Later that evening, at one of our train stops in the middle of the night, Captain Watanabe and his entire family stood on the platform and bowed to us, just as he had promised. What an experience! It touched my mother very deeply that her daughter had earned the respect of these people.

We ended our trip in Tokyo and were able to visit other parts of the Far East before returning home. The return to Japan was a trip never to be forgotten. Then there were the letters I received expressing the happiness my friends felt at meeting my mother and seeing that I was healthy.

Through the years I have continued to correspond with my friends via letters. The letters from Prince Takamatsu expressed his observations about world events during this period. I corresponded with Justice Roling from time to time, as well as Ambassador Nomura, who came to my home in California three times.

John Brannon was always part of my life. I loved him till the day he died. We always talked and corresponded, and I will never forget him. He encouraged me in my law practice from his home in Kansas City and I always felt close to him.

My legal career had its highlights and moments of great interest as I continued to work in this infinitely challenging and complex field.

Many years have gone by. I know I am approaching the end of my life and career. Writing this story of my many experiences has meaning if it can help us know that world leaders are still people with hearts and souls. We hope those who govern will have the clarity and vision to anticipate the results of their actions. A very wise man—Abba Eban, said, "History teaches us that men and nations behave wisely once they have exhausted all other alternatives."

In closing his dissent, Justice Pal said:

When time shall have softened passion and prejudice, when REASON shall have stripped the mask from misrepresentation, then justice holding evenly her scales, will require much of past censure and praise to change places.

John Brannon asked that I not forget his words.

What country in all this vast world would send its own citizens to defend the war leaders of a cruel and hated enemy – only America! For her justice revere her – for her greatness, respect her – for her principles of Godliness, love her. Lest you forget the heritage that is yours as a member of the greatest family of free people in the world, gaze upon this war torn, war sick populace and be thankful.

Having been an eyewitness to the destructive aftermath of the war, I finish my story remembering the beauty of Japan, the perfection of cherry blossoms and the kindnesses and appreciation shown by so many people from so many different cultures to a young American girl who was given the privilege to experience a piece of such a lasting moment in history.

**Cherry blossoms on the road in front of Sugarmo
Prison where the defendants were held**

324

APPENDIX A ~ LETTERS FROM MY JAPANESE FRIENDS

nov. 20, 1948

Dear Miss Fischel,

I appreciate the opportunity of writing you for the first time.

I suppose you have known the penalty for my father. It was so nice for him to have received more light penalty than we had expected. I cannot express my deepest rapture, and I suppose you would be glad as much as I am, for you worked so earnestly for him. He is very healthy and has the quiet life in Sugamo prison.

I have been intending to thank you for your present of cotton. It was so precious in Japan to get as nice cloth as you gave me that I made dresses with my best. I am sorry not to be able to show you it.

November 20, 1948, from Hiroko Shimada Kawano,
daughter of Admiral Shigetaro Shimada

What are you doing now? Your mother must be glad having you beside.

Which is more beautiful the Nature of your land or Japanese Nature? It is getting more cold now, and very beautiful with red leaves.

I have expected if you come to Japan again, because you liked Japan very much. And I wish to visit your land in future.

My mother asks me to give her best regards to you, and please send mine to your mother.

Goodbye for now, and I am looking foward to hearing from you.

Sincerely yours,
Hiroko Shimada

my address —

47 Minami-Cho
Takanawa, Shiba,
Minato-Ku,
Tokyo, Japan.

November 20, 1948, enclosure with letter from Hiroko Shimada

(Translation)

22 September 1946

Dear Miss Fisher,

It is autumn now and the gardenful of insect-musicians comfort us every night with their sweet melody in the fair moon-light. I think you are well and busy all the time.

I thank you very much for your visit on us the other day. We really had a nice time.

It is very kind of you to have sent me such nice wool so soon. I make it my pleasure to knit some lovely wears for my great grand-children.

Please come again, we are all looking forward to seeing you real soon.

Thanking you again, and wishing your good health,

I remain,

Yours sincerely,

Sueko Kido

Sept. 22, 1946, letter from Suiko Kido, Taka Hiko Kido's grandmother

9th Oct. 1946

Miss Fisher,

Here is my grand mother's letter of thanks for your kind present with it's translation. I hope you could understand her most graceful appreciation.

Takahiko Kido
Taka hiko Kido

Oct. 9, 1946, Taka Hiko Kido

330

c/o Maritime Safety Board
Kasumigaseki Chiyoda-ku
Tokyo

April 21 1949

Dear Elaine B. Fischel

How are you getting on? The other day I heard from Miss Hisako that you are unhealthy now. Is that right? I fear, when you were in Japan you worked so hard that you now lost your healthy. I'm other words, Japanese advocation in the trial forced you unhealthy.

Japanese should appriciate you for your devotion in the tribunal, and if Japan should have strong economy she would offer you her

April 29, 1949, from Captain Yasuji Watanabe (page 1 of 5)

2

Kindest thanks. Anyhow I, sincerely, ask you to care and I hope you be well soon.

It has elapsed about 3 months since Mr. Brannon left Japan. and I think he is visiting you now. He wrote me some weeks ago that he is going on trip to East coast and find new job for Japanese rehabilitation. He said he might be back to Japan in this summer.

I am very well and busy as usual. My offices are ordered to minimize personnel according to the "Economic nine prinples", and Tokyo, Yokosuka offices are authorized to retain. But jobs are not

April 29, 1949, from Watanabe (page 2 of 5)

332

3

coming short. However we are enjoying every day. I'm going to have baby in early ~~time~~ May, and now very happy. I know how to content.

I recall last year when cherry trees were in full bloom, we visited Kamakura. Last sunday, the easter day, was the best ~~se~~ time of cherry trees, and many people in Tokyo went out just as last year, and as you know lots of "yopparai" – drunken fellow – trotted streets or gardens.

Now situations in Japan are improving very much. Already we are easy to fooding (Of course

April 29, 1949, from Watanabe (page 3 of 5)

4.

by the U.S support).

Clothing to be recovered soon.

Housing is still hard.

Most anxious point is this;
many people don't remind they should work hard with minimized payment because of defeat. Those people's complains are going to be utilized by Communists to upset conditions to-day. But as we are doing best please be easy and see how the results is.

When I received your last letter, Prince Takamatsu was on trip to Hokkaido for about a month, therefore he read your letter after his trip.

He is busy because he is invited by many assemblies in local,

April 29, 1949, from Watanabe (page 4 of 5)

5

but he is quite well and I think
he will write you. Mr. Brannon
took photos of Prince and Princers
(before he leaves Japan)
in his garden, and he is not sending
its copy yet. (I want) You ask him to have
its copy for you.

Hoping you be well very
soon, and I prey god to recover
your health.

Yours truly
Y. Watanabe

April 29, 1949, from Watanabe (page 5 of 5)

No. 5 Shoto-Machi,
Shibuya-Ku Tokyo
June 6, 1949

Dear Fishel-San and Okā-san,

Your letter dated 22 Feb. came our family March 17. My family very much pleased with your everlasting friendship. Toyoko is rejoying at your very useful gift. She asked a tailoress to make it just fit her. She usually puts it on when she goes out for a walk. We have now splendid weather day after day.

State of affairs in Tokyo is getting better gradually except high prices of commodities. We can expect restoration of social order in a near future. This must be attributed to the wise and lenient policy taken by the G. H. Q.

I am to leave the 2nd Demobilization Bureau by Order. After more than 30 years service to the Country, I must leave

June 9, 1949, from Juji Enomoto (page 1 of 3)

't without any reward. Yet I do not regret of it. I have done all that I could. I believe I have discharged my duty to my country.

I am afraid of I would not deserve the words of praise of your mother. However, I honour myself by knowing that my affidavit was read by your good mother.

I envy your lucky situation. You have good mother with whom you live and are studying a favourite subject. But I advice you not to study too hard; you should take care of your health. I know very well that you work very hard on every thing which you ought to do. I saw your manner of working and excellent ability, with admiration at Ichigaya. This is why I have some anxiety about influence upon your health

June 9, 1949, from Juji Enomoto (Page 2 of 3)

337

resulting from over work.

All of my family wish to have some good chance to see you together with your good mother.

I must beg your pardon for the terrible delay in writing to you. This was caused partly by my bad health affected by the sudden death of my son, partly by my lack of experience in writing a letter in English. Any how I have no good reason of excuse for my fault; I only beg your pardon.

Please remember us for ever. Our best wishes for your mother and your happiness.

Very sincerely

Juji Enomoto

Okā-sama ni yoroshiku o-negai shimasu.

June 9, 1949, from Juji Enomoto (Page 3 of 3)

Dear Miss Fischel,

Tokio
Nov. 6. 1949.

Thank you ever so much for your welcome letter of October 30. which reached me this morning. Altho I have full confidence for your doctor and medicine such as streptomycin yet I was often thinking of you and I am very glad to know your remarkable improvement. Anyway, you are very young. Please be patient and don't move too quickly. To be too much in hasty temper, is not good, I believe.

As you often wrote me, I would like to visit your country once more. Such good friends as Admiral Pratt whom I admire and respect and very good friend since 1915, former Ambassador Mr. Castle, and Mr. Frederick Moore who write to "the Foreign Affairs" I wish to see them once again. As to travel there are much difficulties, especially we are very poor after this war.

For Japan, if Japanese make mind to make democratic improvement and refuse to become communistic country, there is no other way for Japan's existence, than to be honest and trustworthy partner of u.s.a. people here are gradually understanding what is democracy and what is communism and ofcourse majority prefer the former. peace-treaty or no peace-treaty or peace treaty with democratic countries only, Japan, without having any defensive power even against a small enemy, needs the protection from u.s.a. Japanese can never think of sovereignty in the sense, used in the past. Today there are only two countries, u.s. & and soviet-Russia which are sovereign and independent in the absolute sense.

Please convey my best wishes and regards when you make correspondence with Mr. Bannon.

Again with my best wishes for you and your Mama.

P.S. My wife is now in hospital since September but she has recovered and returning home next wednesday.

Yours very sincerely
K. Nomura

November 6, 1949, from Kichisaburo Nomura

339

19 Dec. 1949

1, Nishidai-Machi
Takanawa, Minatoku
Tokyo, Japan

Dear Miss E. B. Fishel:

I am very much pleased to received your nice letter of Oct. 31, 1949 through Mr. Y.Watanabe.

I was not aware of that you were so ill, but I am sure with the wonderful modern medical care such as you have in your country, you will be on the sure way of recovery within the shortest possible period. I am sure the teachings of Japanese philosophy will help a great deal preparing yourself to assume such an psychical attitude which influences one's health greatly.

I pray that before long you will visit us again in Japan, and enjoy the regenerated Japan and things in general.

I desire to see your country again which provides many a valueable instructions for us.

I pray that this letter will find you already on your high way of recovery. Both Takamatsu-no-miya-hidenka and myself enjoy very good health - nothing better could be wished.

With the best wishes and compliments of the season, both from myself and my wife,

I remain,

Sincerely yours,

Nobuhito

(Prince Takamatsu)

December 19, 1949, from Prince Nobuhito Takamatsu (brother of Emperor Hirohito)

Dear Miss Fischel, April 17th 1950.

Your letter of April 11th reached me on 15th to my great delight. How quick it is! Taking into account one day difference of date, it took really only 3 days.

First of all, I am indeed very very glad to know that you are recovering wonderfully well altho I was of strong belief that your stamina will win surely over any drawbacks.

Like you I do not lose hope for peace in future. Reminiscent of horrible tragedies in the last great war, only five years since its end, any sane reel statesmen will not begin more dreadful atomic war.

Don't you think that once wide and separated world is becoming more compact and closely-connected small world by the quick development of aero-planes and radio-communication? Dont you think that this world is developing to become one-world in spite of many obstacles, principally attributable to several countries' traditions, feudalistic ideas and heresies. I am not pedantic but I am rather optimistic, so that peoples in this world will be wise enough to find reasonable and healthy way of living in this quickly changing world by atomic bomb and hydrogen-bomb.

Mr. Brannon is, as you praise him, brilliant lawer. While he is industrious, he is very humane and sympathetic. I am very glad to hear from you that he is showing his ability in a big "trust" case. I will write him but please convey my best regards and best wishes for him.

When you come next time to Japan with your mother, it may be better to cross the pacific via Honolulu. It is indeed pleasant cruise especially for recuperation and rest. This route is always calm, very very seldom to be rough.

With best wishes and regards to you and mother

Yours very sincerely

Kichisaburo Nomura

April 17, 1950, from Kichisaburo Nomura

Takanawa, Tokyo,
April 19, 1950.

Dear Miss Fischel,

Very many thanks for your good letter, and I am particularly pleased to hear that you are getting much better now. As for the Princess and myself, I am happy to say we are faring pretty well, busy all the time attending all sorts of gatherings to assist in the welfare and sport activities all over Japan.

I am surprised to be told that you had a snow storm in your district at so late a time of the season as the beginning of April, and have never imagined that yours is such a cold State.

Talking about "Sakura no Hana," they came out a little earlier this year. The single-petaled flowers were at their best in Tokyo and around a few days from April 7th, and for the double-petaled the season is just about over now. I have read in the papers that the flowers on the Tidal Basin this year failed to bloom on the annual cherry festival day, much to the disappointment of many visitors to Potomack Park, Washington. We had the good fortune to see them in full blossom on April 16th about twenty years ago, when we travelled in your country. At that time, I remember well, they told us that they came into bloom about ten days later than usual for that year.

It is a pleasure to learn that Mr. Brannon is doing a good job back in the States. I am seeing Mr. Logan here from time to time.

The Princess joins me in heartily wishing that you may soon be restored to full health.

Yours very sincerely,

Nobuhito

(Prince Takamatsu)

April 19, 1950, from Prince Nobuhito Takamatsu

Dear Elaine,

How's your E.Q.? It refers to the American Economic System,
being the "Economic Quotient", says the ad on television. At first
I thought it was "Elaine's Quim." Quim is old English slang for
the female lower cleavage. Guess I'm so involved with your suffering
that it fogs my mind, even makes me draw odd cartoons (which I
enclose).

———

I finished Foreign Minister Togo's book. Again I thank you for
sending it to me, and I will return it after I've made some notes.

Strange, but I enjoyed going over the events of Japan that led
to the war again. I wish I had read the book before I made my
last trip to Japan in 1958, at which time Ben Bruce Blakeney had me
to dinner at his house in Tokyo where we spent a very pleasant
evening discussing most everything but the trial. Now, with him
gone, I will never be able to talk with him about Togo.

If I had the choice to made in retrospect, I think I would have
elected to remain in Japan and taken part in its economic revival.
Surely it would have been financially rewarding as well as very
interesting. I never found what I was looking for (whatever that
might have been) when I returned home after the war. Probably I
would not have found it in Japan either. But that is unknown.

As I try to review the several years I was in Japan, I realize
how well taken care of we were. Our food was prepared for us; we
were given a place to sleep; we were respected by the Japanese,
actually catered to, and we had free medical attention. With our
off-limit passes, we were able to travel anywhere we wished without
interference. We had no fear of walking the streets. Most of all
there was there for us to see real results of war amidst the awareness of the enemy subdued and at peace.

It was difficult not to be superior to the Japanese in thought.
We had won the war; that made us better, didn't it? Yet I did not
consciously let myself feel this way. But this attitude of defeat
on the part of the Japanese was all but gone when I returned ten
years later. Still it was a special thing we could enjoy for those
few years we were there at the time of the Occupation. It was a
brush with history.

Materialism was setting in then. When Ambassador Admiral
Nomura would call on me in my little room at the Dai Ichi Hotel, it
was not to see me or talk with me. It was to have his fill of
hamburgers which the room boys and girls would bring up from the

1950, from Brannon (page 1 of 2)

Snack Bar below. Good food was a real problem for the Japanese, especially meat. And there were those wonderful American cigarettes the Japanese craved so much. And we had so much, at hardly cost prices. /$6.00 a cartoon is a cutrate price for a carton of cigarettes today in Kansas City--we paid 50¢ in Japan at the PX, which was 5¢ a package as compared to 60-65¢ a package today/

I don't think I had ever been so well taken care of as I was in Tokyo in those days. I had a maid that changed sheets every day and looked after my slightest wish, and even if I lived in such a tiny little space it was a real home. Maybe, as Frances Way tried to tell me, Sachan was not as in love with me as I thought, but she made me feel that she was. It would have been hard for her to pretend for so long. But that's not important; she made me feel wanted. There was warmth in her that I had never seemed to feel before. And in a way I miss that couple of years with her most of all.

There was death all around. Kids running in rat-packs and raiding the hotel garbage cans when nightfall came. Men of great dignity practically begging for food, while undoubtedly tearing themselves between wrestling with their pride and being happy that the victorious enemy had not slaughtered them. There was the process of getting acquainted with our clients and other of the former leaders of Japan, of finding out that they were delightful men holding up well under the most humiliating and dangerous conditions imaginable. Then there was Admiral Osami Nagano's death, which affected me greatly.

I've mentioned it before, but since I am reminiscing I can't help but recall The Admiral getting a cold and complaining to me that he caught his cold in prison when he went through the daily procedure. That procedure he said was taking off their court clothes, all of them, when they came back from the trial to Sugamo, walk down a long cold hallway in their bare feet (and bare everything else) to where their prison garb was, redress and go to their cells. "Also," he said, "it is not dignified for men our age." He wanted me to do something about it, but I never did. And he died a few weeks later. That's why I have a guilty conscience.

Togo died in July, 1950, while in a U.S. hospital there. Many of these defendants, whom I thought so old then, were not as old as I am now. It is good to take this moment to think about them again from this distance in time and appreciate the strain on them. It adds understanding too. An understanding impossible for me as a young man. So I reminisce, thanks to you.

Sayonar, hisho darling san,

Buranon

1950, from Brannon (page 2 of 2)

Tokio
Sept. 16. 1950.

Dear Miss Fickel.

How are you? I believe that you are enjoying better health near your beloved mother and in beautiful environment of your home. My wife who was 11 years younger than I, passed away very peacefully after many months hospitalization. She had the pleasure of seeing you here. My marriage life with her was 42 years during which she helped and supported me wholeheartedly. The loss of better half is indeed irretrievable. Miss Way was so kind as to send beautiful flowers on the occasion of her funeral service and she must have written to Mr. Brannon who wrote me a letter of condolence which is full of his noble humanism and good heart and touched my heart most deeply.

North Coreans are beginning to crack. General Macarthur is applying his cherished tactics and strategy to crush them at once, at first opportunity. This morning we hear that U.N force have landed at Inchon and marching quietly toward Soul. Peace may be restored in he near future. I may be too old to visit your country but my boy, 35 years old and now in the Nippon Bank, tokio and his wife may be able to visit your country and your home. Japan, I may say, is in the better shape in general, than at the time of your departure, thanks to U.S. helps. Any way Macarthur did here most fine job, in broad sense.

Hoping most earnestly that you are in good health. With best wishes to your mama.

Yours most truly
Kichisaburo Nomura

September 16, 1950, from Kichisaburo Nomura

345

Denen-Chofu 3 chome 127.
Dec. 7. 50.

Dear Miss Fischel:

I wish you and your Mama a merry christmas and a happy new year.

I am very much worried over the new development in Korea. I expected that the war will be finished in this year and a new free united Korea will be born. And that U.S and other united nations will help Koreans to build up a new country. Now Communist army of china came in suddenly in great number and outnumbered U.N. force suffered reverses. I have heart-rending sympathy for your boys now fighting in frozen terrains in Korea. Red china supported by Soviet may be most difficult to treat in negotiation. It is just like a bargain between gentlemen and gangsters. Yet I can't expect yet that it will develop to the world war III.

Dear Miss Fischel! My boy Tadashi applied for a scholarship under GARIOA and passed the several examinations. He will study in one of your universities from next July or August. His wife will join later perhaps if circumstances permit. I think they will call on you one day. Any help you may offer, I appreciate immensely ofcourse. I believe you are now quite well. Best wishes to you and your mama.

Yours very sincerely,

Kichisaburo Nomura

December 7, 1950, from Kichisaburo Nomura (inside)

346

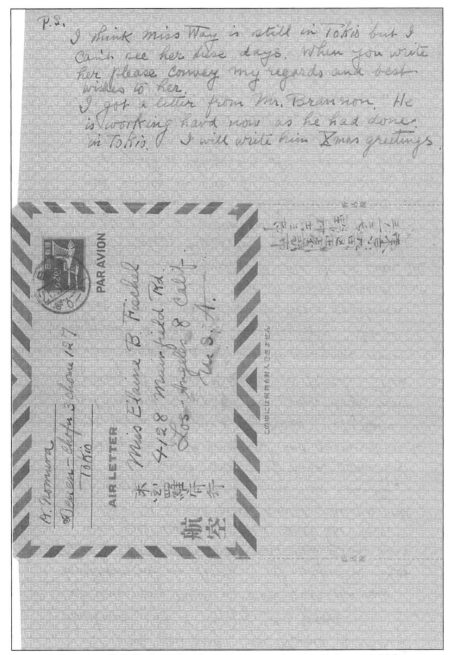

P.S.

I think miss Way is still in Tokio but I can't see her these days. When you write her please convey my regards and best wishes to her.

I got a letter from Mr. Brannon. He is working hard now as he had done in Tokio. I will write him Xmas greetings.

PAR AVION

AIR LETTER

航空

M. Yasmura
Denen-Chofu 3 chome 127
Tokio

Miss Elaine B. Fiedel
4128 Mansfield Rd.
Los-Angeles 8 Calif.
U.S.A.

December 7, 1950, from Kichisaburo Nomura (post script on outside)

347

Tokio
Jan. 12 1951.

Dear Miss Fiebel,

Thank you very much for your letter and a fine Xmas present which Miss Way delivered me.

As to iron ore you mentioned, I inquired several experts about their demands. You will see it will take time in Japan. Hirobata (most modern steel factory near Himeji and recently opened again because it was nearly closed as the object of reparaction) tells me that it is too high price including freight to Japan.

Marunouchi Shoji which is the offspring of once prosperous Mitsubishi, wants more detailed information about ore's composite elements.

Takeshi Terajima, manager of the company (you might remember the name of Terashima because his father one-time vice Admiral and minister of transportation was in Sugamo prison but now he is free) says that the ore seems to be of good quality, including freight the price is higher than prevailing price here but he would like to get more information about ore's analysed analysed composite elements described in percentage.

Will you please give the above information to

Mr. Takeshi Terajima
Marunouchi shoji
Kobiki cho 3 chome 2.
Chuoku, Tokio.

Then, Terajima wants to make direct business transaction with you or your friend.

With best wishes yours very truly K. Nomura

January 12, 1951, from Kichisaburo Nomura

348

Takanawa, Tokyo,
December 30, 1950.

Dear Miss Fischel,

Please accept our very best thanks for
your cordial wishes for the Season as well as a
very good letter with a clipping from a Los Angeles
paper.

I am glad to know that you are all right
again and have taken up your study at the University
of Southern California, and we are looking forward
to the day when you will come back here as a lawyer
in not a distant future.

The Korean situation is indeed a matter
for a grave concern and we all hope it will not be
developed into another world war. We deeply regret
the saddest accident in which General Walker's life
was involved. We really do not know what to say, but
express our deep-felt sympathy in the irrevocable
loss.

As for my activities here, I am expecting
to go into the country for a few weeks to attend
winter sport events and others early next month.

With our kindest wishes for the coming year
filled with happiness,

Yours sincerely,

Nobuhito

(Prince Takamatsu)

December 30, 1950, from Prince Nobuhito Takamatsu

Takanawa, Tokyo,
July 19th, 1951.

Dear Miss Fischel,

Warm thanks for your kind card of sympathy
on the occasion of Her Majesty my dear Mother.

She had never complained about her health
lately, and besides was not so old. Her death was
least looked for. It was indeed a great shock and loss
to us. I, however, am gratified to recollect that her
funeral was performed in a simple but most dignified
manner in spite of the present circumstances, with a
large attendance including representatives from the GHQ
and foreign missions in Tokyo.

Hoping you are well and enjoying your study,

Yours sincerely,

Nobuhito

(Prince Takamatsu)

July 19, 1951 from Prince Nobuhito Takamatsu

Denen-chofu
Mar. 9. 1952

Dear Miss Fischel
Your most welcome air mail of mar. 2. reached me this Sunday morning. Miyoko's mama visited me this afternoon and I told her about your letter's content. I must express to you and your mama our best thanks for so much hospitalities extended to Miyoko who wrote me about the details of your kindnesses and your very charming family. I am convinced that her visit to your country may be very profitable for her future.

I may be depurged in the next future and I may visit your beautiful country if my physical condition and my poor financial condition enable me to travel. I say it might not hopeless. I have not contacted with Mr. Walter Delp yet.

You know very well that our communists are being directed from abroad. Tho they are not many perhaps about hundred thousand, yet they are well organized and death-defying. Our leftist professors and students under them preach that no-armament means no-war. Mothers who have lost their sons in the war and great number of women wish no-war. Those people need enlightenment that we should desire the peace with honor, the peace with freedom and independence, and not the peace of slavery.

We ex-navy men are in very good terms with your navy people. In spite of the recent war, we trust each other. You know very well that Japanese navy was in preparedness for war but our ex-navy men were in friendly mentality toward your navy and your people even before the war.

Thank you again for your most charming letter with every good wishes to you and your mama.
Very sincerely yours
Kichisaburo Nomura

March 9, 1952, from Kichisaburo Nomura

Denen-chofu 3-127
August 3. 1952

Dear Miss Fischel,

Thank you ever so much for your very charming letter of July 13. Tadashi came back on July 10th and Miyo, on July 20th. I was very busy to welcome home them. I have heard very much of you and your mama and that you were so very much warm and kind to them. I wish to express my deep appreciation for your hospitality to make their visit to your country most valuable and profitable. I will not be surprised that you are getting no 1. merit in your class, knowing you in Tokio but I only wish you to be careful to keep your best health.

As in your country, there will be new election for new parliament in Japan. Our politicians are working exclusively to get votes, putting aside our national interests. But I believe that anyhow after new election, Japan is destined to create small, maybe, baby army and naval force, in accordance with the requirements in the mutual security pact between your country and mine. We, Japanese, can't sit idly while your force is fighting in Korea and garrisoning in Japan. We are obligated to relieve your heavy burden as far as our self-help can work out our most moderate self-defence-plan. There is restriction in our constitution for the creation of land, sea and air force. This is hard nut to crack in our domestic politics.

Best wishes to you and your mama with Tadashi and Miyo's kindest regards.

Yours very truly, K. Nomura

August 3, 1952, from Kichisaburo Nomura

Tokio. Otaku, Denen-chofu 3-127
Dec. 29. 1952

Dear Miss Fischel,

Thank you very much for your air-mail of Dec. 25. I am rather behind the time, but I want to reciprocate to you and your Mama the season's greetings. Your letter is full of interests for me. I understand that Mr. Stevenson is a brilliant man. But democratic regimes have lasted 20 years, and your people want now the change of air in Washington and General Eisenhower may be a great leader in politics, as he is a great military leader. Anyway your people are very happy to have so many big men, well qualified for the U.S. presidency.

On the contrary, Japan is very short of big leaders. You know well that Yoshida's administration is unstable. People are tired of Yoshida who is so many years in power, altho he was considered as a puppet of the occupation which ended only this April. Japan is now nominally independent, altho this country is now being defended by U.S. forces. We should do our part in accordance with the mutual security pact and thereby to relieve your heavy burden which your forces are now bearing. I am of strong belief that Japanese people should be inculcated of their sacred duty of defending their country by themselves and that our government should take adequate steps to set up our own self defense. For such purpose, this people should be awakened to stand unitedly, regardless of their political affiliation. After all, we need great leadership now badly.

over

December 29, 1952, from Kichisaburo Nomura

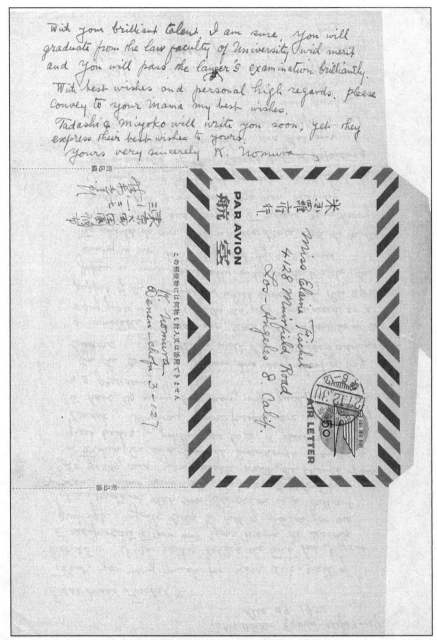

With your brilliant talent, I am sure, you will
graduate from the law faculty of University with merit
and you will pass the lawyer's examination brilliantly.
With best wishes and personal high regards, please
convey to your mama my best wishes.
Tadashi & Miyoko will write you soon, yet they
express their best wishes to yours.
Yours very sincerely K. Nomura

December 29, 1952, from Kichisaburo Nomura

Takanawa, Tokyo, Japan,
January 10th, 1953.

Dear Miss Fischel,

It was very kind of you to remember me
again and send such a pretty New Year card together
with a very good letter. The Princess and I much
appreciated your cordial wishes which we would like
to reciprocate for you.

I am glad to learn that you are steadily
recovering your full health and wish to congratulate
you in anticipation on your graduating soon from the
Law School with honors. The booklet has not reached
me yet. I shall be most pleased to see your picture
and know about your school.

We are now in mourning for the late Prince
Chichibu who passed away on January 4th early in the
morning. We tried what we could do to save him from
his premature death, but all in vain. We are deeply
grieved at the loss of our dear brother.

Wishing you another fine and successful
year,

Yours sincerely,

Nobuhito

(Prince Takamatsu)

Jan. 10, 1953, from PrinceTakamatsu

Tokio

Dear Miss Fischel   Aug. 11. 1953

Thank you ever so much for your very kind letter of July 30. First of all, I want to congratulate your success to be attorney at law in your so young age, altho I have recognized your brilliant brain since I met you. I wish you every success in your new job.

Yes, Miss Fischel, I visited Grand Canyon Ariz. and I went down the St. Lawrence river thru thousands isd, from Niagara to Quebeck and I visited Haryfacks on the way from England to Canada.

I wish to visit your country once more. My idea of travel is to shake hand with my few very good friends who were so broadminded as to renew our friendship after the end of the last war. You know my high age and I am no more interested with social functions and dinners. When you write to mr. Brannon, please be so good as to send my best wishes and regards. With high regards to you and your mama. Yours very sincerely

K. Nomura

August 11, 1953, from Kichisaburo Nomura

356

Takanawa, Tokyo, Japan,
August 17th, 1953.

Dear Miss Fischel,

I thank you very much for your good
letter, and am highly appreciative of your warm
sympathy in the sad loss of my brother Prince
Chichibu.

I am very glad to learn that you are well
and happy in the expectation of your career as
lawyer. Please accept my hearty congratulations on
your passing of the bar examination after your
hard work of the past years, as well as my cordial
wishes for a success in your new life.

I am grateful for your kind words about
our trip to your country. While having no prospects
of visiting the United States at present, I hope
you will be able to come over here to see us again
some time.

With all the best wishes for your future
from us both,

Yours sincerely,

Nobuhito

(Prince Takamatsu)

August 17, 1953, from Prince Nobuhito Takamatsu

Takanawa, Tokyo, Japan,
January 5th, 1954.

Dear Miss Fischel,

I thank you warmly for your beautiful
New Year card and very good letter.

First of all I must congratulate you on
the successes you won in your first law practising
year, and heartily wish you continued good luck in
your career.

We are busy as usual with all sorts of
engagements, official, social, sports, benefit, etc.
The Fashion Show by Groupe Ch. Dior was a benefit
affair in aid of the funds for the relief of lepers
and proved to be a great success.

With cordial good wishes for your health
and happiness in the new year,

Yours sincerely,

Nobuhito

(Prince Takamatsu)

January 5, 1954, from Prince Nobuhito Takamatsu

Takanawa, Tokyo, Japan,
May 1st, 1954.

Dear Miss Fischel,

I thank you very much for your good letter
of April 22nd, and am glad to know you are faring well
and enjoying your professional life so much.

It is a source of great pleasure to me to
learn of the success of the Azuma Troupe who are now
giving performances in the States, and I trust they
have done something to promote the mutual understanding
and friendship between our countries, as well as
international cultural relations.

About your doctor's desire to meet some
players of the troupe back stage, I have at once caused
it to be known to Miss Tokuho Azuma of the troupe, and
if you take him to the theatre where they will play in
Los Angeles and introduce yourselves mentioning my name,
she will be pleased to receive you.

Cherry blossoms this year came out unusually
early, almost over a week earlier, owing to some very
warm days at the middle of March. In fact the weather
is very changeable these days, and we now are having
rather cold days considering the time of the year.
Wisterias, azaleas, peonies, etc., are just in season.
The iris flowers, too, will soon open. Haven't you
ever visited the Iris Garden of the Meiji Park while
you were in Tokyo?

The Princess joins with me in wishing you
good health and further success in your business.

Yours sincerely,

Nobuhito

(Prince Takamatsu)

May 1, 1954, from Prince Nobuhito Takamatsu

June 6, 1955.

Dear Miss Fischel:

I was very glad to receive your letter of December. And I am very sorry not to write you for such a long time.

It has been a great joy for my family that my father was released from prison. It seems for me as if it were a dream to see my father be at home after ten years absence. And we all are very thankful for your great efforts in defending him. He asks me to tell you that he has a discase of cataract and cannot read small letters but is well about his body. The other day when he visited Mr. Nomura's he saw his daughter-in-law and she told him that you were planning to come to Japan when your next large business would be completed. My father is very pleased to hear that and expects to see you as soon as possible.

My elder daughter goes to kindergarden since this April. The younger daughter

June 6, 1955, from Hiroko Shimada

360

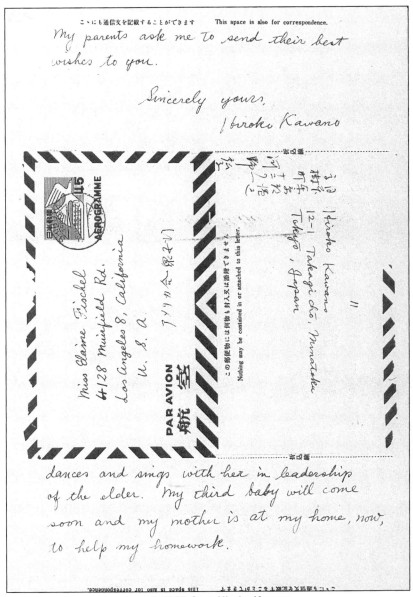

こゝにも通信文を記載することができます　　This space is also for correspondence.

My parents ask me to send their best wishes to you.

Sincerely yours,
Hiroko Kawano

Miss Elaine Fischel
4128 Muirfield Rd.
Los Angeles 8, California
U.S.A.

Hiroko Kawano
12-1 Takagi cho, Minatoku
Tokyo, Japan

この郵便物には何物も封入又は添附できません。

Nothing may be contained in or attached to this letter.

dances and sings with her in leadership of the elder. My third baby will come soon and my mother is at my home, now, to help my homework.

June 6, 1955, from Hiroko Kawano

361

June 22, 1955.

Dear Miss. Fischel

It was my great pleasure to read your nice letter of June 10.

At first I wish to present you my best hearty gratitude for your greatest efforts and kindness to me during the Tokyo Trial. Without your extra-ordinary endeavor with Mr. Brannon I am sure I would be in Paradise now, not in my home.

I have heard about you always from Hiroko by your kind correspon-dence with her. For some time I had been very anxious about your illness supposing your health had been destroyed by too much over-work during the trial in Tokyo But afterwards knowing your perfect recover and graduation of the school, I was very glad and happy, congratulating you from the bottom of my heart.

June 22, 1955, from Admiral Shimada

362

Moreover I have heard about your happy life and success as an excellent lawyer from Admiral Ambassador Nomura who visited you two years ago. I am felicitating you with my wife and daughters for your everlasting happiness.

Admiral Nomura is not the minister of Defense but he is a senator now

Mr. Okuyama is always well and prosperous and I have seen him twice in this year, once in my home after my release.

In my part I am suffering from poor eyesight by cataract, but in general my health is not so bad and therefore kindly keep your mind easy.

As yourself I have also a dream to see you again in Japan with your mother and I hope you would earn sufficient money for your trip not so long before. And my next dream is your happy marriage and we are waiting good news about it!

Hoping your happy success, with the best regards from my wife,

Yours sincerely,

Shigetaro Shimada

June 22, 1955, from Admiral Shimada

Takanawa, Tokyo, Japan,
June 1st, 1957.

Dear Miss Fischel,

Thank you very much for your good letter.
It was quite interesting to me to be told all about your
trip to Acapulco and your water skiing there. In Japan,
too, water skiing is gradually getting popular now. It
may interest you to know that we are now exporting skis
for water skiing to the States and that they are made at
the snow-ski factories in Japan.

I am indeed glad to learn that you are enjoying
your law practice so very much, and do hope it will not
be very long before you are able to come to see us again
here after successfully finishing a great big case.

Talking about the law practice and cases,
what do you think of the recent contention of the Defence
Department to try at the U.S. court martial Sp.-3 Girard
who has been charged with killing a Japanese woman on the
Somagahara firing range? The U.S.-Japan commission had
already recommended a Japanese civil trial for Girard,
since the offence was committed, not in a line of military
duty, but beyond the pale of his official duty. Your
Defence Department's insistence has caused a great
sensation here, and we are afraid this sort of case will
give our younger generation another excuse for their anti-
American movement, particularly at this juncture when we
have heard about a similar case in Taipei. We really hope
this question will be settled in such a satisfactory manner
that the close relations of friendship between the two
countries may be affected in no way.

With kindest regards and best wishes, in which
the Princess joins me,

Yours sincerely,

Nobuhito

Prince Takamatsu.

June 1, 1957, from Prince Nobuhito Takamatsu

Takanawa, Tokyo, Japan,
October 15, 1959.

Dear Miss Fischel,

I thank you very much for your good letter and
the gift of four books, which we have just received. Please
accept our warm appreciation of your thought in always
remembering us in such a kind manner.

We are glad to learn that you are keeping well and
enjoying life so happily. We can very well imagine how good a
time you must have had during your recent tour in Europe, since
you seem to have kept yourself busy with your work all the time.
We do hope you will be able to find time to come to Japan again
next year or in not a distant future.

We are delighted to have these interesting books,
which we shall be sure long to enjoy reading. The "Water Skiing"
particularly interests me, for I have for some time wanted to try
water skiing and actually am still regretting to have missed a chance
of starting it this summer. The Princess is so pleased to have
the "Barbecue Book," as she often likes to entertain guests in the
garden and will find it quite useful every time when she has the
occasion.

With much appreciation and all best wishes to you
from us both,

Yours sincerely,

Nobuhito

Prince Takamatsu.

October 15, 1959, from Prince Nobuhito Takamatsu

Takanawa, Tokyo,
May 19th, 1960.

Dear Miss Fischel,

I have received your good letter of
April 26, and appreciate your sentiment in expressing
kind congratulations on the birth of Prince Naruhito.

I am glad to learn that you are keeping
well and enjoying your work, and also to know that
you and your mother are planning to make a trip to
this country next August, and do hope you will enjoy the
tour. It will be a pleasure to me to see you and your
mother some time during your stay when you come here.

With all best wishes,

Yours sincerely,

Prince Takamatsu.

May 19, 1960, from Prince Nobuhito Takamatsu

3 - 660 KAMiTAKAiDO
SuGiNAMiKu, Tokyo.
Dec. 14, 1960.

Dear Miss Fischel,

Hiroko brought me your nice letter of Nov. 2 with your and your mother's kindest present, a very elegant, smart and agreeable wool-coat, which I received with great pleasure. I am very grateful to you from the bottom of my heart for your kindness.

I had been very happy to see you again and to make the acquaintance of your mother here in Tokyo, and so glad to welcome you in my daughter's home.

It was my hearty joy to know your big success in business, being so rich to enjoy a large journey through the Pacific area. I can suppose well how much delightful you were during whole tour and how much broad views you got in the new places. I congratulate you and your mother on your happiness.

I put on at once your warm present with my wife and Hiroko and we deeply appreciated your excellent choice. I will wear it for a long time as your kind souvenir.

December 14, 1960, from Admiral Shimada

367

My wife is now getting better after a hot-spring cure and asked me to offer her best wishes and thanks to you.

    Wishing for your great success and good health,

        Yours Sincerely,

        Shigetaro Shimada

December 14, 1960, from Admiral Shimada

1960 Christmas card from Juji Enomoto

E. Fishel sama

First of all I must ask you to
convey my best regards to your
good mother. I cannot forget the
forget the happy day when I
was invited by her, to the Imperial
Hotel near Hibiya park.
I will have reached the 86th year
by Jun 16th next year.

I bless you a happy life.
sayō-nara gokigen yoroshiku
Juji Enomoto

1960 Christmas card from Juji Enomoto

Monument Completed For Tojo, Colleagues

By The Associated Press

A beautiful monument built atop a 350-meter mountain in central Japan dedicated to Japanese war leaders hanged for war crimes in 1948 will be officially dedicated at ceremonies Tuesday.

Lawyer Itsuro Hayashi, who defended former American soldier William S. Girard for the shooting of a woman shellpicker in 1957, said Monday "a really beautiful memorial for former Premier Hideki Tojo and six other war criminals has been completed."

Tojo and six others were hanged Dec. 23, 1948 for war crimes by the 11-nation Allied Military Tribunal. They were cremated secretly and the disposition of their ashes was never formally disclosed.

The defense counsel for Gen. Kuniaki Koiso, who was hanged by the military tribunal, Shohei Sanmonji, announced in 1958 that he stole the ashes of the seven and kept them at a Buddhist temple at Atami, southwest of Tokyo. He said a joint tomb will be made at a park near Nagoya, central Japan.

Hayashi, also one of the defense lawyers for the war criminals, joined with Sanmonji in sponsoring a movement to build the memorial.

Hayashi said the ashes of the "Seven Samurai" as he called Tojo, Gen Kenji Doihara, Foreign Minister Koki Hirota, Gen. Seishiro Itagaki, Gen. Heitaro Kimura, Gen. Iwane Matsui and Lt. Gen. Akira Muto have been placed in the tomb.

The memorial was built at the cost of ¥15 million ($41,666) on a 25-acre land atop a 350-meter mountain near Nagoya. Hayashi said the land was donated by the local village.

The mounment itself is on a 1,000-square foot plot of land.

The lawyer has said he was carrying out the project in fulfilling "the responsibility of a Japanese lawyer to look after the welfare of his clients . . . those who want to forget are free to do so. Those who want to remember them are also free to do so. I am one of those who want to perpetuate their memory."

Article regarding new monument for Tojo – date and newspaper unknown

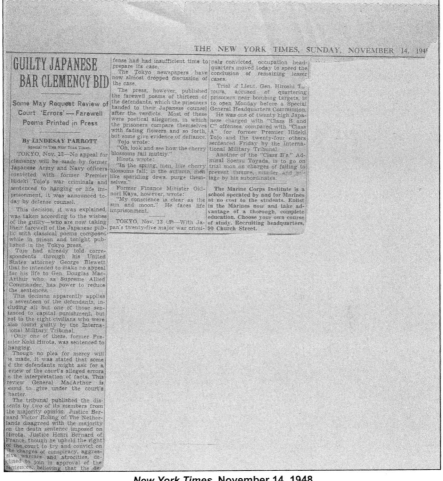

THE NEW YORK TIMES, SUNDAY, NOVEMBER 14, 1948

GUILTY JAPANESE BAR CLEMENCY BID

Some May Request Review of Court 'Errors' — Farewell Poems Printed in Press

By LINDESAY PARROTT
Special to The New York Times.

TOKYO, Nov. 13—No appeal for clemency will be made by former Japanese Army and Navy officers convicted with former Premier Hideki Tojo's war criminals and sentenced to hanging or life imprisonment, it was announced today by defense counsel.

This decision, it was explained, was taken according to the wishes of the guilty—who are now taking their farewell of the Japanese public with classical poems composed while in prison and tonight published in the Tokyo press.

Tojo had already told correspondents through his United States attorney George Blewett that he intended to make no appeal for his life to Gen. Douglas MacArthur who, as Supreme Allied Commander, has power to reduce the sentences.

This decision apparently applies o seventeen of the defendants, including all but one of those sentenced to capital punishment, but not to the eight civilians who were also found guilty by the International Military Tribunal.

Only one of these, former Premier Koki Hirota, was sentenced to hanging.

Though no plea for mercy will be made, it was stated that some of the defendants might ask for a review of the court's alleged errors n the interpretation of facts. This review General MacArthur is ound to give under the court's harter.

The tribunal published the dissents by two of its members from the majority opinion. Justice Bernard Victor Roling of The Netherlands disagreed with the majority on the death sentence imposed on Hirota. Justice Henri Bernard of France, though he upheld the right of the court to try and convict on the charges of conspiracy, aggressive warfare and atrocities, declined to join in approval of the sentences, believing that the de-

fense had had insufficient time to prepare its case.

The Tokyo newspapers have now almost dropped discussion of the case.

The press, however, published the farewell poems of thirteen of the defendants, which the prisoners handed to their Japanese counsel after the verdicts. Most of these were poetical allegories, in which the prisoners compare themselves with fading flowers and so forth, but some give evidence of defiance. Tojo wrote:

"Oh, look and see how the cherry blossoms fall mutely."

Hirota wrote:

"In the spring, men, like cherry blossoms fall; in the autumn, men like sparkling dews, purge themselves."

Former Finance Minister Oldnori Kaya, however, wrote:

"My conscience is clear as the sun and moon." He faces life imprisonment.

TOKYO, Nov. 13 (P)—With Japan's twenty-five major war crimi-

nals convicted, occupation headquarters moved today to speed the conclusion of remaining lesser cases.

Trial of Lieut. Gen. Hiroshi Tomura, accused of quartering prisoners near bombing targets, is to open Monday before a Special General Headquarters Commission.

He was one of twenty high Japanese charged with "Class B and C" offenses, compared with "Class A" for former Premier Hideki Tojo and the twenty-four others sentenced Friday by the International Military Tribunal.

Another of the "Class B's," Admiral Soemu Toyoda, is to go on trial soon on charges of failing to prevent torture, murder and pillage by his subordinates.

The Marine Corps Institute is a school operated by and for Marines at no cost to the students. Enlist in the Marines now and take advantage of a thorough, complete education. Choose your own course of study. Recruiting headquarters, 90 Church Street.

New York Times, November 14, 1948

(Signal Corps RADIOphoto
via International SOUNDphoto)

'BOUNCED,' GYPSY SAYS...

Alternating between smiles and sobs in her 153 E. 63rd St. home, stripper Gypsy Rose Lee fingers the "unmentionables" which went with her when the G-string Girl turned a cold shoulder—fully covered—on $2,500 job just before debut at La Martinique. Gypsy, who says she made costumes with her own dough, claims she was fired.

(Story and Other Photo on Page 5)
(Mirror Photo by Art Sarno)

TOJO HEARS DOOM...

Poker-faced Hideki Tojo, Japan's Pearl Harbor premier, hears himself sentenced to be hanged for war crimes as punishment is handed down against 25 Nipponese warlords by international military tribunal in Tokyo. Six others were ordered to the gallows with Tojo; 16 more received life imprisonment.

(Story and Other Photos on Page 2)

Article regarding General Tojo sentencing – 1948, date and newspaper unknown

AMONG SEVEN JAPANESE WAR CRIMINALS DOOMED BY ALLIED TRIBUNAL IN TOKYO

Ex-Premier Koki Hirota (left), who was present at pre-Pearl Harbor conference when war plans were made; Gen. Iwane Matsui (center), Nanking commander during Rape of Nanking, and Lt. Gen. Akira Muto (right), chief of staff in Philippines, are three of seven Japs sentenced to hang.
(AP Photo)

Koo Says Whole of Asia May Fall To Reds Unless U.S. Speeds Help

By JOHN L. STEELE

WASHINGTON, Nov. 12 (UP).—Chinese Ambassador Wellington Koo said tonight the "whole of Asia may fall" to Communist domination unless China receives "more and speedier aid" from the United States.

His appeal came as Defense Department officials revealed 5,000 tons of small-

Daily Mirror, November 18, 1948

375

Tojo, 6 Aides Weigh Appeal From Death

TOKYO, Nov. 12 (INS).—Ex-Premier Hideki Tojo and six other former Japanese leaders conferred with their attorneys tonight on possible appeals to their conquerer, Gen. Douglas MacArthur, from war crimes death sentences handed down by the 11-nation allied Far East military tribunal.

Like pleas for clemency were under consideration by 18 other defendants sentenced to imprisonment—16 of them for life.

Some attorneys predicted, on the basis of the appeals time limit set by MacArthur, that Tojo and the six other doomed men would be hanged Dec. 7—the anniversary of the sneak attack on Pearl Harbor.

MacArthur, as Supreme Allied Commander, alone has the authority to lessen the sentences.

EMPEROR HIROHITO
Minority opinion would pin guilt on him.
(Other photo on Page 1)

He fixed Nov. 19—one week from today—as the deadline for the filing of appeals.

Emperor Hirohito, although not tried, was declared by Sir William Webb of Australia, president of the military tribunal, to be "a leader" in Japan's war crimes.

Sir William said immunity for the Emperor "no doubt was decided upon as in the best interests of the allied powers."

He asserted, however, the fact that Hirohito acted on advice of his ministers was not a valid defense. Sir William declared:

"No ruler can commit the crime of launching aggressive war and then validly claim to be excused from so doing because his life otherwise would have been in danger.

"The emperor's real power was displayed when he intervened in 1945 to terminate the war and 'save Japan.' In this instance he was acting as an absolute monarch. Previously he had refrained from exercising his real power."

**Article regarding sentencing appeals –
1948, date and newspaper unknown**

376

New York Daily News, November 13, 1948

The Mainichi

No. 9233   TUESDAY, DECEMBER 21, 1948

Communist Troops Within 63 Miles Of Chinese Capital

Strong Reinforcements Rushed By Government To Huai Defense Line

By Joe Jacobs
United Press Staff Correspondent

NANKING, Dec. 20.—Communist troops today were reported within 63 miles of this capital, and the Government rushed strong reinforcements to its vital Huai River defense line in anticipation of a major Communist thrust toward the Yangtze.

Communist forces under General Su Yu were reported by pro-Government sources in the vicinity of Kayu, 68 miles northeast of Nanking, and within 45 miles of Yangtze waterway which links Nanking with the Northwich.

Says Reds Tightening Noose Around Peiping

United Press

NANKING, Dec. 19.—The Communists in North China are reported to be tightening the noose around Peiping and at the same time threatening to cut off the only sea outlet for Gen. Fu Tso-yi's forces through the corridor at Tangku.

On the Central China front, Communists today again disrupted rail contact between Nanking and Peng-pu—major Nationalist bastion 110 miles northwest of the capital.

Reds Enter Tangku

Kyodo-AFP

NANKING, Dec 19.—The Chinese Communist forces entered Tangku, an important port in North China, yesterday.

Gen. Huang And 3 Others Taken Prisoner By Reds

Kyodo-AFP

NANKING, Dec. 19.—A Communist force communiqué claimed today that General Huang Wei, commander of the Government Second Army Group, was taken prisoner when the Government troops were annihilated at a point southwest of Suhsien on December 15.

According to the same report, the vice-commander of the Second Army Group and two Army commanders were also taken prisoner by the Communist forces.

Sun Tenders Resignation

Kyodo-Central News Agency

NANKING, Dec. 20.—Sun Fo, new President of the Chinese Executive Yuan, tendered his resignation to Generalissimo Chiang Kai-shek yesterday because the formation of his Cabinet had been deadlocked, according to today's issues of two leading newspapers here.

Hirazawa Pleads Not Guilty To Charge Of Bank Murders

— Trial Opens At Tokyo District Court —

SUPREME COURT HEARING TODAY RE APPEALS OF WAR CRIMINALS

United Press

WASHINGTON, Dec. 19.—The first hearing of the Supreme Court on appeals of seven Japanese war criminals will be held December 20 (December 21, Japan Time).

Keenan's Assistant Confers With SCAP

United Press

TOKYO, Dec. 20.—The United States Supreme Court action on the appeals from Japanese war criminals was presumably discussed at a meeting between Gen. MacArthur and Willis Mahoney, Executive Assistant to Allied Chief Prosecutor Joseph B. Keenan.

Mahoney called on the Supreme Commander and spent 80 minutes with him prior to Mahoney's scheduled departure for the United States today.

_____ to say whether they discussed the appeals of the Japanese war criminals.

He said the call was "just a friendly one."

Mahoney officially closed the offices of the International Prosecution Section before his farewell call on Gen. MacArthur.

The prosecution official had been in Tokyo 33 months and directed the _____

Report On US Supreme Court Hearing:

All Justices Seem Very Attentive; Listen Closely, Ask Many Questions

Editor's Note—John G. Brannon, who acted as an American defense council for Nagano, Shimada, Oka and Sato in the trials of the International Military Tribunal for the Far East in Tokyo, is now in Washington to appear before the United States Supreme Court in appealing on behalf of the sentenced Japanese war criminals. Mr. Brannon, who was the youngest of the counsels at the recent trials, being only 35 years old, is acting in cooperation with other defense counsels in the Supreme Court appeals.

By John G. Brannon
Defense Counsel, International Military Tribunal for the Far East

WASHINGTON, Dec. 18.—(Exclusive to the Mainichi through United Press)—It was a quick trip across the ocean from Japan to the United States for George Yamaoka, counsel for Hirota, George Furness, Shigemitsu's lawyer, and myself.

After an initial stop in New York City to confer with William Logan Jr. who had been handling the Supreme Court case from the American side, we journeyed on to Washington D.C. where we met David Smith who is also acting on behalf of the condemned Hirota.

It was Thursday morning about 10.30 that we entered the spacious white-marbled Supreme Court building. We held a hurried conference preparatory to the Supreme Court opening at noon.

Great Interest Shown

Newspaper cameramen and reporters exhibited great interest in the proceedings, attesting to the fact that great interest in the unusual judicial hearing prevailed in America, almost on an equal plane, with that in Japan.

In the Supreme Court building we met Michael Levin, former American counsel for Koga, and A. Lazarus who had represented Hata in Tokyo, as well as C. Williams, former counsel for Hoshino, and Naval Captain Beverly Coleman who has been the first of the American counsels for the Japanese accused at the beginning of the trial.

All of these men were excited and extremely interested.

There was a hasty dictation of many notes to Mr. Logan and myself in the War Ministry building in Tokyo and the many lady who contributed so much toward our efforts.

It was not until 3.30 in the afternoon, Thursday, December 16, that the case was called—for argument.

Keenan, Avener Present

The courtroom was packed and many of the prosecution staff who participated in the Tokyo trial including Chief of Counsel Joseph B. Keenan and his able assistant Frank Avener were present.

We decided among ourselves to have Mr. Logan explain the background of the case to the High Court. As he approached the lectern

Autonomous Regime Planned In Szechwan

United Press

HONGKONG, Dec. 20.—The usually reliable newspaper Takung Pao reported from Chungtu that officials in the Central China province of Szechwan are planning to establish an autonomous regime there.

The dispatch said discussions have been going on for weeks among officials interested in separation from Nationalist China.

Formal discussions in the Szechwan capital will begin Tuesday, it said.

According to the report, a healthy plan calls for establishment of a provisional army of 20 divisions.

Szechwan would not pay taxes to Nanking.

Chengtu was a wartime American B-29 base.

Opposition Requests _____ Of Government Wage _____ Will Submit Own Am_____

Representatives Of Oppositi_____ Hoover, Whitney At GHQ In _____ Way Out Of Deadlock In Po_____

TOKYO, Dec. 20.—The Opposition p_____ ernment to withdraw the Government wage _____ anew its amendment to expedite the Diet de_____

The request was filed in reply to th_____ earliest deliberations on the Government b_____ Opposition by Speaker Komakichi Matsuok_____

Yoshida Asks Speedup Of Bill D_____

Earlier, representatives of the _____ Opposition parties met Chief Hoover _____ of the Civil Service Division, GHQ, _____ today to hear his views on the wage _____ scale problem.

In the conference, it is said, the _____ SCAP representative stressed the _____ need for wage stabilization and administrative readjustment.

Although the Democratic Party is _____

Nationwide Strike Is Staged In Italy

19,500,000 Govt. Workers Walk Out For 24 Hours

United Press

ROME, Dec. 19.—Ignoring Premier Alcide de Gasperi's last minute appeal against strike, some 19,500,000 Government workers left their jobs for 24 hours in a nationwide work stoppage one minute after midnight this morning.

Strike leaders of the Communist-led National Confederation of Labor issued a communiqué an hour beforehand, blaming the Government for necessity of walking out demanding higher wages.

There were no reports of any incidents as heavy patrols guarded postal and telegraph buildings.

All state workers were affected by the stoppage.

Italy-Hungary Accord

Radiopress

BRAZZAVILLE (Radio), Dec. 19. —A commercial agreement will be signed between Italy and Hungary, probably tomorrow, in Rome.

Austrian Treaty

Russia Agrees To Negotiate With Big 3 West Powers

United Press

VIENNA, Dec. 19.—Russia agreed to try again to negotiate for the Austrian treaty sometime in mid-January with the Big Three Western Powers—United States, Britain and France, sources close to Chancellor Leopold Figle said.

The latter countries have already replied favorably to the Austrian request for Four-Power talks. But Austria complained that a possible division of the country into four Occupation zones would impose a heavy burden on her.

Prepares New Transmitter For Use Of Radio Berlin

AFP

BERLIN, Dec. 19.—Following the demolition by the French Military Government of the two aerials of the Soviet-licensed Radio Berlin at Tegel in the French sector, a detachment of Soviet engineers, aided by German radio technicians, has started to dismantle the building of the

Article regarding U.S. Supreme Court Hearing the Mainichi, December 21, 1948

War Trials articles, *New York Star*, December 10, 1948

Articles regarding the sentencings, *New York Herald Tribune*, 1948 date unknown

Article regarding the death of Prince Takamatsu, *The Daily Yomiuri*, February 1967

Old book has advice that is new again

By TONY PERRY
Times Staff Writer

TIMELESS: *"The Iraqis have . . . differences among themselves," the handbook says.*

MICHAEL PERRY For The Times

SAN DIEGO — The book will never rival Harry Potter for sales, but in the rarefied world of university publishing a Chicago outfit has a somewhat unusual hit this season.

The University of Chicago Press, publisher of scholarly works since 1891, just filled a rush order for a third 5,000-copy printing of "Instructions for American Servicemen in Iraq During World War II."

Previous printings sold out quickly, which publicity manager Levi Stahl attributes to a fortuitous meeting of past scholarship and present public interest.

The original pocket-sized volume was given by the Army to GIs sent to Iraq during World War II to help British forces thwart any German military drive toward the Persian Gulf. The reprint, priced at $10, is available on the Internet and at some bookstores, often placed near the checkout counter.

"It seems to have struck a chord with the public, which surprised all of us," Stahl said. "It looks like and is priced like an impulse buy, so we've had good luck through all the usual channels."

Although it contains language that today would be impermissible, such as slang references to the Japanese and homosexuals, much of the advice is the same given to modern Marines and soldiers sent to Iraq.

Don't be boastful or arrogant when talking to Iraqis. Never stare at or try to talk to Iraqi women. Be prepared for a country that is blisteringly hot and dusty in the summer. Learn a few Arabic phrases. Remember that Arabs are some of the most relentless guerrilla fighters in the world. Use your best manners.

"American success or failure in Iraq may well depend on whether the Iraqis (as the people are called) like American soldiers or not," the book says on its opening page. "It may not be quite that simple. But then again it could."

The 44-page book is just as it was when given to the GIs with one exception: a foreword by Army Lt. Col. John A. Nagl, who served a year in Iraq after the April 2003 fall of Saddam Hussein. Nagl also wrote a foreword to one of the University of Chicago Press' other bestsellers, the newly updated "U.S. Army/Ma-

rine Corps Counterinsurgency Field Manual."

The idea of reprinting the book on Iraq came as a result of the success Britain's Bodleian Library had with two other instructive volumes from World War II: the U.S. Army's advice for troops going to Britain ("NEVER criticize the King or Queen") and Australia (Aussie football "creates a desire on the part of the crowd to tear someone apart, usually the referee"). The University of Chicago Press handles U.S. marketing and sales for Bodleian.

The books involving troops bound for Britain and Australia are quaint, but "Instructions for American Servicemen in Iraq During World War II" includes several passages that are ominous in the context of the current war.

"The nomads are divided into tribes headed by sheiks," the book says. "These leaders are very powerful and should be shown great consideration."

Nagl writes in his foreword that if more attention had been paid to the sheiks after the toppling of Hussein, that "might have prevented the fervent insurgency from being raised to the fever pitch it has taken recently."

Of the schisms in Iraqi society, which have contributed to much of the violence since the U.S.-led invasion, the book advises, "The Iraqis have some religious and tribal differences among themselves."

It's a sentence, Nagl concludes, that is best described as a "stunning understatement."

tony.perry@latimes.com

Article regarding book given to U.S. servicemen during WWII – date and newspaper unknown

Tojo on the cover of *TIME*, scant weeks before Pearl Harbor

SELECTED BIBLIOGRAPHY

Agawa, Hiroshi. *The Reluctant Admiral*. Kondansha International Ltd., 1969.

Benedict, Ruth. *The Chrysanthemum and the Sword*. Houghton Mifflin Company, 1967.

Bix, Herbert P. *Hirohito and the Making of Modern Japan*. HarperCollins Publishers, 2000.

Brackman, Arnold. *The Other Nuremberg—the Untold Story of the Tokyo War Crimes Trial*. William Morrow and Company, 1987.

Brown, Courtney. *Tojo, the Last Banzai*. Holt, Rinehart and Wilson, Inc., 1967.

Craig, William. *The Fall of Japan*. Dell Publishing Company, 1967.

Minear, Richard. *Victors' Justice—The Tokyo War Crimes Trial*. Princeton University Press, 1971.

Pal, Justice R.B. *International Military Tribunal for the Far East Dissentient Judgment*. Sanyal and Co. India, 1953.